SUCCESSFUL SCHOOL BOARD LEADERSHIP

Lessons from Superintendents

Edited by
Gary Ivory
Michele Acker-Hocevar

Rowman & Littlefield Education
Lanham, Maryland • Toronto • Plymouth, UK
2007

Published in the United States of America
by Rowman & Littlefield Education
A Division of Rowman & Littlefield Publishers, Inc.
A wholly owned subsidary of The Rowman & Littlefield Publishing Group,
Inc.
4501 Forbes Boulevard, Suite 200, Lanham, Maryland 20706
www.rowmaneducation.com

Estover Road
Plymouth PL6 7PY
United Kingdom

British Library Cataloguing in Publication Information Available

Library of Congress Cataloging-in-Publication Data

Successful school board leadership : lessons from superintendents / edited by
Gary Ivory, Michele Acker-Hocevar.
    p. cm.
Includes bibliographical references and index.
ISBN-13: 978-1-57886-630-4 (hardcover : alk. paper)
ISBN-10: 1-57886-630-8 (hardcover : alk. paper)
ISBN-13: 978-1-57886-631-1 (pbk. : alk. paper)
ISBN-10: 1-57886-631-6 (pbk. : alk. paper)
1. School superintendents–United States. 2. Educational leadership–United
States. 3. School management and organization–United States. I. Ivory,
Gary, 1947– II. Acker-Hocevar, Michele, 1948–
    LB2831.72.S83 2007
    379.1'531–dc22   2007011504

©™ The paper used in this publication meets the minimum requirements of
American National Standard for Information Sciences—Permanence of
Paper for Printed Library Materials, ANSI/NISO Z39.48-1992.
Manufactured in the United States of America.

To our spouses—Irma B. Ivory and Fritz A. Hocevar—who have appreciated our involvement with this project, endured our endless phone conversations, and supported our collaborative work: Thank you.

CONTENTS

Preface   *Gary Ivory and Michele Acker-Hocevar*   vii

1   Challenge: Leading in an Era of Change
       Kathryn Whitaker and Sheldon T. Watson   I

2   Success Strategy: Sell the Vision
       Edith A. Rusch   22

3   Success Strategy: Prioritize and Decide
       Judith A. Aiken   41

4   Challenge: Fostering Student Achievement
       Robin Dexter and William Ruff   52

5   Success Strategy: Base Decisions on Data
       William Ruff and Robin Dexter   67

6   Success Strategy: Recruit, Keep, Develop, and Rely on
          Good Staff
       Faye E. Patterson   83

7   Success Strategy: Learn About Education and Your Role
       Ramón Domínguez   99

8   Challenge: Shortages of Resources
       Rhonda McClellan, Adrienne Hyle, and L. Nan Restine   119

9   Challenge: Mandates and Micropolitics
       Cynthia I. Gerstl-Pepin   135

10 Challenge: Understanding Your Superintendent's Perspective
       L. Nan Restine, Adrienne Hyle, and Rhonda McClellan   149

11 Challenge: Needing to be Reelected
       Thomas L. Alsbury   164

12 Success Strategy: Obtain Meaningful Community Input
       Eduardo Arellano   185

13 Success Strategy: Maintain Good Relationships
       Mary E. Devin, Teresa Northern Miller, and Trudy A. Salsberry   199

References   213

Index   223

About the Contributors   233

PREFACE

Gary Ivory and Michele Acker-Hocevar

School board members commit to leadership in one of the most important functions of our society—educating the young—and they commit to doing so in a world of unrelenting tensions. Serving the multiple and competing interests of constituents, staying abreast of the many changes in education, and simultaneously ensuring that schools improve are formidable tasks under the best of circumstances.

School leadership today comes with increased pressure for accountability, demands to improve student achievement, and calls to upgrade technology. Often a school board member is expected to do these things with shrinking resources. We believe this book can help *you*—a current or potential school board member—lead more effectively. We do not believe it will eliminate or alleviate all the tensions; the tensions are inherent in American education—in fact, are embedded in American culture. This book represents our profound respect for you and everyone else who values education leadership and who works to improve education despite the excruciating tensions you encounter.

One of the tensions educational leaders face is between the roles of superintendents and board members. These roles represent an unavoidable tension between the responsibility and authority you hold to oversee education on behalf of your community (or communities) and the specialized knowledge the superintendent holds to run a school system efficiently. Superintendents often express frustration with boards. Some superintendents may resent having prepared and studied for years to lead school districts, only to find they must have their decisions reviewed by a committee of nonexperts. Board members, on the other hand, may be frustrated by a superintendent's perceptions of them as mere rubber stamps for the superintendent's decisions. Some board members seem to believe the school district is a place for them to exercise their will wherever, whenever, and however they please. We believe that position also is unacceptable.

We suggest that in many ways board members and superintendents are in the same boat: You have similar ideals, and you face similar problems. We believe your role as a leader of education in your community is legitimate, and we believe that you can learn from superintendents how to do it better. So what we offer here is advice for board members based on the perspectives of superintendents. We hope this book helps you lead your school district with commitment, imagination, and courage and also within legitimate legal and ethical constraints.

A DOZEN TENSIONS

Let us first attend to the tensions. If you have already been a board member and you are given to careful thought, then you have already experienced many of them. We spell them out here just to set the stage for the rest of the book.

The first tension is this: A value embedded in the concept of locally elected boards is that this system allows for more voices to be heard and more viewpoints to be considered. But the more viewpoints that are considered, the more obvious and possibly problematic disagreements become. The harder you work to be a democratic leader, the more difficult it will be to arrive at simple decisions. This dilemma is inherent in democracy. Since school boards are in place to promote democracy, you will regularly experience this tension. Kowalski (2001) predicted, "Inclusive decision making at the district level will magnify and personalize philosophical, cultural, and political differences in

American society. The resulting conflict will require skillful facilitation so that necessary compromises can be forged" (p. 184).

The second tension is related to the first one: In deliberating before arriving at a decision, you should gather as much information as you can, listen to as many points of view as possible, and then make the most rational decision you can for the good of the students. As political scientist Kenneth Strike (2003) put it, policy should "be shaped through reasoned discourse rather than manipulation or indoctrination" (p. 38). Martha Nussbaum (1997) wrote of the value of "a democracy that is reflective and deliberative rather than simply a marketplace of competing interest groups" (p. 19). But some people who present their viewpoints will not do so rationally. Some will count on emotional appeals and other propaganda, manipulation, or even intimidation to win you to their side. So your second tension is committing to rational consideration of viewpoints that may be presented irrationally.

The third tension is between leading our school system to promote common values and beliefs while also leading them to an appreciation of diversity of background, experience, and perspective. Every society probably needs some common beliefs and values to survive and maintain itself, but a society that attempts to impose orthodoxy on those disinclined to accept it will generate substantial resistance to that orthodoxy.

A fourth tension is in your responsibility to lead schools in ways that meet the needs of your local community in the face of federal and state mandates about what schools should accomplish—often without additional resources to accomplish what is expected.

A fifth tension is between excellence and equity. Excellence may require you to expect the best from students, to push them to higher and higher levels of performance, and to refuse to accept mediocrity. Equity, on the other hand, may require you to be sensitive to obstacles students have to overcome and to offer students multiple opportunities and ways to experience success. It is very difficult to do both. For example, universal free public education brings everyone in to participate but is regularly criticized for not producing excellence. A counter example, high school football, often requires excellence of students, but only a tiny minority of students gets to participate on the football team. Society now asks you as a board member to lead your district to produce both excellence and equity.

A sixth tension is the one we alluded to above: the need to place one's faith in the expertise of the superintendent versus the importance of having the superintendent's work be overseen by and be accountable to a strong body that is representative of the community. Kowalski (2001) noted three benefits of local control:

(1) Increased flexibility. Schools are able to respond more quickly and directly to changing needs when important programming decisions are made locally. (2) Effective use of human resources. Those who must implement change can participate in the process of planning change. (3) Increased relevance. Decisions are made at the level closest to the problems and real needs of students. (p. 185)

Let us move quickly through the last few: seventh is the tension in any organization, including school systems, between the need for stability and the need to change, or at least to adapt to change. Eighth is the tension between communication or action toward efficiency and communication or action toward relationship building. Ninth is the tension between being a trustee or a delegate. Trustees work to make decisions for the good of the entire community and often to present a united front in support of that good; delegates make sure their own constituents (who may have in the past been underrepresented) get to share in the benefits of society. Tenth is the tension between acting rationally versus acting politically. Eleventh is that, even in acting politically, there is the tension between needing to ally with the faction whose values you agree with versus allying with the faction that seems likely to be in power.

The twelfth tension is the challenge of monitoring student learning through standardized testing without becoming so obsessed with test scores that you make them the point of public education. On the one hand, if you do not monitor achievement, you cannot be sure that your district is fostering learning by all students. But on the other, you must realize that standardized tests assess only a fraction of the learning students need, and that therefore a school system that produces *only* good test scores is selling children short. As almost all our chapter authors emphasize, the No Child Left Behind Act makes it more difficult than ever before to negotiate between these two points.

LEADING WELL AMID THE TENSIONS

This introduction provides both bad news and good news, and then more good news: The bad news is that you will probably never get to a place in your school leadership where you will not have to deal with excruciating tensions. The good news is that you do not have to feel alone in your struggles. Many of the tensions you see or will see in your community appear in communities like yours all over the United States. In fact, as we said above, they are inherent in democracies. So when you face these maddening frustrations of providing good leadership to your school system, know that they are not unique to your school system and that you are not alone in having to deal with them. Dealing with these frustrations and tensions is contributing to democracy in your community for the sake of the young people of your community. And that is a very good thing.

The additional good news is that there are ways of dealing with these tensions. These are not secret recipes that work 100 percent of the time; there are no magic bullets to slay the monsters you have to deal with; but there are guiding principles that over the long haul will help you deal more effectively with the challenges of leadership. Superintendents often know these principles and have talked to us eloquently about them. That is why we think this book, a book for school board members based on the words and thoughts of superintendents, is a good idea. We believe school boards have legitimate roles to play in education, but we also believe they can learn from superintendents how better to play those roles.

Thus, we have organized this book around themes that superintendents talk about when interviewed, and we often use superintendents' own words to illustrate points we are making. We believe a strength of this book is the vividness and energy with which superintendents describe ideas and the concrete examples they provide. That does not imply that we agree with their every word or their every perspective. Nor does it imply that you should. But we do believe the ideas we have gotten from them can help you be a more effective educational leader in your community. We also believe that as you increase your understanding of how superintendents perceive public education, you will grow in effectiveness at working with superintendents to improve education for all children.

THE ORIGINS OF THE IDEAS IN THIS BOOK

This book grew out of a collaborative longitudinal project of the University Council for Educational Administration (UCEA). UCEA is a consortium of nearly 80 doctoral-granting universities that produce school administrators. In the mid-1990s, UCEA researchers set out to interview superintendents and principals to improve understanding of their "'most vexing' problems of practice" (Pounder, 1999, p. 5). The project began with the name "A Thousand Voices from the Firing Line," which was eventually shortened to simply "Voices." In the first phase of Voices, researchers interviewed 29 superintendents. Since 21 of those superintendents mentioned school boards in their interviews, we used the ideas in their interviews to guide the writing of this book. A second phase of Voices involved conducting five focus groups with superintendents, and a third phase began with three pilot focus groups. So, in all, 82 superintendents have been interviewed for this book, 21 of them one-on-one and 61 in focus groups. Researchers began interviewing in the mid-1990s and finished in 2003.

Not all interviewers reported their superintendents' gender and ethnicity, but we know that 20 of the superintendents were female and 57 were male. Sixty-three were white non-Hispanic; seven were African American; and one was Hispanic. Fifty-one of them had doctorates. Thirty-one of the superintendents reported that they worked in rural districts, 19 worked in suburban districts, and 8 in urban districts. We wish we could tell you where all of these superintendents served, but to ensure confidentiality, interviewers often concealed superintendents' locations. We can tell you that 18 states are represented, from Connecticut to New Mexico, and from as far south as Alabama and Tennessee, to Wisconsin and Wyoming in the north.

So, the bottom line is that we do not claim to have represented every superintendent or even every kind of superintendent in the United States. But we do believe we have input from superintendents in many different kinds of situations. And we are grateful to them for their willingness to talk with us about the rewards and challenges of their work in public education.

The two of us, Ivory and Acker-Hocevar, then spent months coding the interviews and talking to one another about how we might organize our findings to make sense of them. For example, Acker-Hocevar developed codes that included professional development, career advancement, change, preparation, decision making, challenges, learning over time, motivators, public relations, communication, resources, detractors, leadership, school board relations, student achievement, community, negotiations, listening, social context, personnel, politics, ethics, role behavior, and teaching and learning. At the same time, Ivory was developing his own codes, and we spent many hours over the telephone comparing our insights and arguing over which seemed to make the most sense and be most consistent with the interview data.

Then, Ivory took the coding from both researchers and identified 13 categories, the six challenges and seven success strategies you see as themes of chapters in this book. During the next several weeks, we spent more hours considering and discussing which portions of the interviews seemed to fit best with which challenges and success strategies. We rethought and recoded during this time to get the best possible fit of topics with superintendent quotes. Next, we divided up the coding work, with Acker-Hocevar coding the data for the six challenges and Ivory coding for the seven success strategies. The entire process took us well over a year. Then, we invited our colleagues who had interviewed the superintendents or contributed in other ways to the project to write the chapters you see here. The chapters are laid out as follows:

Chapter 1 describes a challenge, the maelstrom of internal and external changes districts face. Then, chapter 2 presents a success strategy, developing a vision and propagating it to the community. Chapter 3 is about another success strategy: prioritizing and making decisions in line with that vision.

Chapters 4 and 5 elaborate on the challenge of fostering student achievement and the strategy of basing decisions on data. Chapter 6 relates a fourth success strategy: making sure you have staff in the district who can do the jobs that need to be done. Chapter 7 presents yet another success strategy, one that will take you through the rest of your career in educational leadership: learning about education and your role in it.

Chapter 8 describes a challenge that bedeviled the superintendents interviewed: shortages. Chapter 9 explores the complexities of yet another challenge, the myriad of competing voices who want a say in how education should proceed in your community. Chapter 10 follows with yet another challenge, understanding where your superintendent is coming from. Chapter 11 presents a final challenge that haunts many elected officials: anticipating the next election and wondering whether you will be reelected to continue the work you have begun. The book ends with two final success strategies: getting meaningful input from the various voices in the communities (chapter 12) and maintaining good relationships (chapter 13).

We are delighted to report that the variety of perspectives from superintendents is buttressed by the variety of perspectives from which our chapter authors wrote. A brief report on each author and his or her education and experience appears at the end of this book.

We thank all the superintendents who gave of their valuable time to be interviewed, and all the researchers who interviewed them. We thank two school board members who provided insights to us at the beginning of this project, Dan Wever and Dr. Lorraine O'Donnell. We end this chapter by also acknowledging the tremendous contribution of Jim Earley, graduate assistant at New Mexico State University. Jim is a superb writer and editor. He has gone out of his way to take responsibility for the completion of this project. We could not have finished it without his help.

❶

CHALLENGE:
LEADING IN AN ERA OF CHANGE

Kathryn Whitaker and Sheldon T. Watson

Change has always been a part of education and, in fact, of human experience. Today, however, the pace of change and the number of areas that such changes touch upon are dramatically altering the way public education is administered and delivered. Vaill's words in 1991 seem to describe the life of educational leaders today: "No sooner do you begin to digest one change than another comes along to keep things unstuck. The feeling is one of continuous upset and chaos" (p. 2). Despite our discomfort with upset and chaos, it is important for us to be wary of the lure of *presentism*, of thinking that our contemporary conditions are somehow extraordinary, and that once the change passes, we can return to some "normal" way of doing things.

Change is with us, and school district leaders must deal with it. Though there is no clear delineation between the origins of the changes, we can say this: Some seem to originate externally, though their effect is felt internally; others seem to originate internally, though one could trace their origins to events external to the district. Our categorizing changes here as external and internal may seem somewhat arbitrary, but it provides a framework to organize our discussion of the variety of changes you face.

Changes that in our view originate externally are as follows:

1. Declining confidence in public education. This has given rise to calls for accountability mechanisms, culminating most recently in the No Child Left Behind (NCLB) legislation, and increased expectations of educational leaders especially with regard to instruction.
2. Population movements that change dramatically the demographic makeup of a district, often in terms of ethnicity, culture, language, or economics. The changing composition of a district can change the level of political activism in a district, so we treat political activism as a "local" change.
3. Fluctuations in the national and state economies that affect a community's ability or willingness to tax itself for education.
4. Increasing legal constraints and students' needs for more services.

Changes we think originate internally are these:

1. Increasing political activism
2. Reductions in the deference paid to individual leaders
3. Increasing reliance on technology
4. Increasing concerns over school security and safety
5. Reductions in the availability of human resources

These changes—those of both internal and external origin—can affect your responsibilities as a school leader and your ability to lead effectively. You and your superintendent must develop a shared vision of the challenges that these new conditions bring to school districts and of the strategies that can be used to address them. Along the way we suggest strategies to deal with change based on the leadership literature we have read and the experiences of America's public school superintendents.

EXTERNAL CHANGES

In looking at the impact of external changes on school district leadership, we cannot help but run into the idea of *power* again and again. Power means very different things to different people (Watson & Grogan, 2005). For some, it involves holding a certain position and exercising authority over others. For others, power refers to specific responsibilities, such as agenda setting or the allocation of financial resources. Yet others think of power more broadly, as simply the capacity to *influence* others to perform certain actions. All of these perspectives on power reveal themselves when we look at the external forces that are having an impact on superintendents and school boards as they administer school districts. The interconnected web of influences that shape district decision making are very much about power—who has it; who does not; how it is distributed, shared, and taken away; and how it evolves as school districts move into the 21st century.

Declining Confidence in Public Education

In recent decades, Americans have consistently given their local schools high marks for quality yet scored the nation's schools very low (Rose & Gallup, 2005). Superintendents we spoke to characterized this as a "public confidence" issue. One veteran urban superintendent noted,

> We [in education] are really in the bash in public education right now—everywhere from the presidential election right on down the line. It's a problem in our local communities. I've had to deal with it here on a yearly basis. It doesn't go away.

Widespread concern for the quality of our public schools (from a national perspective) became commonplace during the 1980s as policymakers, pundits, and the media developed a narrative (some might say a *spin*) that our schools were in decline and that our students were falling behind those from other nations (Berliner & Biddle, 1995; House, 1991). This critical view of public education has largely persisted since then and has contributed to many of the education reforms of the past few decades. Cronin and Usdan wrote in 2003, "International reports that placed the U.S. 15th or 20th in mathematics and science were viewed as indictments of local control and confirmed widely held notions of school system mediocrity" (p. 185). A Midwestern superintendent reflected, "A talk show in [a large city in a neighboring state] has implications for public opinion about [schools here]." In this way, an external change morphs into an internal one.

Disaggregation of data by subgroups, as is required by NCLB, has contributed to this by formalizing our recognition of diverse groups of students that have traditionally had less success in our schools. And thus does the ability to shape public opinion play a role in who shall have power over education: national leaders or local ones. Policy initiatives and public opinion have been moving hand in hand in a steady march toward the current condition of external intervention in the local control of schools.

One of the most dramatic instances of this march has been to pressure schools to show evidence of student achievement. In a district that is being scrutinized for low test scores and accountability issues, leaders must focus on raising test scores, and this requires district leaders to be better instructional leaders than they ever had to be before. According to a recent poll of 813 superintendents, they are playing more assertive roles in shaping instruction (Archer, 2005). The top instructional leadership practices identified by these superintendents include training for teachers and principals on the use of performance data; initiating and maintaining a common district curriculum, especially in mathematics and reading; standardizing school improvement plans; conducting effective induction of new teachers; promoting common planning time for teachers; supervising instruction; and administering their own districtwide assessments and adjusting instruction accordingly (Archer, 2005, p. S5). A superintendent from a suburban district remarked, "The superintendent's role in instructional leadership is becoming more and more pronounced. . . . [My colleague] and I were joking recently that we were at a social gathering and we were talking about instructional methodology!"

The heavy focus on the instructional leadership role of superintendents has also created changes that affect school boards. In past decades, much of the conversation at board meetings centered on transportation issues, athletics, and facilities. In many cases these were the areas that board members knew the most about. One small district superintendent summed up the change of priorities reflected at board meetings:

At last month's board meeting there was a conversation between the board and the audience about the use of calculators and the style of math curriculum. The discussion used to be the football fields and new uniforms. There has been a change of focus. Before I couldn't even get academics on the agenda, and if I did, it was, "You'd better hurry through it."

Currently, board members have to understand test results, achievement gaps, reading and math programs, and NCLB mandates. This need for increased understanding means that you have to make it a priority to educate yourself on these instructional matters.

Despite the public relations difficulties that school districts currently face, recent polling indicates that almost two-thirds of Americans would like to see their children become teachers (Rose & Gallup, 2005). Ultimately, there is still a foundation of respect and appreciation for our educational system that we can build on. An important external change and an aspect of power that affects schools is that some leaders in our society have learned better than others how to sway public opinion. Politicians and the media are experts at this. Educational leaders have been less savvy and more poorly positioned to exercise such influence. Despite the steep public relations learning curve that must be climbed, boards and superintendents must work together to promote public perceptions of the positive aspects of our schools, not just the shortcomings. Perception *can* become reality in relationship to public support for education, but the positive message of what is happening in successful districts and schools must get out there for this to happen.

Public Perception and Accountability: The Need for Transparency

Struggles over how education should be controlled manifest most clearly today in accountability procedures. In recent years, sources and mechanisms of accountability have both shifted and intensified. Power that was once more diffuse, and often quite localized, has now become centralized in state and federal agencies.

The NCLB legislation represents an unprecedented expansion of federal power and influence into the core operations of public education. When combined with the already-existing web of standards (local, state, national, and professional), standardized testing (local, state, and national), and comprehensive school reform frameworks, the federal policy creates a superstructure of accountability that frames public education. Districts struggle to work within this complex framework to advance the needs of their students while complying with external policy mandates, first from the state and now from the federal government. Unfortunately, despite good intentions on all sides, these multiple masters are not always easily served equally. In fact, some of them may contradict each other.

Again, communication with all stakeholders in a district is an important part of dealing with these issues. A superintendent from a rural district said,

> We have become much more accountable, but we have worked at that. We are better at telling people what we are doing. What happens is when you tell people what you are doing, when you involve them in the planning, they expect you to also show them that you are doing it.

Transparency, or letting people in on what's going on in a school or district, is a fundamental part of what greater accountability measures are calling for. With all of the internal changes taking place in districts at the same time, it becomes even more critical to have open lines of communication and involvement with families, teachers, staff, policymakers, and the public at large. We have entered a new era of openness regarding our schools. Superintendents and school boards must become more accustomed to conducting business and making instructional decisions in public, and with public input.

Population Movements Shifts

Growth or Decline in District Size   District leaders can be challenged both by rapidly growing and by rapidly shrinking districts. Many school districts have experienced huge population growth that has exceeded their capacity to build enough schools and to staff the schools once they are built. One issue facing a growing district is having the ability to build new schools or expand older ones. Closely related to building or expanding schools is managing class sizes. When schools are crowded, class sizes increase and teachers become frustrated with trying to manage these huge classes instructionally and behaviorally. Parents become dissatisfied as well. Keeping class sizes at an acceptable level poses challenges. In a rapidly growing district, the numbers continue to increase; district leaders must offer assurances to constituents that the class size issue will be taken care of next year, and oftentimes next year is many months away. One superintendent commented that this situation can create anxiety and frustration, which can cause a lot of positive feelings to "go right down the drain."

School districts have to go to the public to urge them to vote on bond issues to build new facilities. This responsibility is huge for district leaders, who must spend time providing the community specifics on why they need increased property taxes to build new facilities. You may spend many hours speaking to individuals and groups about the need for new or upgraded school facilities or recruiting others to do the speaking for you.

Conversely, other districts face shrinking populations (and tax bases), which makes it difficult to provide the funding necessary to provide services. After all, when a family leaves a district, they stop paying taxes in that district, but the cost of maintaining the building they attended remains the same. And, ironically, districts may face declining growth in one part of the district and huge enrollment increases in another part simultaneously. Such a situation can create jealousy among different communities and also among board members who represent those communities—another challenge that can result in a power struggle. When new schools are built in one area of the district while another area continues to deal with older, more outdated facilities, people can complain about being treated unfairly. But you may find this to be an opportunity as well as a challenge. A superintendent from a suburban district stated,

> In our area, one magisterial district has all brand new schools in it, so they are all state-of-the-art bells and whistles. The advantage is that we can use this situation to create a climate for equity that enables us to go back and modernize the other schools and I'm not sure that we would have had a lot of the funding approved to renovate and upgrade [the older] schools had there not been new schools on the scene that sort of presented the new benchmark.

On the other hand, you may have to sell the public on the fact that some variation among schools is desirable, at least with regard to programs. In reflecting on the future of new schools and new programs and the need to be fiscally responsible, a superintendent from a large district commented,

> We have three high schools right now. We have a fourth one on the books and we have a fifth one in our vision. We have great programs available in the first three schools and I expect to replicate that in the fourth school. But there has to be a day when the leadership of the community agrees that what we will do is focus our efforts on exemplary programs in certain centers within the county and make that available to all students as opposed to expecting that we can spend [money] to replicate everything the exact same way in each school.

These two examples demonstrate how the creation of *model schools*, combined with long-term strategic planning, and skillful selling of ideas can help deal with population growth.

Racial, Cultural, and Linguistic Diversity   Coupling rapid student population increases with increased diversity poses additional challenges for district leadership. A superintendent from a suburban district summarized the quandary of increased diversity and rapid growth that can lead to student behavior problems:

> When you combine more [diversity] with overcrowding, there is a tendency to believe that there are more problems than there really are. We want to sort of demonize certain people or attach those problems to certain people and the fact is, when you put 50 percent more kids in a building than belong there, I don't care who they are. When they are bumping one another constantly and they are 13 years of age, the types of behaviors that do erupt will erupt. It doesn't matter who the children are.

These diversity issues affect school board members as you try to be respectful and responsive to different constituencies in the district. English-speaking parents who might be upset with low test scores brought about by students lacking English proficiency and ethnic-minority parents who are disillusioned with huge achievement gaps between minority and Anglo students both have concerns that need to be heard. These achievement-gap issues can create community splits and often cause groups to look to charter or private schools to address their concerns. Such community conflict presents huge political challenges for board members who must maintain support for the public schools while trying simultaneously to address the concerns of different factions in the community.

Another diversity challenge faced by district leadership is finding highly qualified teachers, particularly minority teachers, to serve as role models to minority children. A superintendent stated,

> I'm not sure we are seeing good teachers in all the schools. I think over a period of time, we see the good teachers gravitate to the good schools and so we end up sometimes with a lot of poor teachers at schools that are not performing well, and that only exacerbates their problem.

In many communities, minority parents are demanding that districts hire more minority teachers and administrators. This is a great example of how district leaders need to be responsive both to external mandates of the federal government (such as NCLB's highly qualified teacher requirements), to which we will return shortly, and internal community expectations (such as a more diverse faculty). Leaders who fail to meet their responsibilities to either group are likely to face an uphill struggle in creating and maintaining high-quality schools in their districts.

Fluctuations in the National and State Economies

A parallel trend to that of increased accountability and public attention over the past 5 years has been that of general economic decline. As the nation has grappled with economic malaise following repeated cycles of recession, so have school districts across the country. Educational leaders have had to deal with reduced funding, the need for budget cuts, and local conditions that are not supportive of tax increases. Local reluctance to bond and levy initiatives is common, despite the public identification of lack of financial support as a problem facing the schools (Rose & Gallup, 2005). Such conditions create perhaps the greatest challenge that superintendents and school boards currently face. In the words of one frustrated superintendent,

> We have high expectations and more demanding people. . . . We have an eroding tax base. A mill today brings in $100,000; a mill five years ago

brought in $105,000. We are losing hundreds of thousands of dollars a year in tax base while the cost of running the operation is going up. I do not see any way out to correct that situation.

Correction may indeed not be possible, but *adaptation* is a necessity. Eroding tax bases were common complaints from many of the superintendents we interviewed. Even in situations where the tax base was not in decline, increasing costs often exceeded existing resources. This was particularly true in rural and residential areas. A superintendent of a rural district remarked,

> There are only two towns [in the district] and there are less than 6,000 people in each town. There is only the personal property tax base, there's no industry in either town—none. In each town there's only one place where you can even use a charge card, and those are gas stations. No commerce here—it's just a very rural—affluent—but rural setting.

These economic trends, of increased expenses paralleled by tightened local budgets, are often compounded by shrinking slices of state funding going to public education. The result is that many districts face extremely high performance expectations imposed from state and federal sources yet often have significantly reduced revenue for financing their efforts.

Increasing Legal Constraints and Students' Needs for More Services

Often, in trying to help students, districts can put themselves at risk from lawsuits from those for whom they are trying to provide. Rather than thinking of what is best for the child, the family, or the school community, district leaders often have to make decisions based upon legal necessity or expediency—at least, they often feel as if they must. Ironically, these concerns over running afoul of the law or opening oneself up to a lawsuit come at the same time that superintendents and school boards find themselves in the position of needing to provide more services to students. Our public schools are asked to provide an increasingly broad range of services to students and families, often within the context of shrinking budget resources and these increased legal constraints. These services often go well beyond the "three Rs" and may present great legal obstacles to schools as well. Districts must often tread lightly in trying to further the interests of particular students while working within a rather limited legal framework.

Superintendents note that legal conditions regarding public education have intensified over time. Some go so far as to classify legal concerns as *constraints* upon their action, as this quote from a superintendent shows: "We just live in a litigious situation in our society and rather than becoming the risk takers that perhaps we would have been, it's always with the caution flag up. 'How might this get us in trouble?'"

In addition to being concerned about how they work with individual students and families, districts must also be vigilant regarding their compliance with state and federal policy mandates for many other areas of education. From curriculum to student performance to teacher quality to student safety to special education, school districts must "walk the line" and adhere to policy. Failure to comply or perform may lead to serious consequences and sanctions that affect everyone in the district. Few districts have the internal expertise to interpret every complexity and legal nuance of the intensified policy environment in which they find themselves. This environment is also constantly changing as state and federal guidelines are modified and adjusted.

Finally, in many districts, particularly those in urban areas, powerful teacher unions wield great influence over district operations. The legal context of contractual relationships between teachers and districts is often such that district leaders feel yet another limitation on their capacity to initiate needed reforms and changes. Unions exist to protect the professional interests of teachers, yet they can create another challenge to leaders trying to respond to conditions that are already quite complex and rapidly changing. District leaders in these contexts must strive to develop strong collaborative relationships with teacher unions in order to facilitate positive change for the benefit of students.

INTERNAL CHANGES

Increasing Political Activism

One of the most obvious manifestations of power struggles is that political activism, especially local political activism, seems to be on the rise, and as we noted above, this may stem from movements of people into and out of the community. Activism may wax and wane, as Thomas Alsbury explains in chapter 11, but it will not go away. Activism affects how you will lead. Its bright side is that it can support you in leading the way to better schools. Its dark side is that it can buffet you "on every side with bolder, more powerful special interests that challenge every innovative policy idea" (Fullan, 2001a, p. 2). Your challenge is to build on the support and to deal intelligently with the buffeting.

As many of the upcoming chapters emphasize, one primary consequence of demographic change is a need for greater accommodation of community involvement and diverse input in our schools. For decades educators have called for more community support and participation. In the past the public, as well as policymakers, have often deferred to district leadership to maintain and develop our schools. That has changed a great deal. Education is very much in the public eye now. It is also a prominent and visible theme in local, state, and national elections. District leaders often find themselves scrambling to meet the needs and demands of parents and community members who now have more information and more choices about how their children are schooled. A veteran superintendent working in an urban district noted,

> I think school superintendents have to be more involved in the community now than they used to. I think community involvement is critical because you have to look at the entire community, not just the school from the standpoint of just being part of the school.

A superintendent from a small district said,

> [The superintendent is] talking with the commissioner, mayors, the lawyers, and the people coming into the town who are going to be big players on how the school district is running this way and all that. The superintendent has to be very alert. . . . Everyone is going to be looking to [the superintendent] for leadership.

In a rural school district, leaders should look to local sports, church, and other community events as opportunities to monitor and respond to changes. A superintendent from a district of 5,000 students stated,

It's getting to the point that we're going to have to change how we do business in the district and recognize that there's a constituency out there we
have to answer to; whether the board likes it or not, we have to at least respond back.

District leaders have the responsibility of facilitating the development of
a shared vision for education around fundamental interests that we all
share. Diverse groups of people watch schools more closely, advocate
for their interests more vocally and with better information, and expect
schools to listen. Individual school board members must balance their
representation of their own constituents with their need to decide as a
unit for the benefit of the entire district. Thomas Alsbury will develop
this idea more in chapter 11.

Weaknesses, shortcomings, and outright failures are bound to be seen
and responded to much more vocally by concerned groups. However,
this level of participation in our schools by a broader spectrum of citizens offers an opportunity to harness the benefits of this increased attention for the good of the children. A public that scrutinizes the schools
and is invested in the outcomes is more likely to attend to school district
success stories. They are more readily available for input, dialogue, and
support. The audience is there; it is up to district leaders to engage the
public meaningfully. Eduardo Arellano develops this idea in chapter 12.

Engaging people plays out differently in communities. One rural superintendent told a story about his puzzlement, during his initial training, at having to accompany an experienced superintendent to breakfast,
to eat sausage and grits with several community members. After the
breakfast, the experienced superintendent remarked, "Now you understand, we just sealed the budget and I just took care of three or four
other problems and did more business at that diner than I will accomplish the rest of the day." The neophyte learned an important lesson that
day about a way to do business effectively in his community.

A superintendent from the South told how he established ties: "I go
to about 62 churches and it is rare that I am not asked to sing a song."
Ramón Domínguez writes in chapter 7 about how board members and
superintendents can support each other in learning how to work with
the community. Mary Devin, Teresa Northern Miller, and Trudy Salsberry provide more helpful advice in chapter 13.

A superintendent shared with us his experience taking a course entitled "Power, Politics, and Conflict: Daily Medicine of Superintendents." This course included panels of superintendents who spoke about their daily experiences in power and politics. The course's greatest value, he pointed out, was in conveying the message that conflict and power is what leadership is all about. For example, one superintendent related this story:

> We had a conflict over who was going to be in control of the athletic program, whether to turn it over to the Booster Club or not. I've never had to bring attorneys to meetings with parents before, but these were wealthy and powerful voices in the community and they brought their personal attorneys with them. The most helpful thing that happened was that many other community members got involved and told the group to back off. I'm not sure the board and I could have done that alone.

Superintendents get fired and board members lose elections over politics—over not being able to read the politics of the community and not engaging in coalition building. There are many groups that compete for time, attention, and dollars. A successful board and superintendent team must be able to read the signs and build partnerships in and across communities.

Reductions in the Deference Paid to Individual Leaders

The evolution from appointed school boards to elected school boards has created a change in their composition. This changed school board composition has altered the role of the superintendent as well by reducing the power he or she once had. An experienced superintendent from a large district commented, "The biggest change I've seen is the respect in which people in a bygone time held positions of authority."

Although superintendents are compelled to be much more collaborative now than in the past, they are still ultimately responsible for the success or failure of a school district; and school boards, of course, hold superintendents accountable. A superintendent from a large district summed up the role change:

> Every now and then somebody will say something [foolish] like, "It must be a pretty isolated role." It is the most crowded role I have ever had. The

traffic is pretty heavy. But a lot of that is needed because it is a group of people—not a person—anymore.

In the current era, leaders are expected to work collaboratively with parents, community, and politicians, oftentimes in communities that are split philosophically about the direction of the district. A superintendent from a large district commented on the leadership style necessary today:

The leadership style that superintendents have now is somewhat different from past years. My mentor, for example, was a very autocratic gentleman, a superintendent for many years, [who] taught me many things. I don't think he would survive in today's world.

Another veteran superintendent pointed out that both boards and superintendents have lost the power to act alone:

It seems to me that with the adoption of education in everybody's political agenda, our role has changed depending upon whose agenda we are a part of. . . . I spent much more of my time in 1991 working directly with the local board—[a board] that felt like they were more in control of goal setting—direction setting—in the mission of schools.

There are, however, certain areas where it is still acceptable for superintendents to be somewhat autocratic. In areas such as school safety or health and welfare issues facing the district, superintendents are expected to be strong and decisive. The challenge for board members is how to react when superintendents find that they must make a quick decision on a safety issue or other crisis without consulting board members. It is important to superintendents that board members have confidence in them and respect that there are times when this kind of situation occurs. At times, it is crucial to demonstrate that the board is unified and behind the superintendent.

Increasing Reliance on Technology

Many educators and community members expect big things of technology and judge a district by how well it seems to use technology. As Montoya and Ivory (2005) pointed out,

On the instruction side, some expect technology to (a) give students access to a greater wealth of learning materials and opportunities for productive interactions with others, (b) foster more engaging and challenging forms of pedagogy, (c) enable longer and more flexible work periods and more cross-disciplinary learning, and (d) facilitate students demonstrating their learning in a greater variety of ways. (p. 321)

On the administrative side, they expect technology to help with "accounting for funds, supplies, pupils and their grades; helping them plan and manage time better; enabling them to update their knowledge of research and best practices; facilitating the analyses of management information; and improving communication among educators and learners" (p. 321). The potential impact of board and superintendent decisions about technology can overshadow many other decisions because of the high visibility and high costs of technology integration (Radlick, 1998). Equity concerns and fears that our nation faces a "digital divide" further complicate your task. One superintendent said,

Technology is just encompassing all of our schools and the schools that are not going to become high tech are not going to be around . . . and that creates other inequities with the students that have technology and students that don't, so [the gulf between] the haves and have-nots gets bigger.

Coupled with other inequities, such as in programs and achievement, perceptions of technology inequities create tensions within the district among various constituencies and you must address them.

Boards and superintendents must also consider how technology will change the classroom of the future. The important point for you in the integration of technology is to make sure that whatever approach you take, you have given sufficient thought to your district's needs and financial capabilities and what you intend to accomplish with technology. A disjointed technology plan that is not well integrated with curriculum, instruction, assessment, and administrative needs can cause more problems than not having enough technology (Wiburg, 2001).

Increasing Concerns Over School Security and Safety

School leaders have probably always had some concern for school safety, but recent school shootings, reports of educator sexual misconduct with children, and incidents of bullying and predation over the Internet have raised people's concerns about the possibility of their own children being victimized. There are other safety concerns besides school violence. Increased environmental hazards such as asbestos, radon gas, lead, toxic air, mold, and other hazards have an impact on the safety of school buildings. These hazards require you to find additional monies to remove such hazards. Moreover, heating, ventilation, and air conditioning systems must be repaired and updated.

In chapter 7, Ramón Domínguez advises you on how important it is that you strive to learn all aspects of your role. We believe that environmental- and climate-control considerations represent additional issues where you must take charge of your own learning and spend time reviewing the issues and determining the priorities for your district.

It is important that community members perceive the schools as safe, and, in fact, most schools are safe most of the time. But as one superintendent pointed out to us, incidents of school violence are like airplane crashes. Once an airplane crashes, it is on everybody's mind and everyone is panicked. This is one more area where you may need to involve school staff, parents, and other community members in discussions about school safety, despite the enormous amount of time this can take. District leaders must frame school safety in a way that shows that most students are safe most of the time and that educators are working to keep them that way. You have to figure out how best to raise safety issues without causing panic.

Reductions in Availability of Human Resources

As Faye Patterson notes in chapter 6, district leaders face increased challenges related to human resources. With the NCLB legislation, securing highly qualified teachers becomes more urgent. Teacher contracts, teacher retirements, and induction programs for new teachers challenge most school districts. Shortages of principal candidates exist in many districts and states, creating a leadership vacuum (Whitaker, 2003). The fact that large numbers of teachers and administrators are retiring compounds your problem. A superintendent from a large district shared the quandary that he and the board face in the next couple of years:

> I have almost 30 years in the state retirement system; I have five assistant superintendents who are in their mid- to late fifties; all of them are eligible to retire at any time. Coupled with board turnover in the next couple

of years due to term limits, I have to really focus attention on succession concerns.

You must think not only about the leaders you have now but also about who will succeed them. As school district and community leaders, you must work to ensure continuity of leadership, meaning that you have to nurture and encourage and provide experiences for those who are identified as promising administrators and board members. A superintendent commented, "The quality of administrators today coming in to the profession is not as strong, and certainly not as many people are even applying for the vacancies that were, at one time, considered plum positions."

One reason for a lack of administrative candidates includes salaries that are too low for the responsibility. If prospective administrators stay too long as classroom teachers, at a certain point, they are likely to make a lower per diem salary as administrators than they would if they continued as classroom teachers. Then they question whether they want to work longer hours and during summers for less money per day. Board members must be astute in keeping up with the salaries within their state and regionally so that they can attract and retain high-quality administrators. This can create a delicate balance when so many other competing issues also require additional dollars. At this point, we refer you to Faye Patterson's advice in chapter 6 on ways to make the most of district human resources.

RECOMMENDATIONS

One highlight of this chapter, based both on our own understanding of change and the words of the superintendents, has been the necessity of tailoring solutions to specific local contexts. Therefore, leaders must be intimately aware of the stakeholders in their districts and in particular must be aware of the learning needs of their students. That has always been the justification for having districts led by lay boards of local citizens. But, despite the importance of context, we also call your attention to some generalizations.

Leaders may differ with one another over how tightly they should hold on to authority and power, how much information they should share, and how much they should include others in decision making. We argue that whatever one's beliefs, changes inside and outside the district have redistributed authority and power, access to information, and people's ability to insert themselves into district decision-making processes. We suggest that the following general principles can lead to more successful leadership in such a world.

Our suggestions revolve around the related ideas of communication, collaboration, proactive vision, and facilitation. In the area of *communication*, district leaders must work to establish and maintain a focus on student learning, and must facilitate the articulation of knowledge throughout the district. In addition, leaders must also promote coherence within a climate that is also receptive to diverse input. Coherence means bringing people to common understandings of what is at stake in public education and how they can contribute to better education. Receptivity to diversity can be developed by modeling an attitude of inclusion in all of one's professional actions and through engaging diverse elements of the community in conversations about the schools. These strategies of communication serve to convey a clear message of the vision, goals, and objectives of a district focused on the learning of all students.

Communication is critical, but it must also be tied to clear structures and values of *collaboration*. What is communicated must be a collective product of the educators and citizens in a district, not simply a commanding vision from above. To build a culture of collaboration, involve faculty and staff in short- and long-term strategic planning; actively seek the input of others; build partnerships throughout the organization and the community; implement models of distributed leadership (Spillane, 2006) throughout the district and schools; seek common ground on district goals through collaborative interaction; and link all efforts to student learning.

During times of dramatic change, leaders must possess certain personal qualities as well. One critical personal quality is *proactive vision*. Although clairvoyance would be helpful, in the absence of such an extrasensory power, there are still some things that leaders can do to be more prepared for future developments. Simply being a *news junkie* can be helpful. Staying aware of social, economic, and political trends keeps us aware of major policy, financial, and cultural issues that are likely to eventually affect schools. Leaders can, to a certain extent, see change coming and incorporate this into their long-term strategic planning.

Along similar lines, it is also important to be a lifelong learner and not neglect one's own professional development. Leaders who keep seeking out new learning experiences are able to stay more up to date and in tune with new research, programs, and technology. Based on their learning, these leaders are in a better position to make tough decisions aligned with district objectives—and to back them up with a sound rationale grounded in awareness, knowledge, and logic.

A final component of proactive vision is for every district leader actively to plan how he or she will balance personal life with professional. District leadership can be incredibly time consuming and personally draining. The long-term planning of leaders needs to include how their personal lives will not become marginalized by their professional responsibilities. Colleagues need to be supportive and facilitative in helping their peers achieve this balance.

Finally, once the lines of communication are open, a spirit of collaboration has taken root, and a proactive vision has come to characterize district leadership, the hard task of implementation must occur. Implementation of goals and objectives is ongoing, but the earnest work of program development and enactment requires special efforts in the area of *facilitation* from district leadership. Strategies that our superintendents identified in this area included the alignment of training and collaborative activities with goals and objectives related to student learning priorities; the development of model schools as exemplars for districtwide school improvement processes; the visible promotion of district goals through hiring and staffing decisions; striving to maintain stability and continuity in district and school leadership positions; avoiding micromanagement of individual schools and classrooms; expecting that district leaders will demonstrate strong interpersonal and human relations skills; and active support and facilitation of the success of other district leaders.

It is in these areas of leadership that superintendents, school board members, and other district and community leaders must concentrate their energies in order to develop the capacity to meet many of the challenges of this era of change. We hope that this long list of strategies does not overwhelm you. It is meant, instead, to be viewed as a source of encouragement and inspiration. There *are* district leaders across the nation who are successfully dealing with aspects of the difficult challenges outlined in this chapter. Change is not easy, but it is likely to be handled more effectively when district leaders actively communicate with others, encourage and model collaboration throughout their district, develop a proactive vision for responding to change, and facilitate the development of programs and practices aligned with district objectives that have emerged from such a culture of cooperation and informed planning.

The internal and external changes school boards and superintendents face are daunting. School district leadership in an era of change engages leaders in problem solving perhaps through a wider lens and with more people engaged in decision making than does leadership in more stable times. Within the view of controlling information and limiting access to who is engaged in decision making, dealing with unrelenting and multi-faceted change is overwhelming. However, if we juxtapose an emergent model of leadership in which control becomes secondary to dialogue about how to define and solve problems around an agreed-upon set of principles and values, then the job becomes less formidable. As Michael Fullan wrote, you will find yourself leading more powerfully than ever before, and "the rewards and benefits will be enormous" (2001a, p. 11).

2

SUCCESS STRATEGY: SELL THE VISION

Edith A. Rusch

Developing a vision for the future is exciting work. Dreaming forward, imagining ideal states—not hard tasks for people who live in a country that made it to the moon and back. We tend to be great at ambition, but a quick look at the poor results from early vision statements developed in the 1980s suggests that our first efforts to dream forward did not include the hard work of selling our educational dreams. Essentially, selling a vision is comparable to an Olympic quest. We can envision an ideal such as standing on a platform and receiving a gold medal, but the actual work of getting there is not a dreamlike task. It involves hard work and heartbreak, constant surprises and adjustments, intentional and targeted growth, and, usually, a great deal of money.

This chapter focuses on the challenging work of selling a vision of extraordinary educational outcomes to a community. The chapter begins with a short history of school district *vision work* in order to explain how the *selling work* has changed since the passage of No Child Left Behind (NCLB). Next, drawing from superintendent voices, school websites, and published accounts from around the country, you will find ideas, examples, and suggestions for the actual work of *selling* educational ideals. Finally, following the premise that the marketing and selling of an educational ideal is decidedly different for today's school board members from what it was in the past, you will find some thoughts on what a superintendent from Virginia described as "the need for a statesmanship role" from civic leaders who care about the quality of education for our children.

A SHORT HISTORY OF VISION WORK

The development and selling of a vision is a recent phenomenon in the history of school governance. In fact, until the release of *A Nation at Risk* (1983) and the establishment of over 270 school reform task forces and commissions, most school boards worked with the superintendent to develop, or merely approve, a set of yearly goals and objectives to guide district operations. That all changed when *A Nation at Risk* led others to release a barrage of reports that documented declining test scores, decreasing skills in the workforce, and defeat in international scholastic competition. Within a few short years, school boards and school leaders across the country responded to the barrage of criticisms by adopting the private sector practice of strategic planning.

Public schools gained familiarity with and expertise in strategic planning through the American Association of School Administrators (AASA), which advertised strategic planning as "a concentration of school district efforts and resources on agreed upon goals" (AASA, 1988). The organization suggested that, through strategic planning, a microcosm of the school community could define common beliefs and reasons for being and then identify the key objectives and strategies that would "control their future—to direct, rather than be tossed by, the winds of change" (AASA, 1988).

The process of strategic planning fostered two practices that, for most school districts, were not commonly used. First, strategic planners began to engage a wide variety of district stakeholders in a common conversation. For many educators and community patrons alike, this was the first time each had had a serious conversation with the other. Second, the planning process required the stakeholders to create an "ideal vision" for schooling in order to project a desired state that would guide the direction and actions of the district organization for, at least, the next five years. School districts who engaged in strategic planning

2 4   EDITH A. RUSCH

interpreted the process as creating "imperatives," "blueprints," "visions," and a "recasting of problems as opportunities" (Rusch, 1992). The statements below, collected for a nationwide study of strategic planning, are examples of the visions derived in a variety of school districts during the late 1980s.

- Our children are the message we send to the future.
- We are preparing productive citizens for the 21st century.
- The future is not some place we are going to but one we are creating.
- The paths are not to be found but made, and the activity of making them changes both the maker and the destination. (Rusch, 1992, p. 1)

Few of us would argue with these lofty visions, and despite our complex and often large-scale community efforts to envision a better future for schooling, few of these plans led to major improvements in the achievement of our children. In fact, an analysis of 1,134 belief statements, the guiding frameworks for these blueprints of the future, found that only 34% of the statements actually related to the education of children. The remainder of the visions for schooling and education either reflected the relationship between school and society (for example, educated citizens are essential for a democratic society) or our values (for example, joy is essential to the quality of life; Rusch, 1992).

In essence, when multiple and diverse stakeholders came together to develop a common vision for the future of our schools and the education of our children, we generally found it easier to agree on fundamental value statements and the connections of schooling to our social fabric than to agree on a vision for educating all of our children to high levels. A review of the action strategies in the vast majority of the plans found an overwhelming focus on the business of schooling: finances, governance, marketing, and efficient operations. While most plans identified graduation as a high priority (for example, 100% of our students will graduate by 1992), few identified comprehensive learning or teaching strategies to achieve that goal. In fact, a few years later, a superintendent identified community (students,' teachers,' parents') expectations for achievement as one of his most vexing problems.

Selling visions was not totally ignored in the 1980s. Districts produced slick and businesslike documents, provided employees with business cards imprinted with the vision text, painted the vision statement on schoolhouse walls, added the statement to all school publications, and in some cases, had everyone memorize the statement so it could be recited on demand. However, implementation of strategic actions that would lead to actualizing the visions was spotty. The failed efforts were described by one superintendent as "not so much as [not] having a plan but putting it on the shelf and not following our plan."

Despite a vast number of visions to graduate 100% of our high school students (Rusch, 1992), the messages we were sending to the future included disparate achievement for students from lower-class backgrounds, inequitable achievement in math and science for women and minorities, burgeoning dropout and graduation rates for nonwhites, and dramatically different postsecondary routes for some minority populations (Good & Brophy, 1987; Oakes, 1985; Winfield, 1986). To a large degree, our weak visions of the 1980s, or our less-than-fruitful efforts to sell these visionary ideas, may have fostered the passage of NCLB, a policy that has totally changed vision work for local school districts.

A NATIONAL VISION REPLACES LOCAL VISIONS

Today we face a scenario not unlike the responses to 1983's *A Nation at Risk*. Once again, NCLB has led to an avalanche of criticisms and reform strategies; however, this time, the criticisms reflect actual data about student achievement. In fact, the data are about our local kids. *A Nation at Risk* was far easier to dismiss because we could believe it reflected experiences in schools outside of the local district. NCLB's stringent reporting requirements, on the other hand, do not allow any of our schools or districts to withhold achievement data from public view, thus exposing our local successes and failures in ways quite unlike any other policy change.

This event alone has redefined the work of school boards and superintendents across the country. A superintendent from the Mid-Atlantic region referred to "the myth of local control." When one compares visions/missions set in the previous decade with those emerging since 2001, the shift is stark. Jim Hager, former superintendent of Washoe County Schools in Reno, Nevada, noted that national and state legislative actions now require a focus on product/accountability instead of process/opportunity (personal communication, 2006). Essentially, NCLB has established a national vision that local school boards are expected to sell and enact. While local boards still engage in long-term and strategic planning, vision statements now reflect a national goal: to increase the achievement levels of all children, ensuring that, indeed, no child is left behind.

Several examples of contemporary vision/mission statements follow:

- Tucson Unified School District is a professional learning community that ensures every student learns, exceeds all expected performance standards, graduates, and is able to compete and succeed in a global economy.
- Naperville Community Unit School District Vision: Building a Passion for Lifelong Learning—Our mission is to educate students to be self-directed learners, collaborative workers, complex thinkers, quality producers, and community contributors.
- Cherry Creek School District Vision: Dedicated to excellence—To inspire every student to think, to learn, to achieve, to care.

For most of us, the educational vision established by NCLB represents a far greater *sales* challenge. While few argue the merits of this goal, it presents today's school board members with a twofold challenge. First, your task is to sell a vision that some would argue is an impossible ideal and not always in the best interest of our children. Second, you are charged with selling an ideal that was determined by policymakers in Washington instead of local stakeholders. Several superintendents in our study spoke about a sense of powerlessness among local officials because, as a superintendent from the Mid-Atlantic region said,

So many others are dictating the agenda . . . and that has changed our role because now we are responding to people that we don't interact with, we have no communication with, and literally have no influence over, and I think it has made us a little less powerful.

Any of you with sales and marketing experience know that successful selling requires a sense of influence on and connection to the vision and goals of the organization. So selling this highly politicized vision to yourselves and to your local constituents is challenging.

In an effort to assist you with selling a vision that has been set outside the local school community, next you will find a variety of strategies that school board members, school administrators, and community groups have used to move their districts toward a highly desired state of education. First, you will find suggestions for engaging your community in an idea that they did not dream up. Next, you will see strategies for connecting local interests and needs to the national vision. Finally, you will find a vision for your role as school board members in this important endeavor.

STRATEGIES FOR MARKETING AN IDEAL

Any of you who have experience with marketing a new and unique product know that long before you actually sell anything you have to create a need. Once the public perceives the potential of "33% fewer cavities" or "fewer carbs," selling is easy. Many of you also understand how difficult it can be to champion new and unfamiliar educational notions. You know that if there is anything that makes school patrons nervous, it is change in their most familiar and treasured institutions.

Any of you who have ever proposed or supported changes in school calendars (for example, year-round schooling) have experienced how difficult it is to shift the public's mental models of schooling. Most often, an understanding of the need for change is lacking and the benefits of the change are too far into the future to be perceived as important. One superintendent suggested an approach, noting that communities and school districts are

> rooted in tremendous traditions. . . . If you're going to do anything at all, in terms of making progress or making change, you have to validate those traditions and then work with people to begin to move ahead, while not totally casting them aside.

The most challenging part of marketing a vision is helping a community to understand the importance of supporting a pathway to an uncertain future. The primary task of marketing educational visions is convincing community members, both inside and outside the schoolhouse, that change is a continuous process. One barrier is that the general American populace today, from ages 5 to 85, has known schooling only in its present organizational form. With few exceptions, everyone attended an age-graded school until mid to late teens, studied specific subjects, and progressed from an elementary to a high school setting. Not many realize that the schools we know today were once a vision that evolved over several decades, pushed by changing demographics, economics, social concerns, and (yes) laws and policies. The story itself can be a useful tool for moving a community conversation into unknown and unpredictable territory.

You can start by thinking about the conversation in families, among teachers, and between administrators and school trustees at the turn of the 20th century. From 1850 to 1930, the landscape of the country changed almost daily with a burgeoning immigrant population, the rise of industry, and massive population shifts from rural areas to rapidly growing cities. New laws and policies, such as compulsory school attendance laws and child labor reforms, also changed the landscape and the mission of schooling. Political objectives varied. One goal was to decrease the class disparities between the haves and the have-nots, another was to Americanize the ever-increasing immigrant population, and still another was to foster the education of a workforce that could keep up with the rapid industrial changes.

Responses to these well-intentioned efforts, such as compulsory schooling, were not always positive. Again, try to picture an economically impoverished immigrant family's consternation over the loss of family income because the children were now required to stay in school until age 14 or 16. At the same time, more privileged parents probably wondered how their children could possibly relate to non-English speakers or children of factory workers. No doubt there were teachers and principals agonizing over how to teach children with different aspirations in the same classroom. These were the quandaries that faced school board members and policymakers 100 years ago. People like you had the vision to create and sell what we now govern. Your task is the same one—no less challenging, no less daunting, and no less crucial.

Somehow, between 1867 and the end of the Depression, a schooling system emerged that was widely accessible and responsive to diverse types of interests. By 1910, 13.5% of the population had completed high school, and by 1940, seven out of ten teens were attending high school, and 51% of them had graduated. That is the story of a well-marketed vision.

Several elements of this story provide hints for marketing today's vision to leave no child behind. First, consider the amount of time it took to modify hearts, minds, and organizational structures to develop the schooling system we know so well today. The work we face will be no different; it will encompass multiple terms of office for multiple board members or trustees. Second, try to comprehend the enormously complex social, educational, and organizational issues that had to be addressed and puzzled through in order to move from educating only a few in a classical manner to educating masses of children with divergent interests and needs. History books are filled with stories about the professional, policy, and community groups that met, deliberated, and designed a system of schooling. The work was accomplished by elected and appointed officials and educators intentionally engaging the community.

The standard system that emerged included age-defined grade levels, Carnegie units, separate subjects, self-contained classrooms, and professionally trained administrators. Today, criticisms of this highly developed system suggest it meets the needs of an industrial era that no longer exists. Those critics may be correct, but at the same time, if we take time to look at the activities of this historical time frame and reflect on the accomplishments of the collective, we may be awestruck by how this vision evolved into a reality. This brief slice of history also points out to us the need for widespread community engagement in order to evolve a new vision in a new century.

Engaging the Community

If anything stands out in our interviews with superintendents, it is their awareness of the changing nature of our communities and the need to actively engage the community. A veteran urban superintendent described the shift in school governance as moving from decision making and acting as a go-between for the different people and groups in the community to now working as a team in order to be effective. He described the community shifts as

More poverty, more wealth; we have more right-, more left-wing philosophies; we have the churches involved in terms of their beliefs and what they would like to see taught. We have lots of different legal things that we have to deal with. I just think the thing I notice most is our population that we serve is becoming more diverse, not only culturally, but socioeconomically, philosophi[cally]. . . . I think school superintendents have to be more involved in the community now than they used to. I think community involvement is critical.

The Annenberg Institute and the National School Boards Association have excellent ideas and resources for developing a community team and increasing public engagement. According to each of these groups, engagement and team building involve much more than sending out district newsletters and holding occasional advisory meetings.

Communication

Far beyond newsletters and brochures, the superintendents in our focus groups used media to reach a wider community audience. In the Southern region, a school district leader indicated that her "newspaper [was] willing to let [them] have a whole page once a month" to communicate with her public. High school journalism students wrote most articles; this cost-effective approach probably increased readership. What parent or grandparent—or student, for that matter—will resist reading an article written by an acquaintance or family member? In her view, this practice supported communication with a growing nonparent population, whereas a district newsletter reached only parents. In the Mid-Atlantic, one superintendent scheduled "a live presentation on our budget [in order to] sell it to the public." Both strategies open the door to an increased information flow that is essential if you want community members to engage fully in understanding the need for an extraordinary vision.

Building Trust

In light of more federal and state control, the essential purpose and work of community engagement is to rebuild the public trust in public and local education. To a large degree, efforts to reengage citizens in schooling are more critical now than ever in our history. Once again, populations are on the move—across the borders of states and nations. Once again, the world of work is changing faster than the world of preparation for work. And once again, new laws and policies are troubling our citizens and diminishing support for public schools. A Midwestern superintendent described how, as communities change, school boards and administrators are challenged:

> The issues of those people who have been here and consider themselves the founders of this community and feel that they have a voice and should be running things when, in fact, there is a new group of leadership in the community and there's resistance to accept that new group of leaders in our community.

Part of the vision-selling work is the development of trusting relationships among groups with competing interests.

In the Mid-Atlantic and Southern regions, district leaders described complicated relationships between school boards and county boards of supervisors. In some cases, the county board appoints school board members and plays a key role in determining budget resources. The Southern superintendent noted that the two groups "were never accustomed to sitting down in the same room." She scheduled a series of dinner meetings where "[both groups could] ask all their hard questions about the budget." She concluded, "I realize it's going to be a real challenge to keep that dialogue progressing . . . so they both feel they can trust each other."

Trust was also key for a superintendent from the South who described extensive efforts to communicate her vision by engaging civic groups like "the Lions Club and discussion of SOL's [student learning objectives] . . . using the example that all students will take Algebra II." She saw the notion that all students needed Algebra II as "a mind-boggling concept for some of the constituents in [her] community." In order to create a vision of high levels of math achievement for all students, she invested in creating a realization of the need among the people responsible for juggling limited local resources so they would make it a priority. That same superintendent also invited representatives of all local businesses in to discuss work ethic. Seeing the issue of work ethic as a joint concern, she proposed that collectively they "could come up with something that was mutually beneficial" and "would produce better employees" who understood the responsibilities of regular attendance and the importance of graduation.

A Vision Sales Force

Some superintendents and school board members still see *selling* as a superintendent's responsibility. Several superintendents we interviewed expressed personal ownership of the vision process, describing themselves, as one did, "as the person who has to be accountable. I don't think that you can count on the board or I don't think you can rely on other administrators. I think the superintendent has to do that." However, a recent study of school-community engagement by the Annenberg Institute for School Reform (Mediratta, 2004) found that school leaders who were too invested in their own power and authority to be secure in collective and collaborative engagement had great difficulty in attaining and sustaining community support. The examples that follow come from superintendents who have successfully outsourced the work of selling their vision by strategically engaging a variety of individuals and groups.

Engaging Teachers   Distributing responsibility for vision work was most prominent among superintendents of small school districts. A Southwestern superintendent was blunt, noting that the view of his role as the sole public relations (PR) person and seller of the school district vision was "unrealistic." In his view, teachers needed to be part of the process. He encouraged teachers to become familiar with policy and policymakers in an effort to make them "politically knowledgeable." His strategy focused on engaging a wider circle of people in the education of state legislators who were "making regulations and deciding on how much money you get to teach kids." A district administrator from the South noted the importance of directly engaging the key principles of major industries, describing the support and lobbying provided by high-level managers of a large high-tech firm. "They all won't come to a public hearing," he said, "but they will pick up the phone . . . to underline the importance of high-quality, first-class public education in a community."

Engaging Kids   Several Midwestern superintendents described strategies that engaged past and current students. After engaging the typical civic groups, one intentionally sought out "kids who did drop out of high school and [were] still in the community" and former students who had run-ins with the law in order to reflect with them on what would have made their situations better. Another individual in the same region engaged in discussions with students about test scores and discovered that few were taking testing seriously. In his view, students "have very good ideas about what is effective . . . and that's another stakeholder that we don't tap into nearly as we should." Keeping in mind that a vision is a long-term effort, selling future voters and policymakers the ideal of high achievement for all is a very wise sales strategy. This strategy may also *sell* young people a vision of future civic duty, even one day as school board members.

Engaging Advisory Councils   Advisory councils were another community-engagement strategy. Far beyond small issue-based community committees (typically focused on textbook oversight, sex education, or programs for the gifted), the advisory groups our superintendents described played a key role in selling the district vision. In one case, a Southern school leader interviewed "almost 200 people" to find community members who were interested in and supportive of the school district. She wanted "truth-tellers and . . . wanted it to be a real diverse group of people, not just the people who say good things but the ones who have axes to grind." She saw the diversity of viewpoints as helpful to surface issues and then in "communicating some of the solutions and generating support for . . . initiatives."

Another strategy described by one district leader was a community foundation formed to find additional funding for schools, but also to "cheerlead" for schools. Describing an "outlying board," a superintendent from the South talked about the contrast between her school board and this community group. In her view, "[The foundation's] cheerleading . . . allows the school board to take that hard look at what's happening in schools." To a large degree, these two complementary groups had built a bridge over the gap between process/opportunity and product/accountability, which was described above by Hager (personal communication, 2006).

The voices of superintendents have been consistent in the past decade; they see opportunities in the midst of chaotic change to bring communities back into education. One of our participants spoke to the current opportunity:

> There are things bringing adults back to school now in terms of technology and lifelong learning. So it's an opportunity for schools to get back to

an audience that has been disconnected for a while. So I think finding common ground, that's an approach I use. . . . If you sit and talk to people about change—"You've got to change, you've got to change"—they say, "Why do I have to change? I don't want to change; who likes change?" But if you talk with people about learning and if through learning they can see how things are different, then in effect you've accomplished what you set out to do when you said, "Let's change."

One superintendent provided a stark example of a serious community issue that had educational ramifications. He took advantage of the moment to

let people know that public education is an investment. . . . Not much thought was given to the dropout rate here, because it's a way of life in [our community]. But when we started talking about the fact that those dropouts stay in the community and now [a well-known appliance manufacturer] isn't taking dropouts anymore and you have to have some very refined skills to go to work for [that company], even if it's in the plant. You have to be able to do some things that dropouts can't do. So once we raised the level of awareness, people started to say we've got to do something about this and we ended up with a wonderful partnership.

This is a clear example of the vision-setting/selling partnership among schools, municipal leaders, and communities. You can learn more about such approaches from the Annenberg Institute for School Reform and the National School Boards Association.

FROM IMPETUS TO OUTCOMES

Community engagement efforts often begin when someone is farsighted enough to see the uncertainties of the emerging future. Here are some examples of how school districts engaged the community to prepare for the future.

In Gwinnett County, Georgia, a projection of dramatic enrollment growth and a decline in socioeconomic status led district officials to create a 24-member community planning group to identify standards for success at graduation in the district's schools. The group gathered input from over 3,000 parents, community members, and teachers; they identified key knowledge and skills and put a local assessment program in place in anticipation of NCLB standards. By all measures, Gwinnett County children are achieving at record levels, despite the changing demographics. More than 10,500 citizens now have been engaged in school improvement efforts (Georgia district, n.d.).

Rapid growth was also a key to Chula Vista (California) Elementary School District's efforts to increase community involvement. Chula Vista is a rapidly growing district that spent 18 months engaged with a diverse group of community members to "shape the future of the school district." Initial efforts led to a "Vision and Value" statement that includes the following:

- Families, staff, and our entire community are full partners, actively working in a collaborative manner for the benefit of each child's education. Together we have an investment in our District's Vision and believe a child's success equals our success. We ensure an environment in which everyone is valued and treated with dignity and respect.
- Everyone assumes responsibility for the success of the school community. The entire educational community accepts the challenge of change and is motivated to acquire skills and values for a rapidly changing world. We create dynamic learning experiences by supporting and encouraging excellent teaching and the educational growth of family and staff.
- The Chula Vista Elementary School District community is dedicated to instilling hope for the future so that today's children will share their vision with future generations. (Vision, values, n.d.)

With this as a guiding vision, students have support for achievement despite the challenges the district faces with its rapid growth. According to the superintendent,

We know that students who have been assessed in our District for three years or more score 36 percent higher than those who were assessed just one or two years on the California Standards Test. [Chula Vista Elementary School District] English learners with three years of state assessment results scored 73 percent higher than their counterparts with less school experience in our District. (Superintendent's welcome, n.d.)

Some efforts to engage the community in a vision start on a very small scale and grow in surprising ways. In Westminster, Colorado, board members began having conversations in people's homes in order to find out why so many families were leaving the increasingly diverse district. The key issue turned out to be a lack of emphasis on postsecondary attendance. As district officials responded to that need, they discovered that parent engagement increased. Now they hold suppers in schools, bring in facilitators to increase cultural understanding among new populations, and provide child care. At a recent meeting they ran out of food because attendance was so high. At each meeting, board members ask, "What can the schools do to make you feel more comfortable?" and responses to that question have led to connections with community services and academic events like family math nights (Small groups, n.d.).

Some efforts intentionally use both short- and long-term visions to change a culture. The San Jose Unified School District, suffering from a loss of community support, established a short-term vision to "attract and involve citizens in schools." Once community members began to participate and respond, the board set a long-term vision to "engage the public and produce higher student expectations, ongoing school community conversations, strategic communications planning, and user-friendly communication tools" (Public engagement, n.d.). Yearly community conversations and annual climate surveys with resulting action plans have paid off in annual increases in student and parent satisfaction, significant increases in student achievement, and the passage of bond issues.

In Chicago, a board president envisioned programs that would engage parents in urban school settings. A Power of Parents Conference, with parent workshops, motivational speakers, and community resources, drew 5,000 attendees. The next year, workshops were focused on teaching parents the district's standards for promotion to specific grade levels. The results: "In 2005, the district had the lowest number of students held back a grade since 1997 and record high test scores in reading" (Power, n.d.).

Not only are these powerful examples of how districts are achieving the vision of NCLB, each of these community engagement efforts was led by school board members who saw their role as civic rather than political. In fact, envisioning your role as a civic responsibility may be a key to moving beyond the sense of "powerlessness" that many local education leaders feel due to NCLB mandates.

A VISION OF STATESMANSHIP

The public service nature of board work provides you with a civic platform; you can raise expectations within the community and encourage citizens to engage in the community's future. Yet, your oversight role and the political nature of the work often overshadow the need for building a learning environment for the community. The work of schooling is so very public, and often emotion bound, that board members and administrators often get trapped into reacting and responding, thus losing sight of the important work of guiding and expanding the community's perspectives. When you look critically at how you spend your time as a board member, do you sometimes discover that you invest the most time in things that will least affect a vision for quality education for children?

"We have to in some way present to everyone around a bigger vision," one superintendent from a rural district said, observing, "In essence the arena we operate in [education and schooling] supports many systems within a system." An administrator from a Southern state expressed the goal as "looking for statesmanship." The superintendents we interviewed were fully aware of and increasingly troubled by the political challenges school board members face, particularly when reelection is at stake. But more than one superintendent expressed a desire to work with board members who have let go of their personal agendas in order "to assist all children." As described earlier in the chapter, this is a time when leadership and statesmanship are paramount if we are going to sell and enact a vision of all children achieving at high levels. Statesmanship and leadership require a shift in your views of power and authority, solid efforts to do active listening, and a commitment to collaborative thinking and doing.

MIND SHIFT: POWER

As noted earlier, the Annenberg study concluded that a sense of loss of power was the most prominent reason community engagement efforts moved so slowly. Large sections of communities may feel disenfranchised when community engagement is used as a political tool directed only to powerful constituents. Too often, this approach deprives many constituents of a voice. One superintendent talked about

> a few key people whom you really should listen to because they probably do have a pretty good pulse on what's going on. . . . Depending on the communities you're in, it can be someone with a lot of wealth. It can be somebody who owns a lot of land; it can be someone with a certain political position in the community; it can be someone who is a lifelong resident who has a lot of ties with other people, related-wise, in a lot of communities.

This may be an efficient approach, but it also runs the risk of ignoring important voices. While you may sell your vision to the powerful, a Mid-Atlantic leader pointed out that today we need "to understand . . . the way in which many individuals operate in society, from those that are very wealthy [to the] poor, and think [about] racial differences, class differences."

Jim Hager, former superintendent of Washoe County Schools in Reno, Nevada, asked his board members to develop personal visions. In his eyes, board members needed to express "a strong set of personal values—getting beyond the right words to a deep belief set." Once the board members had a sense of their own inner dreams, they were better prepared to "treat people with dignity, [do] right for each child and each employee—show an intensity. Not let anything get in your way to support students excelling" (personal communication, 2005).

SKILL SHIFT: LISTENING

The majority of superintendents we interviewed identified listening as a key skill and they acknowledged how hard the work of intentional listening can be in our increasingly politicized community environments (see

Eduardo Arellano's chapter 12 for suggestions on listening). Board members who truly have a vision of community engagement will find that a majority of superintendents understand the importance of practicing patience and quality listening. In fact, our data suggest that district leaders are actively seeking school board members who will partner and support expanding the voice of the public by being "good listener[s]. Keep communication lines open. Find ways to get people involved."

Based on the demographic changes across our country, I believe getting people involved requires new communication skills. In fact, vision selling today requires the same multicultural competence exhibited by leaders and statespersons during the last century. A Midwestern superintendent was clear that he "would rather have people knocking down [his] door to share concerns than stepping back and not being involved. They [the public] just want to be informed." The majority of superintendents interviewed recognized, like this Southern superintendent, that "people have a major need to be listened to and heard. All of us want to think that the things we believe and say are important. I think the need to be heard is the cry I hear."

ACTION SHIFT: GROWING AN EFFECTIVE COLLECTIVE

One other caution came from the Annenberg study: If the engagement process is experienced as superficial, temporary, or merely an image-enhancing effort, the end results will be ineffective for either selling or enacting a vision (Mediratta, 2004). Successfully selling a vision requires community engagement from the very beginning of the process. Kimpton and Considine (1999) concluded that promoting collective responsibility and accountability through leadership is about orchestrating the ideas, people, visions, and potential of diverse organizations into a program of educational improvement. To lead engagement efforts effectively, leaders should be concerned about who *is not* at the table as well as who *is*.

As a board member, you have the power and authority to set a new value: listening to and engaging with your community. You can establish an expectation that your sitting superintendent will increase community engagement and then intentionally and actively support his or her efforts or, if you are searching for a new district administrator, you can look for candidates who have demonstrated valuing community engagement and the ability to foster it.

Part of your statesmanship work may entail a reeducation process with your constituents about how a visionary board functions. In fact, a board can adjust its approach to governance by persistently and publicly asking how all decisions affect student outcomes. Members of the public may be used to bringing operational concerns to board meetings, expecting full discussion and resolution of a concern. Thus, you may experience criticism from public entities that have lost their open forum for complaints. It may take the public a considerable amount of time to change their expectations. Patience is key during this transition, but it is not the only thing that will help. The entire governing team must examine the communication links between the community and the district. Remember, the work of shifting a community's mind-set about schooling to a visionary concept of educating is akin to teaching a child to walk or coaching a teen to become more independent.

A role model and some instruction for the work can be found in the work of Mary Parker Follett, who initiated community engagement with the new immigrant population at the beginning of the 20th century. She had a passion for public life and democratic engagement, which she fostered using her *principle of unifying* (Follett, 1918). She established community centers in schools, giving her insights into the potential of education to support her views. She was convinced that the actions of unifying were dependent on citizens of all ages learning to practice interdependence, genuine discussion of differences, collective thinking, social consciousness, and self-direction.

Follett wanted schools and centers to promote an "attitude of learning to make them see that education is for life" (Toth, 2004, p. 370). Her experiences with group processes in the community centers led her to posit that a set of skills for "unifying" or "integrating" multiple ideas was a "secret that would revolutionize the world" (Follett, 1918, p. 97). You, as a board member, have the same opportunity today to revolutionize the world if you join forces with your administrators and community members to dream forward and work hard to achieve a new vision of educational excellence.

3

SUCCESS STRATEGY: PRIORITIZE AND DECIDE

Judith A. Aiken

I think it's important to step back and keep focus on what the district has identified as priorities, and you can always hang your hat on that instead of always trying to be everything for everybody . . . keep focused on your district priorities.

—Superintendent of a rural district

Decision making is the primary function of everyday leadership (Chance & Chance, 2002). Given the complexity of school organizations and changes occurring in the political, economic, and social life of many communities, boards and superintendents find themselves faced with many demands from multiple interest groups who want a stronger voice in school-related decisions and policy matters. Often, these demands come from interest groups who maintain dramatically different perspectives from yours (Bagin, Gallagher, & Kindred, 1994). Thus, you constantly have to decide among competing goals. No matter how wise and well crafted your district vision is, your success as a school board member and educational leader depends on your ability to make decisions under difficult circumstances.

Decision making involves allocation of limited resources (time, money, human resources, and knowledge) and organizational politics that often result in conflict among individuals and groups. Faced with strong demands from state and federal governments and from special interests, superintendents expressed concerns about how they were frequently pushed into mediating roles in conflicts where the quality of education in the community depended on their decisions. As a board member, you will also be placed in such situations when you are called upon to make key decisions on behalf of education in your school district. A superintendent from a medium-sized school district asked rhetorically,

> Where do you find that common middle ground? . . . How do you act in a moral and ethical fashion . . . and still find a place where you can work for the common good? . . . [In] every community you have people who say, "You've got to do it my way. Kids aren't learning the right things." . . . Sometimes you get to be the referee or umpire to sort all that out about how schools are going to run.

The superintendents in our study shared their views on the challenges of decision making. In our interviews, we heard how to make quality decisions in turbulent times while working to maintain the professional relationships with other leaders, staffs, and communities. The ability to stay focused on the vision or what is most important and to maintain your commitment to core values and beliefs about education and what is "good for kids" surfaced over and over again.

I argue in this chapter that all the tactics you use, all the "success strategies" spelled out in chapters in this book, should be in the service of decisions that will further the accomplishment of the district vision. Above all, you will need to know how to set priorities (vision) and how to stay centered as you work through the challenges of school governance. All of this also requires that the vision serve as the driving force for your planning, decisions, and actions.

To help you, this chapter develops four themes. First is the board's role as policymaker. Policies are most effective when written to reflect "ends" or outcomes (Carver, 1990; Oliver et al., 1999) that are consistent with the district's mission and with laws or other government mandates. Once articulated, you can base most, if not all, policies on the agreed-upon vision. As stated by Carver (1990), "Testing everything against mission becomes the standard check of organizational direction" (p. 195).

Second, every decision you face and action you take should be considered in light of policy and also of the district vision. One superintendent voiced how her own clarity about values served as "personal anchors" in order not to risk what Johnson (1996) referred to as "being swept away by professional fads or political currents" (p. 286). Third, you and all district personnel should consider what evidence is available to show how well you are doing at fulfilling the vision. Fourth, running across these three efforts must be your striving to create a culture that supports decision making. Major components of such a culture are trust and courage.

POLICIES THAT REFLECT YOUR DISTRICT'S VISION

As board members, you need to develop policies and procedures that are based on ends or the goals and outcomes you hold for the school district. In other words, such "ends policies" (Carver, 1990; Oliver et al., 1999) define what results an organization holds itself accountable for. In the flow and rush of events, it is easy to feel compelled to churn out policies that respond merely to federal or state mandates or to problems that have sprung up in your district or in the news. Sometimes, you must do that. But your decision making will be more coherent and should come more easily if you consider policies in terms of the big picture, your district vision.

DECISIONS AND ACTIONS IN LIGHT OF POLICY AND THE VISION

Given that crafting good decisions can be a "daunting task" as well as a "constant, if not relentless dimension of school leadership" (Davis, 2004, pp. 621–622), board members and other school leaders must have a sense of the goals or "ends" that they hope to achieve. It is this image of what "can be" that we call vision (Bennis, Parikh, & Lessem, 1995, p. 50). Once you have a vision, you promote it within the community, as Edith Rusch describes in chapter 2. But you promote it, not merely as part of a public relations campaign, but so that it can guide decisions and

actions within the district and influence all "practical functions of the
school" (Starratt, 2002, p. 20). In other words, you must be able not only
to articulate a vision for your school district but also to effectively communicate that vision throughout the organization and to make decisions
and take actions that are aligned with and in support of the vision.

Although making sure that the vision is printed on all school corre-
spondence and contained in all handbooks and manuals is important, as
a board member you must also test all decisions—about budgets, resource allocations, hiring, or curriculum changes—against the vision
(Carver, 1990, p. 195). One veteran superintendent put it this way:

> I think another piece—how you . . . create a vision and communicate that
> vision—then have all the pieces in place so it can be accomplished. And
> have the right people to help you get there. And I think that part is criti-
> cal because through the ups and downs of the daily work, if that vision is
> still out there and communicated, and the things are in place to make that
> a good place to work, you can accomplish it.

Faye Patterson writes in chapter 6 about how to get and develop "the
right people to get you there." I want to emphasize in this chapter how
important it is for you to align your decisions and actions with the vision.

The superintendents talked to us about the importance of converting
vision to action through strategic planning processes or action planning
and encouraging as much participation among school members as possible. For example, a number of superintendents in our study voiced
how "you need to be schooled in some good consensus-building
processes and in the best practices of strategic planning" in order to
make decisions that lead to positive changes. One superintendent described his growth in understanding this process:

> My first year was whatever came to the desk was a crisis and we had to
> deal with it. And now we're able to say: "Keep a focus on what we're try-
> ing to do as a district, and does that fit into our philosophy and goals, and
> if so let's deal with it. If not, then we can put it to the side . . . and let it
> ferment for a while."

One superintendent of a district of 1,650 students, for example,
talked about priorities as follows:

I learned long ago that you can't be all things to all people. For people like me, who are basically the type of individual that has a "pleasing" personality—that wants to do the right thing and please people—you can't always do that. You choose the course that you are going to pursue and, after whatever study or consideration you need to make, you move ahead with it.

Other writers in this book have developed the ideas of getting input, building consensus, and maintaining good relationships in your communities. I agree with their suggestions, but I argue that even these efforts involve decisions. After all, your success at meeting priorities often depends on your ability to make connections with those individuals who can help you meet your priorities.

Jinkins and Jinkins (1998) suggest that one way to consider how to make connections with others is to think of building networks that cultivate relationships with those who have a vested interest in the school and the particular priorities you have articulated (p. 155–156). Thus, as a board member you will need to make time for networking while being judicious with regard to the parties with whom you network so as to not spread yourself too thin or be at odds because of participating in networks with competing interests.

As board members, there is no doubt that you will need to engage in negotiation and bargaining. Skills in negotiation and bargaining are central to decision making. Negotiation is needed whenever two or more parties with some interests in common and other interests in conflict must reach an agreement (Bolman & Deal, 2003, p. 212). Successful negotiation skills are based upon some key principles, two of which received particular mention from our superintendents. One was to separate the people from the issue, and the other was to focus on common interests versus engaging in positional power struggles.

Often we heard how the superintendents try to stay positive and help people refocus on the issues versus the personalities involved in the conflict. Eduardo Arellano in chapter 12 develops these ideas more fully. As board members, your ability to stay focused on the "ends" you have defined and to engage in the art of constructive politics is critical to your success and can ensure that you will make the kinds of decisions needed, even in the heat of a politically charged environment.

CONSIDER EVIDENCE OF SUCCESS

"The most important work of any governing body," writes Carver (1990), "is to create the reason for organizational existence . . . which is the production of worthwhile results" (p. 56). Thus, it is critical that you work together to set out a plan for how you will monitor results. The evaluation and assessment of results is an integral responsibility for both the administration and governance of the district and needs to be "precise, systematic, and criteria-focused" (Carver, 1990, p. 76).

Your capacity as a board to engage with your superintendent in honest conversations requires that your entire board have opportunities to receive and consider important information through data-driven leadership (Rubin, 2002). In today's school districts, leadership and accountability are hand-in-hand. This means that as a school board member, you must peruse data and be willing to ask questions that evaluate the data in light of the priorities of the district.

Many of the superintendents discussed how quality decisions often resulted from using important sources of information or data for consideration. Thus, it is important that all board members have access to and use data, including data on student achievement, demographics, enrollment, and so forth, to shed light on important decisions that might need to be made, are being made, and have been made. By using such data, you will ensure that the trustworthiness of your decisions can build your capacity to work as a team with respect to setting priorities and acting in ways that are congruent with what the data tell you about your school district and are aligned to the vision.

Not only do you as board members need to adopt, evaluate, and update board policies that are consistent with the district vision as well as local and state standards, you also should adopt monitoring policies and processes for the superintendent and for yourselves to stay accountable for reaching desired ends or outcomes consistent with the vision. As Tom Alsbury notes in chapter 11, your actual evaluation of the superintendent can be less political and more helpful to both parties (board and superintendent) if it also focuses on the district vision and desired outcomes associated with that vision. Ealy, Hogan, Skrla, and Hoyle (2000) made it clear that tying evaluation to "political, subjective, and interpersonal relations with individual school board members" is unacceptable and that "improved training for board members on what the superintendent's job is all about and how to judge the success" (p. 257) of that work and job is needed.

I suggest that there needs to be a clear understanding among board members about the evaluation process and the criteria upon which the superintendent will be evaluated, and these criteria must be tied to the vision and outcomes upon which you, as a board team, have agreed. Ultimately, your success is tied to the success of the superintendent. As a team, you need to craft specific indicators of success that are both data driven and student focused. The identification of these indicators as criteria in which to gauge your success can help you as a board member, and the overall board as well, focus clearly on what you want to achieve so that both you and the board can engage in productive and purposeful evaluation.

Many of the superintendents talked about student success as the driving force for action and the need for aligning executive actions and decisions with vision. Your most important responsibility as a board member is to set a vision, commit to decisions and actions in accord with it, assess your success at achieving the vision by collecting and studying reliable data and perhaps adjusting decisions in light of the data.

Critical to your success as a board member is the ability to explore current data and use these data for decision making within the context of local community vision and values. As we listened to our superintendents, we learned that many have set out on a quest to research and gather data to illuminate what was "really going on" with students in their districts and to look for patterns or practices that might put some students at risk for failure. Several expressed their desire to work with others (such as administrators and teachers) to examine and interpret data.

For you as a board member, this could enhance collective inquiry and good decision making and make the data more meaningful. A superintendent of a suburban district said it this way:

> I look at the data that you mentioned earlier. We have periodic assessments over the course of the year. I ask the . . . director of assessment . . . for reports. . . .We look at the [assessments]; we look at the . . . preceding year. We make adjustments here; we make adjustments there. . . . For me, I'm looking at data. . . . I have meetings with the principals in those buildings.

. . . I want to know what they're going to do to fix it. . . . They need to utilize their staff and if they need assistance from central office, we're there
as a resource.

Thorough examination of data can lead to your facing hard decisions
in the interest of students. A veteran superintendent of a suburban district highlighted such a hard decision:

When you ask, "What can a superintendent do to foster student success?"
I think [there is] one we're overlooking, because this is the time we should
be looking at the data. If you're not seeing the success in certain buildings,
then we, as superintendents, have the responsibility in order to foster student success . . . to make adjustments to the staff. . . . So that's one thing
we can do as superintendents to foster student success. If the principal is
not getting the job done, get a principal in who will get the job done.

In addition to monitoring the district's success, a board might consider how to evaluate and improve its own effectiveness as well. For you
and your board colleagues, this accountability is what ties you back to
your communities—it is inextricably connected to your role as a leader
and how you prioritize and make decisions. It fosters trust by providing
the evidence community members need about the degree to which your
efforts attain results.

Since many superintendents in our study shared insights into the politically charged arenas in which they find themselves and how they
must engage in "constructive politics" to advance what is recognized as
the common good for all students, you, too, as a board cannot escape the
political arenas in which you govern. You will need to work within a
complex network of individuals and groups in your district to attain results and make decisions.

Since many administrators depend on their communities for resources to do their jobs, they are often enmeshed with external constituents who may or may not speak with one voice, thus making their
jobs as administrators difficult (Bolman & Deal, 2003, p. 229). Thus, by
constructing clear performance criteria and monitoring the performance of the school superintendent, as a board, you may actually help
yourselves and your superintendent navigate the political terrain you encounter each day and speak with one voice about what is important to

the community and district. At the same time, you can educate the community about how focusing on priorities succeeds in ways that promising everything to everyone cannot. (See William Ruff's and Robin Dexter's chapter 5 for further development of the idea of data use.)

CREATING A CULTURE FOR EFFECTIVE DECISION MAKING AND A CULTURE OF TRUST

The school board is the governing body in charge of the school district and is the body that hires the superintendent to run the district. Although most district leaders are well intentioned, sometimes complex situations can cloud your understanding of how to act on your good intentions. For example, perhaps you were elected to your board position feeling that you had to represent the interests of particular groups of students or parents in your district.

What often surfaces, you quickly come to understand, are narrow or more individualized perspectives or viewpoints with respect to important issues and problems. Efforts to govern according to what is best for the whole community may get lost as you attempt to intervene in the routine decisions about running the schools (Carver, 1990). First and foremost, as a school board member, you need to recognize and accept that you are obligated to govern effectively and that you sit in trust for the entire school district in which you serve, not just the community that elected you.

Board members realize quickly that their responsibilities can be daunting and that decision making in educational governance does not follow neatly in a well-structured and linear process. Board members and administrators occupy positions that are influenced by pressures and expectations that contribute to tough decision making. Often these situations eventually affect the public's perception of professional competence and quality (Davis, 2004, p. 625). More importantly, the ways that decisions are made set a precedent, affecting how people will choose to influence the system in the future to get what they want.

Your effort to foster trust and maintain courage in saying no to people develops the ability of district leaders to make the tough decisions needed; they know that you are supporting them behind closed doors.

Trust and courage can be seen as two sides of the same coin. People trust you if they believe you are reliable, and being reliable in the face of difficulties requires courage. In district leadership, courage plays out as making and sticking to decisions you believe are right and being forthright with people about your position.

If teachers, parents, school board members, and community citizens are going to support the vision defined for the school district, there must be a culture of trust among all participants. In order to engender trust, members of the school community must have no qualms about the openness, honesty, and trustworthiness of the board and superintendent; the community must feel the board and superintendent are working as a leadership and governing team together to achieve the same priorities (Fiore, 2001, pp. 136–137). One superintendent said,

> I have learned that it is better to tell someone the truth first than to say, "We will think about it." I've learned that over the nine years. If I know I am not going to do something it is better to say so up front. If you don't want someone back, the fairest thing is to tell them, "We don't want you back next year." I have learned that.

Quality decision making depends on you as board members and the superintendent working collaboratively as a leadership and governance team. While attending to your separate concerns, the board and superintendent must work jointly in an atmosphere of mutual trust and respect for each other's role. Your ability, together with that of the superintendent's and the overall board's ability, can serve to build and inspire trust in all members of the school community. This trust will be linked to your ability to be successful as a leadership team. Such trust evolves when you deal with important issues and attend to critical problems using honest communication and clarity about roles. Ramón Domínguez in chapter 7 develops this notion further.

To restate, superintendents in our study talked about how important it is to engage in open and honest dialogue and to work from a shared understanding of roles and responsibilities that would lead to clarity, consensus, and commitment to a district vision for student success. The first point to understand is that to achieve such trust, it is important that roles and responsibilities are clearly understood and adhered to by both parties—board and superintendent. As stated by Carter (1990), fundamental to success in government is "Clarity about roles and responsibilities between the board's job, the superintendent's job and the critical link between them" (p. 109).

As board members, it is important for you to examine such roles to ensure they are congruent, as far as possible, with state mandates, community perceptions, and district norms. In particular, it is important for you as a board member to delegate administrative and management functions to the superintendent as appropriate and not get "caught up" in the everyday management of the organization. In this way, you are in a better position to support what superintendents talked about in keeping the vision out front and being able to make difficult decisions by aligning actions with the agreed upon and shared vision.

Putting into practice all the ideas in this chapter may seem a tall order, but at no time in our history has the role of the board member been more critical to successful decisions that affect the outcomes of their schools. As the superintendent stated above, boards must make critical decisions about vision and potential course corrections. Superintendents benefit when boards act decisively and inclusively. We hope that the voices of the superintendents will help you define new learning and leading strategies so that you and your superintendent may become more effective decision makers, always with a goal of contributing to the growth, well-being, and learning of students.

4

CHALLENGE:
FOSTERING STUDENT ACHIEVEMENT

Robin Dexter and William Ruff

One way to think about education is to look at the connection between schooling and the needs of society. In the late 1700s and 1800s, America was an agrarian society. Americans thought of formal public education mostly in terms of basic reading and writing skills and sufficient knowledge of math to pay taxes and conduct business transactions. In the late 1800s and 1900s, we became an industrial society; more jobs required literate and skilled workers, schooling became compulsory, and vocational programs and elective subjects were added to secondary education. In the last half of the 20th century and early in the 21st century, we moved from an industrial society to an information- and knowledge-based society. How will schools meet these changing workforce requirements?

The increased demands of an information- and knowledge-based society require that all members of society be literate, have access to technology, know how to interpret data, and have the knowledge to use data in the decision-making process to increase the overall productivity and effectiveness of the work in which we are engaged. Everyone must be fluent in reading, writing, and problem solving. To achieve this, our public schools must develop a capacity unheard of in the generations that preceded us. It is not enough that all our children attend school and achieve minimal functional literacy; children must also achieve mastery in a variety of subjects—reading, writing, math, science, and social studies, among others. Recognizing the needs of an information and knowledge society, the No Child Left Behind Act of 2001 (NCLB) was created and implemented to improve public schools through standards and accountability measures to assess progress.

This chapter addresses the challenges of fostering student achievement. Some of our insights into these challenges come from interviews with superintendents, and we will often use superintendents' own words to illustrate our points. Understanding the challenges can help you work with your superintendent to ensure students achieve literacy and numeracy. In addition, understanding these challenges can help you lead students to develop critical problem-solving skills for the workplace, for citizenship, and for life in general. The superintendents' voices reveal their perspectives on the challenges of improving student achievement. We present these perspectives in four themes: (1) creating a vision and mission focused on instruction and learning; (2) exercising instructional leadership to implement the vision; (3) assessing student learning; and (4) building the capacity for equity, that is, ensuring a quality education for all students.

THE CHALLENGE OF CREATING A VISION AND MISSION FOCUSED ON INSTRUCTION AND LEARNING

As a board member, you should play a key role in the district by working with your fellow board members and the superintendent to formulate a vision and mission for the school district and then articulating the vision and mission to the rest of community. The vision is a statement of what you, as a board, expect students to know and be able to do after being educated in the district. For example, Ramaley (2005) defined an educated person as demonstrating these attributes:

- an ongoing love of learning and a curiosity about the world
- an ability to find creative and adaptive solutions to newly emerging problems as well as ones that are ever with us
- an understanding of how we know what we know and how to construct a warranted foundation for the claims we make about what is true

- an ability to use knowledge and acquire new understanding in a responsible way, mindful of the effects of our actions on others—a moral imagination, meaning the ability to take seriously the lives of other people and to be concerned about their well-being (pp. 66–72)

Your role as a school board member is to provide an appropriate education for *all* students that ensures the student can function as an educated citizen in society. Ramaley's definition can be the basis for engaging in dialogue with the superintendent, other board members, and members of the school community to define what it means to develop an educated person. The superintendent's role is to lead your board through a purposeful process of defining what educating all students means and determining what academic success will look like for all students in your community.

The mission is the road map for the district to follow to make the vision a reality. As Kathryn Whitaker and Sheldon Watson noted in chapter 1, one factor that makes this challenging is that federal and state mandates have taken away some of your ownership in this process. Anne Loring (2005), a former school board member in Nevada, believes, with regard to student achievement, that control has been taken away from the local school board. She believes this has happened for four reasons: (1) there was a loss of focus on the mission; (2) school boards failed to focus on results; (3) boards were reluctant to compare their district's results to those of other districts; and (4) local boards were not accepting responsibility for poor results. Turning this situation around begins with establishing a clear vision and mission. As one superintendent from a rural district put it,

> The ability to structure schools so that schools have optimum performance from your students . . . has to be visionary. It has to go past what you're doing and you have to take all that and have some mission for what you want your schools to look like—where you take your children.

Petersen (1999), in a study of superintendents as instructional leaders, found that superintendents strongly supported the establishment of a vision or goals as of paramount importance for the district's success in improving instruction. Superintendents need your help to establish your district's vision for instruction and learning. Visionary words in a well-articulated statement are a beginning, but the words alone do not create the vision. The vision statement must come to life by being continually shared and practiced. In the words of an experienced superintendent, "As a superintendent you have to capitalize on every opportunity to share why you are doing what you are doing." Your role as a board member is to ensure that your superintendent is sharing what he or she is doing and why, and connecting work in the district to the district's vision and mission of improved student achievement.

You may feel great pressure from state and federal governments to improve student achievement, but countless studies demonstrate that this alone seldom leads to increased student achievement (Fullan 1999; Hall & Hord, 2006; Sarason, 1990; Tye, 2000). As Larry Cuban (2004), a recognized educational researcher and former superintendent, writes,

> Without local expertise and commitment no sustained improvement can occur. More often than not, state and federal policymakers opt for compliance. It is simply easier to have regulations requiring higher standards, more tests, stricter accountability, or more choice than to improve classroom teaching and learning. (p. 112)

Board members and superintendents affect student learning partly by how well they articulate policy and put it into practice in both the community and schools. A superintendent with 17 years of experience voiced the importance of you as a board member, collectively with other board members, developing expectations for student success by stating, "The board should be able to articulate clearly [its] own beliefs and values to the superintendent."

A vision and mission statement that clearly outlines the direction to be taken by all stakeholders in the district and the will to enact the vision and mission are critical to building the capacity required of our schools. Without a clear vision to focus the use of resources and efforts of people, the mission will become diffused, efforts will be scattered, opportunities will be lost, and you will not get the improvement in teaching and learning that you want. Every district needs a plan to ensure that all children are educated. This plan will need to address the quality of instruction provided in every classroom. This is where your role as board member in supporting the superintendent as an instructional leader comes into play.

THE CHALLENGE OF EXERCISING INSTRUCTIONAL LEADERSHIP TO IMPLEMENT THE VISION

Instructional leadership makes teaching and learning the priority, establishes shared expectations and commitments to the ideal that all students can learn to high standards, and ensures that teaching and learning standards are coherent and are tied to assessment tools that guide instructional practices (Darling-Hammond et al., 2005). Responses from superintendents emphasized the importance of strong instructional leadership but expressed frustration with the lack of support to fulfill this role. This frustration was specifically expressed by a group of rural superintendents from the West who believed that their efforts to take on instructional leadership roles were blocked. For example, one superintendent voiced her frustration:

> I have very strong opinions on [instructional leadership] because a super-intendent should be the instructional leader of the school system and everything that occurs in that school system should be around the super-intendent that oversees the instructional program; I don't think we are allowed to do that.

Another rural superintendent voiced his frustration in different words with the challenge of focusing on instructional leadership:

> You have to be the insulator between all this garbage [political, personnel, and financial issues] and the learner. It wears on you, that part you want to hold sacred—instructional time for the people that you got that are good at doing what they do—and that is teaching children.

As a board member, it is difficult to maintain focus on the district's vision of improving student achievement when so many mandates come from federal and state policymakers and from your own constituents.

Another superintendent in the West expressed frustration at having his efforts fragmented, detracting from what he saw as his role as an instructional leader:

> I think it is amazing what the state and federal governments expect out of superintendents, that our focus and what we are tested on and financed by is student learning and achievement. This is just why we are all here. We want people learning and we want people literate, happy, and providing back to the community, but we are divided, fragmented, so much putting out fires here or remembering politics—whose toes you're stepping on—and where in the world did your vision go focusing on the kids?

A superintendent who took on the responsibility of a district with 82 schools labeled as failing shared that he dealt less and less with instructional matters and more and more with political and financial issues when trying to get buildings in shape and the community engaged.

Staying focused on the role of instructional leader is difficult for the superintendent, and it will be for you, too. It is crucial that you, as a board member, understand the importance of the superintendent's role as an instructional leader. In promoting the superintendent's role as an instructional leader, Petersen (1999) noted that you play a pivotal role in the successful promotion of instruction within the district. This focus works reciprocally in that effective superintendents encourage you as school board members to learn about district instructional strategies, involve you in the establishment of district instructional goals and objectives, and guide you in articulating a philosophy aligned with the district vision and mission about what has to be accomplished to have an academically successful school district.

Once you and other district educational leaders have defined and set expectations for what an educational experience is for all students, including how educators approach teaching and learning and the tools for measuring what their students need to know and be able to do, the board can then work to align resources and strategies to improve student achievement. The school board and superintendent must work together to focus the business of school on teaching and learning to ensure the academic success of all students.

THE CHALLENGE OF ASSESSING STUDENT LEARNING

One of your roles in the area of student achievement is to evaluate programs of instruction and learning based on assessment data and, based
on your findings, to help decide where to allocate scarce resources.
This policy-level decision requires the superintendent to provide you
and other board members with a wide-angle view of general indicators
of student achievement summarized across large numbers of students,
across all grade levels, and across all content areas. You are entitled to
see indicators of student achievement in your district, and your superintendent should provide you with sufficient information to allow a
view of the entire teaching and learning situation from a variety of perspectives. The information should be disaggregated and placed in context by comparing it with benchmark groups. Disaggregation means
that it must be broken down so that you can see how different groups
of students have performed. Comparison with benchmark groups
means that you can compare district achievement results with national
or state achievement results, or with results from demographically similar districts.

You, as a school board member, should ask to see data on student
achievement. Mary Fulton (1998) suggested in the *American School
Board Journal* that school board members should ask the tough questions about teaching and learning initiatives:

- What are the intended goals?
- How can we know if they are achieved?
- How do we gauge progress along the way?
- What do we do if we seem to be off track?
- How long do we allow a program to operate before deciding
  whether to continue, expand, or abandon it?
- How do we build in rigorous, periodic evaluations to measure
  the progress and impact of education initiatives on our students?
  (pp. 1–2)

Information exchange should not be in one direction only, from the
superintendent to you and other school board members; it should be a
two-way exchange in which the superintendent gets input from the

board. A suburban superintendent with four years' experience expressed the need to include input from school board members as meaningful data by stating,

> We're exposed to a great deal of data, and on review of data, we can identify, along with our staffs or by ourselves, what we may perceive to be achievement issues, student achievement issues. They can jump out on the page for us. I think there's also a political level to this, too, and that can come from the perspective of listening closely to our school board members and supervisors who can be free to identify problems for us as well.

In partnership, superintendents and school board members need to examine student achievement, monitor student learning over time, and determine how to take responsibility for the academic success of all students. You will need to make the review and discussion of evidence of student learning a priority.

NCLB stated that all schools must have clear, measurable goals focused on basic skills and essential knowledge, and that annual testing in every grade will provide the information that stakeholders need to ensure that every student experiences academic success. A 20-year veteran of the superintendency from a Western rural state noted, "[NCLB] has helped us focus on how we will be accountable. It forces us to focus on the subgroups and really pay attention to their progress. We will always have high expectations for all of our kids." Another superintendent from a rural district shared his thoughts about how the policy helped clarify priorities for his board and district administrators: "NCLB is about accountability and focus. It is not necessarily bad. I see the lack of funding as the negative part. I think it aided administrators in painting a picture in how to move forward." A superintendent in a large district in the western United States shared a belief that NCLB creates leadership opportunities, "It has given us some leverage to improve in some areas we have always wanted to address. [NCLB] forces us to use data to make changes." Using data to make changes helps you as a board member support resource allocation and staffing decisions that have a direct effect on student achievement.

The NCLB-mandated disaggregation of student achievement data helps you target resources to the students who need extra support. A rural superintendent with 20 years in the superintendency supported NCLB as highlighting the need for equity:

> [NCLB] forces you to look at kids who need more help. This group that needs the help is a larger percentage than we realized. I was the only guy who found it positive in my district. This whole plan is to help students who are not getting it. It is a good platform to advocate openly for students who are not getting it.

And finally, a rural superintendent shared his belief that NCLB redefined the role of district leadership in child-centered terms: "I like [NCLB] because it put out there what we are all about. It spells out a plain national platform to do things for kids."

Superintendents also exhibited frustration with NCLB. One area was the lack of funding necessary to fully implement the NCLB mandates. A superintendent from the Southwest and new to the superintendency stated, "It is an unfunded mandate and many parts of it are not realistic." Several superintendents voiced frustration with the unintended consequences of NCLB. This comment about the policy's impact on curriculum provides an example of the frustration felt when standardization is confused with standards, "A significant problem is that in the end NCLB will narrow the curriculum and will stifle what we have had in education. . . . NCLB is too prescriptive." Whether or not the superintendent agrees with NCLB mandates, the superintendent is the vital link between the development of an action plan to improve student achievement, effective use of an accountability policy, and the outcome of improved achievement for all students. The superintendent and the board need to work together to focus the district's human and fiscal resources on the goal of improving instruction and learning.

You can monitor progress toward improved student achievement. Superintendents have the monumental challenge of getting data on student growth and then conveying information on the growth in a meaningful way to stakeholders throughout the community. A veteran suburban superintendent conveyed this challenge by saying:

> I think we have a better understanding of what learning is all about, student learning and how to assess it. We're on the way to establishing standards that we can all uphold, but I think that we also need to be held ac-

countable for some of those standards and making sure that kids are assessed appropriately so that we can say that learning has occurred.

Federal and state officials have developed frameworks for school accountability, for what achievement is to be measured, and for how it is to be measured. Yet it is essential to keep in mind that local educational leaders, including superintendents and board members, and their communities must interpret the evidence and use it to guide efforts to meet the goals set for students to be prepared for life in a democratic society.

Superintendents in our study emphasized the importance of focusing on results and using achievement data to improve learning. One superintendent from the West summed up the need to monitor student achievement results to ensure success for all students by stating:

> If we take a realistic look at our data and try to analyze that data, then we have to take a look at how our students are performing and have discussions with our teachers. If you have a long-term vision and you base your decisions on that and do not waver, your students will improve.

NCLB makes it clear that educational leaders today must understand measures of student achievement and how to articulate the results of these measures to community members. Board members can expect their superintendent to be well versed in assessment of student achievement and then expect to see a plan of action to address how the district will improve student achievement results.

THE CHALLENGE TO ENSURE A QUALITY EDUCATION FOR ALL STUDENTS

Ensuring High Standards

The demand for improvements in student achievement requires that schools set high standards for the quality of instruction that goes on in the classroom. NCLB requires that schools have highly qualified teachers in every classroom. To be deemed highly qualified, teachers must have (1) a bachelor's degree, (2) full state certification or licensure, and (3) documentation that they know each subject they teach. The literature on improving student achievement supports the need for quality teachers in the classroom and for quality principals in the buildings. The superintendent will need your trust to make personnel decisions to improve student achievement based on the vision and mission of the district.

A major reform issue is how teachers are recruited, supported, and evaluated. This will require administrators, with your support, to work with local universities, offering contracts as early as possible, and recruiting in other states. A superintendent from the Southwest, in his first year, reflected upon how districts compete for the better teachers and therefore must get ahead in the hiring process, "We used to interview teachers. Now they interview us."

Once staff is hired, it is essential that boards of education support their professional development. The single most important determinant of how students achieve is their teachers' qualifications (Darling-Hammond & Ball, 1998). Schlechty (2000) strongly recommended that district resources to support professional development should be at least 2% of the school's operating budget. As a board member, you have the responsibility to allocate scarce resources. This requires you to keep your focus, as well as the superintendent's focus, on the district vision and mission toward improved student achievement.

You, as a board member, can make professional development a priority for educators at all levels of the organization. Superintendents voiced the need for quality professional development in order to support and retain the staff currently working in the district. This means that you will have to restructure professional development from how it has been provided in the past. The big in-service day at the beginning of the year provided to all staff is not enough. A suburban superintendent from the Northeast shared,

> I think we know more than we have ever, ever known about how children learn. . . . We need people now to go in and mentor teachers and get that process moving and start making a difference, but we cannot do it with the current form [and] structure of education as we see it today.

According to a new rural superintendent from the West, to make change happen, "You have to retrain staff and give them support to make the changes necessary to improve student achievement." Professional development needs to be provided on an ongoing basis and this will require your support, even when you hear complaints about school schedules being changed to accommodate professional development during the workday and throughout the school year. As a board member, you need to understand that educators have differing levels of expertise and confidence. Change is more difficult for some than for others.

Meaningful school and district improvement initiatives must include professional development that is well planned, implemented, and evaluated. District leaders need to provide growth opportunities that meet the needs of principals, teachers, and everyone who can affect student achievement. Professional development is about teachers and principals designing individualized professional development plans that include working with other colleagues and outside consultants who work with teachers in classrooms to improve instruction and learning. One of the most powerful strategies being implemented in school districts currently is providing peer coaches and mentors who work directly with teachers in the classroom on instruction and learning strategies. Boards can ask district administrators to produce professional development plans and explain how they are developed, implemented, and monitored for their effect on student achievement.

The Challenge of Ensuring Equity

The pressure to produce year-to-year increases in student achievement (Adequate Yearly Progress [AYP]) and to achieve equity challenges districts to close the achievement gaps between students in different socioeconomic and ethnic groups. "Assessment for learning and assessment for equity are two complementary principles, both of which are essential for getting assessment right at the classroom level" (Shaw, 2005, p. 343).

Consider these three purposes of assessment: It enables you to monitor student learning, to share information on student learning with the larger community, and to recognize when programs must be improved because learning is unsatisfactory. A superintendent from the rural West reinforced this by stating, "There is increased pressure to focus on student achievement for all groups: Equity is important." NCLB has given schools 12 years to move all students to the state-defined proficiency level in reading and math. Districts are required to produce AYP reports reflecting student achievement on performance standards established by their state for students across all student groups. *All* means students from all socioeconomic levels, all racial and ethnic groups, all males and females, all grade levels, all students on different post–high school tracks (to work, to college, to trade school), regardless of first language or disability.

The intent of NCLB is to guarantee each child the right to a quality education. This could have a negative effect if all students are not taught the content on which they will be tested and if they do not have access to quality programs to prepare them to meet the standards. As a board member, you are responsible for ensuring an appropriate education for all students. You will need to continually ask why some groups of students are succeeding at higher levels than others and then expect to see a plan of action addressing the low-performing groups.

Equitable does not mean equal. Equity is about ensuring that every child is learning regardless of ethnicity, socioeconomic status, or disability. That often means that some students will receive more resources because their needs are greater. Equity is about ensuring that every child learns regardless of ethnicity, socioeconomic status, or disability. Superintendents from the rural Southwest voiced frustration with the issue of limited funds to support quality programs for all students, such as

> I think that one of the things we all continually try to do is meet the needs of all kids on a very, very, very limited fixed budget. Trying to implement programs that will address [all learners] from the special ed kids to the top high-performing students becomes more and more and more difficult when you have limited funds to do that.

The following comments from suburban superintendents in the Northeast echoed this frustration with limited resources for diverse student groups:

> As a result, you're seeing competition for internal money that you didn't see in the past—regular ed versus special ed parents taking a look very carefully at the board actions when you send a kid to one of these alternative placements and it costs $50–$60,000. They're beginning to say, "Well, that is what it costs for five or six students; what does my child get?"

A superintendent from the Southwest identified the challenge of allocating adequate resources for the "middle kids," students not targeted for special services, when he shared,

> I think we put so much focus on pulling those outside kids up that sometimes we forget about those kids that don't need that extra help and they'll do fine and we know they will do fine, and you just kind of let them go. They don't get that extra attention and they deserve it.

As a board member you will be expected to support the needs of all students. This means it will cost more for some students to learn and you will have to justify this expense to your community without violating the individual rights of the student receiving the extra resources.

To sum up the challenge of meeting the needs of all learners, the board will decide how resources are allocated in an equitable manner to facilitate learning for our poorest children, children of color, and children with disabilities. The issue of financial constraints will continue to plague districts. The board will need to develop political, educational, and financial policies and structures that will eliminate educational inequalities and achieve AYP. One of your most difficult responsibilities as a board member is to ensure that every child is educated to understand the challenges and opportunities of the future and is prepared to meet them.

SUMMARY OF STUDENT ACHIEVEMENT CHALLENGES

We have presented the challenges of improving student achievement organized around four themes: (1) creating a vision and mission focused on instruction and learning; (2) exercising instructional leadership to implement the vision; (3) assessing student learning; and (4) building the capacity for equity. School boards will need to define and articulate a vision and mission focused on improving student achievement. Every decision needs to be based on what will best promote student learning. This does not make decisions easier, because learning must be promoted in ways that are equitable for all. Furthermore, in an era where federal and state policies mandate what shall be taught and how achievement will be measured, you still need to articulate and implement a local vision and mission that defines the meaning of teaching and learning for your community.

Anne Loring recommends the *Key Work of School Boards* (National School Boards Association, 2000) as a guide to help school boards focus on student achievement. She also recommends that boards need to expect results, focus their conversations around student academic performance, and plan how to improve it.

Staying focused on the role of instructional leader is difficult for the superintendent, and you as a board member can make a big difference if you understand what the superintendent is doing and why. The school board can work with the superintendent in the role of instructional leader by allowing him or her to make instructional decisions about the appropriate placement of individuals in leadership positions and, most importantly, teachers in the classroom. You can also support the superintendent in the role of instructional leader by viewing all issues such as budgets, facilities, personnel issues, tax levies, and public relations through the lens of student achievement. Dynamic boards and superintendents in successful school districts focus on the business of educating all students (Loring, 2005).

According to Rudy and Conrad, successful school improvement efforts are made up of teachers, administrators, and community members working together to address the teaching, learning, and assessment needs of all students. They found that one way to use data-informed improvement is to focus on student achievement results. "Leadership is critical for systemwide implementation of effective data-informed decision making" (2004, p. 41).

This chapter outlined the challenges of fostering student achievement; the next will focus on using data to meet these challenges.

5

SUCCESS STRATEGY:
BASE DECISIONS ON DATA

William Ruff and Robin Dexter

THREE LESSONS FROM DISTRICTS THAT HAVE
SUSTAINED STUDENT ACHIEVEMENT

In the previous chapter, we discussed the challenges of student achievement. In that discussion, we asserted the need for data and data-driven decision making by local education leaders. The challenge of monitoring student achievement directly relates to the collection and analysis of data. In this chapter, we continue the discussion of student achievement but turn the perspective from the challenges of fostering student achievement to how you and your superintendent might deal with these challenges by using data as the basis for your decision making. The board can request data from the district administration, and you, as a school board member, can use data to frame your decision-making processes.

There are countless studies and narratives about how individual schools go from low performing to high achieving. In fact, most of the published research on instructional improvement focuses on the classroom or school level. But to get systemic improvement of instruction, we must focus our attention not just on one school but on systems of schools. In other words, we must focus on districts. That is where you, the board member, play an important role. One study that looks at instructional improvement at the district level identified five districts with high percentages of children in need and children of color that sustained successful student achievement progress for more than three years in all demographic categories. Researchers studied these districts to find common elements to account for their success and found seven common strategies among these highly successful districts:

- Districts had the courage to acknowledge poor performance and the will to seek solutions.
- Districts put in place a systemwide approach to improving instruction.
- Districts instilled visions that focused on student learning and guided instructional improvement.
- Districts made decisions based on data, not instincts.
- Districts adopted new approaches to professional development.
- Districts redefined leadership roles.
- Districts committed to sustaining reform over the long haul (Togneri & Anderson, 2003, pp. 5–8).

From this study, we learn three important lessons. First, instructional improvement requires a commitment from board members, school administrators, teachers, students, parents, and community members. This commitment provides the foundation for accepting the responsibility for prior performance and seeking ways to improve; adopting new approaches, leadership roles, and a student-centered focus; installing a new vision and new methods of decision making; and, finally, sustaining a long-term effort (Zmuda, Kuklis, & Kline, 2004).

Second, the interpretation and use of data propel action toward continuous improvement. Systematically gathering relevant data enables you and other board members to assess program effects and students. "The emergence of public reporting of testing results drove many districts to look at student achievement data in new ways. . . . [T]he courage to accept negative information was critical in building the will to change" (Togneri & Anderson, 2003, p. 10). Your use of data is not limited to providing summative evaluations, such as annual evaluations of school programs that tell the community how well the school district performs. Data should be used formatively as well. Formative data are collected while a program is in progress to let you know how things are going in time to change course, if needed. Think of formative data as progress reports. For example, they provide information to educators regarding the strengths and weaknesses of instruction. They inform you about whether and what kind of staff development is needed. Moreover, they provide you with a reliable basis for decision making based on the current realities of a situation as opposed to personal perceptions and beliefs. Data-based decision making builds accountability into the work processes of the district and establishes internal accountability systems for making improvements.

The third lesson we have learned from studying successful districts is to focus on the strengths of the relationships that govern individuals and organizations and interpretations of events. Only through productive relationships will districts be able to sustain change to meet the challenges of fostering increased student achievement. For example, refocusing the district's vision from a focus on school routines to a focus on teaching and learning requires organizational change; shifting problem solving to data-based decision making requires organizational change; adopting new approaches to professional development requires organizational change; redefining leadership roles requires organizational change; and enacting the common strategies found in high-performing districts requires organizational change. Change requires existing relationships to be rewoven throughout the organization (Sarason, 1990). When district leaders look at problems from a perspective that is systemic and allows for a holistic solution, student achievement can improve. A systemic perspective recognizes the interconnectedness of each component in the district to achieve stated goals. Using a systems perspective, you will understand how interventions can produce a ripple effect that affects the whole district.

Approaches to meeting student achievement challenges described by superintendents from around the country emphasize using data. Superintendents describe using data in three ways. These three ways parallel the three lessons learned from the commonly held strategies of successful districts.

First, you and other school board members can use data to earn commitment and support from key constituents in the district and in the community. Your role as a school board member requires that you garner community support for systemic school improvement. A superintendent from the Northeast claimed,

> I think that it is this matter of keeping before the public not only the good news about education but the right news about education. Also, establishing enough of a dialogue so we . . . as school leaders can afford to surface the problem that needs broad-based support for its solution without feeling like we're attacking our own institution. . . . We have a real responsibility, I think, to establishing the kinds of communication to allow for honest discussion about improving.

Second, you and other school board members can hold people accountable to adjust programs and activities to ensure student achievement goals and objectives are met. This use of data is demonstrated by the following statement made by an experienced superintendent from a suburban district:

> I think our role is to see kids succeed academically, socially, emotionally, and then I do a lot of—I keep track of data on everything so I can measure where we are, discipline referrals, and that just kind of helps me gauge where we're going or if we need to shift our focus a bit.

Third, you and other school board members can use data to reweave patterns of relationships. This includes creating a shared vision and perspective, and building trust, consensus, and capacity within the district and its community, as well as reenvisioning how things get done. A superintendent from a suburban district in the South explained:

> We have invited practically all of the businesses within our community, most of which are quite small—the hospital and two or three of the manufacturing groups are large—but our whole purpose is to say we know that we have a joint concern about work ethic. We think that we can produce better employees if these young people are finishing school and have good attendance. We know that the issue of attendance at work is a concern to business so we'll sit down and work on that and perhaps come up with something that we feel can be mutually beneficial.

In summary, research on the best practices of instructionally focused school districts reveals three trends: successful districts have stakeholders committed to a student-centered focus; leaders use data to monitor progress and to refine efforts; and leaders attend to relationships among people, events, and organizational elements.

You and the other board members can strengthen student achievement by pursuing these three strategies. Put another way, you, together with the superintendent, can use numerical and qualitative data to gain commitment from community members, to evaluate progress and direction of instructional programs, and to reweave relationship patterns to become more effective as a district. Through making information transparent and public, you are engendering openness and inviting public trust.

USING DATA TO FOCUS DIVERSE PEOPLE ON A SINGLE TASK

A number of years ago, one of us went on a family vacation to Disney's Epcot Center. At that time, there was a temporary exhibit there from Brazil. The exhibit consisted of a very large wide-screen video monitor and 100 pairs of circles on the floor. Each was about 18 inches in diameter. The circle on the left of each pair was red and the one on the right, blue. The pairs of circles were arranged in neat rows 10 wide and 10 deep. Every 10 minutes, 100 people would file out and another 100 people would file in to take their place with one foot on the red circle and the other on the blue.

As this was a Disney theme park in the middle of June, there was no shortage of people. After everyone was in place, an announcer explained that standing on the red circle moved the cursor on the video monitor up or left (depending on the game). Standing on the blue circle, moved the cursor down or right. The more people who stand on the circle, the quicker the cursor will move. This was it for the instructions. Immediately following this brief presentation, Pong, a video tennis game, appeared on the screen. Within 45 seconds of the game appearing, the 100 strangers organized themselves to coordinate their movements well enough to keep the video ball in play for several minutes. Halfway through the session, the game was changed. The objective of the new game was to pilot a boat up the Amazon River and avoid a host of obstacles. Again, in less than a minute, a group of strangers coordinated their movements to successfully negotiate the boat up the river.

We tell this story because this exhibit is a wonderful metaphor for the crucial role information plays in the process of focusing a group to accomplish a task. One hundred people assembled as total strangers. They received a brief set of instructions on how to perform their role and a broad objective (win the game). They received instantaneous and continuous feedback on the performance of the group, enabling them to modify their individual performance to meet the group's objective. As a result of these conditions, they quickly achieved and were able to maintain the group's objective. A continuous stream of instantaneous feedback provided the information necessary to achieve group success and sustain individual commitment. In other words, the group used information to self-organize and achieve success.

Now, imagine how this would work in a school district. You and other school board members could bring the community together for information sessions to provide explanations to both the community and the schools about different roles and perspectives to achieve a common vision. The common vision should be developed by the group to focus the tasks performed by each person's role (such as teacher, parent, business partner, student, etc.). In a district, each person could collect and share data, providing a continuous stream of data from multiple perspectives. From this stream of data, each person would obtain the information he or she needed to adjust his or her performance to keep the group progressing toward the common vision. Additionally, through the interaction of adjusting performance to facilitate group progression, each individual would gain greater insight and understanding of the common vision. This greater understanding would be shared and added to the continuous stream of data, creating a positive feedback loop to increase group focus and performance.

It is. one thing to speculate about what happens in the world based upon a metaphor, but before we can trust such speculations, they should be anchored with real experiences and events. Superintendents acknowledge that one of their primary challenges in gaining continued support and commitment is clear and accurate communication. As an experienced superintendent from the Northeast put it:

One of my biggest problems—or challenges, I guess—is clear and accurate communication. . . . I'm convinced that if we could clearly communi-

cate the issues to people, 80 to 90% of them will arrive at the same conclusion that we have arrived at with the same information. How you do
that is absolutely monumental, because what happens is, if you do not
communicate clearly, then what you are dealing with are so many other
social dimensions.

In effective communication, the receiver gets the message the sender
intended, yet diverse values can cause receivers to get messages other
than the ones intended. To prevent this shift, you must find common
ground and use it to enhance the communication of meaning. In the
words of a Southwestern superintendent,

I think we've forgot about some institutions we need to make this democracy work. . . . I think just finding common ground [in differing group values is essential]. . . . I believe you can give people more information. You
can educate people. . . . It's an opportunity for schools to get back to an
audience that has been disconnected for a while. So, I think finding common ground, that's an approach I use.

A superintendent of a growing suburban district in the South stated the
challenge of educating the public more concretely:

They [a board of supervisors] understand that with the rezonings of land . . .
that they have helped contribute to the issues that we are dealing with
[school overcrowding]. But to ask Mr. Taxpayer, with 70% of the population
with no kids in school now, to come up with more and more monies, . . . we
have trouble. To be able to go in and educate folks [about the facts] . . . is
constantly a challenge.

You and the other board members as well as the superintendent cannot ignore the need to provide a continuous stream of information and
data to people throughout the community. Your providing information
helps to ensure that local school administrators, teachers, parents, and
community members work as a team for children. That is the bright side
of our position, but there is a dark side to this. If information is not forth-
coming, people can become distrustful. Speaking to this issue, an experienced superintendent from an urban district said, "We have to communicate this student achievement and this information to the public. I

think if we are going to garner support for . . . instructional support, . . . we have to speak on behalf of and be advocates for our students." Commenting on the need to keep people informed with the facts, another superintendent from a Southwestern suburban district remarked, "I try to keep the board informed and the teachers informed and the community informed of what the situation is. Otherwise, people will be asking for things, and they can't understand why they can't have them." Another veteran superintendent from a rural Southern district elaborated,

> We need to put out as much information as we can, about what actually is, and not cover up anything at all. People will call and say, "This is a problem." If you say, "I don't think there is anything wrong with that," then there are two problems. One is the problem they called about, and the other is that they think the superintendent doesn't have a clue about what is going on. So we have to admit when we have problems. And that is fine, as long as we follow up on it and say, "This is how we are addressing them."

Before going on to discuss how engagement facilitates communication, we need to make one more point regarding the importance of your maintaining a constant stream of meaningful information relevant to governing your school district. Specifically, when you provide a constant stream of information and data to the community, it gives people a broader view of events and may mitigate situations where people might overgeneralize from a single issue. A superintendent from a suburban district put it this way, "That gets back to creating a responsibility for the school system—[the] school board. It becomes very important that we educate the community so that single issues do not drive the election of board members."

Superintendents talked about factors that facilitated clear and accurate communication, the development of a common understanding of information, and the development of commitment to student-centered school initiatives. These factors all revolve around the notion of engagement. Jerome Bruner (1997), a well-known and respected educational scholar, wrote that meaning becomes evident in the application of information.

Superintendents use engagement as a means for improving the accuracy of communication and providing a common understanding of what the information means. One superintendent from a Southern urban district put it in these words:

> Talking about facilitating factors [for clear communication], . . . [a key factor] has become a foundation board [separate from the school board] as well as our business partnerships. . . . They began to provide support for the school board that gives them a greater base. Not only does the school board receive a lot of information about the schools, but so do these other groups, and those people then pick up some of the members of the community who influence the political process. What has happened is there's an expanded base of support for the schools through those co-boards that have community leaders in them.

Just as foundation boards and school-business partnerships facilitate the accurate flow of information, other superintendents find that creating parent advisory boards fosters the exchange of information between home and school. An experienced suburban superintendent from a mid-sized school district put it this way:

> [One] thing I've done—I think quite successfully with my leadership—is to create parent advisory committees and almost compel them to come and listen and exchange, hoping that they would be representative of parents in general. Those are districtwide committees.

A superintendent from an urban district in the South describes how her notion of educating the community evolved:

> It [involvement] used to mean the parent community. It really means the entire community and that change becomes an increasingly larger proportion of that entire community that doesn't have children in schools. A couple of things we have done, and it worked extremely well, our newspaper's been willing to let us have a whole page once a month . . . and I have switched from sending out something to parents once a month to simply printing a page in the newspaper—articles that are written mostly by high school journalism students. At least we have an audience of the whole community.

In summing up how information and data are used to create support and commitment for the school, its students, and policies, superintendents discuss involving others in problem solving as a means of obtaining both multiple perspectives and commitment in the implementation of the solution. This statement from a Mid-Atlantic superintendent is representative:

> When I'm faced with a vexing problem, I'm stressed. My natural style is to revert to a planning mode, and get as many people as I can involved in defining what the problem is, and generating alternative solutions. Also, if necessary, get more information, get back history, do data searches, build people's understanding of the problem, so that we'll move toward a solution, and they'll hopefully be supportive of it.

HISTORY OF DATA-DRIVEN DECISION MAKING

Data-driven decision making stems from the idea that decisions based on facts are often far superior to decisions based on opinion or politics. Mike Schmoker (1999), a school improvement consultant, wrote, "We have been naïve; without the reference point that results provide, experience is often a slow and misleading teacher. Informed changes in practice can produce timely, even rapid, incremental advances" (p. 2). The notion of data-driven decision making can be traced to the management theories of Dr. W. Edward Deming, whose work was largely ignored in the United States until the Japanese credited his work for their rapid rise in the global marketplace during the 1980s. Since that time, quality improvement models have become commonplace in American business, government, and schools.

A fundamental concept underlying the continuous improvement of schools is a focus on checking the results of plans carried out. Plan-Direct-Control, a model used in many bureaucracies, was replaced with a model that focuses on results, Plan-Do-Check-Act (PDCA). Since the early 1990s, this new model has facilitated thinking in schools toward a more student-centered approach. *Plan* refers to a proposed change or solution that might work toward improving a given situation. *Do* refers to a test of the change on a limited scale. *Check* refers to a study of the test's results and effects. *Act* refers to the adoption, modification, or abandonment of the change or solution based on the test results (Quality Schools Consortium, 1995). By using the PDCA model, district leaders can base decisions to implement or expand a change or a solution on fact and can focus on obtaining results.

It is not surprising that data-based decision making is the approach mentioned by superintendents as they discuss dealing with the challenges of raising student achievement and district accountability. Assumptions underlying the No Child Left Behind Act of 2001 (NCLB) as well as the accountability reform movement are closely aligned with the principles of continuous quality improvement. For example, Adequate Yearly Progress (AYP), a key element in NCLB, is synonymous with continuous improvement. Countless schools throughout the country employ data-based decision making with such programs as Data in a Day, where the entire district staff visits a single school and collects as much data as possible during a single day. The information is fed back to the faculty and staff, allowing them to assess their overall progress. Another similar type of program used in schools is Data on the Wall. In this program, teachers, administrators, and staff display current information and data about all the various programs in the school, to include student progress.

Data collection also involves getting input from constituents. Superintendents see decision making based on their own personal views as easier and perhaps more time efficient, but involving people in the decision-making process can earn more support. One superintendent from a Western rural district articulated this as follows: "It certainly is much easier just to make a decision and move on; that's much less time consuming and much easier. But we garner support by listening and giving people the opportunity to at least be heard."

Another superintendent from a suburban Southern district addressed the issue in its capacity-building aspects in these words: "I think that if people have a stake in the decision by helping to craft what happens, and then also because they've had that part in it, they also share some accountability to see that it's done well." Data collection contributes to this process of getting input, because data provide individuals with the ability to make informed decisions for themselves rather than merely carrying out actions based on the opinion of another. An experienced urban superintendent expressed it this way:

> We are constantly aware that we must provide a lot of data and we try to do that. Gathering the data sometimes is a task and it is time consuming,

but it usually works out better when people make decisions if they have a lot of facts rather than giving them the opinion that we are just doing things because the school system wanted to do them or the superintendent wanted it.

Making decisions based on evidence has clear advantages over basing them on other motives, but it requires you to cultivate a climate in the district that allows for critical thinking and its expression. For example, a superintendent from the Southwest illustrated how agreement with decisions based on loyalty could lead to disaster:

> If I say something and everybody out of loyalty thinks that's a hell of an idea, and it may be the stupidest thing that one's ever thought of, but they don't feel at ease to give suggestions or even constructive criticism, some real bad things could happen that could be avoided. I think somehow setting the environment for all people who are in your organization to be able to give feedback . . . is real important.

INTERPRETING DATA: SEEING MULTIPLE PERSPECTIVES

Data are always subject to interpretation, and interpretations can differ. What one person sees as glaring facts indicating problems may be totally missed or discounted by another. As a veteran superintendent from the South put it, "Some educators, when they have been in it a long time, they no longer see those problems. . . . The closer we are to the problem, the harder it is for us to see the problem."

Interpretation involves viewing situations from a variety of perspectives, as another suburban superintendent points out: "Analyze a problem and research it from different angles. I definitely do research to find out what an issue is and what the possible alternatives are." In the words of a Midwestern superintendent, "People hear what they want to hear from their own perspective. I have learned to ask people, 'How did you hear that? What did you hear me say?'"

The way data are disaggregated and presented can alter perspectives, so board members must be open to these different presentations. You also can learn from different sources of data, both quantitative data, such as test scores, and qualitative data, which consist of people's descriptions. An experienced urban superintendent expressed the need for district leaders to make firsthand observations of the teaching and learning that occurs in the schools. "That's probably the strongest thing that school boards are looking for, I think—someone who is out there and knows what's going on in the classrooms." Technology provides another conduit of information. An experienced suburban superintendent pointed out, "With the technology comes more readily information about each student that is at your fingertips."

Many of the superintendents emphasized informal data collection over more formal methods. You should not construe this to mean that hearsay and anecdotal information are automatically to be preferred to data gathered systematically. Informal data gathering should be systematic and include direct observations of events, discussing specific topics with different groups of people, and noting existing beliefs and attitudes held by community members by listening to them. Formal data collection is highly defined and more focused in scope. On the other hand, informal data can provide important and unexpected insights and can be accomplished without a special effort. The differences between informal and formal data collection lay in the rigor of how they are collected.

An example of collecting information informally is shown by a rural superintendent with two years' experience: "All you really have to do sometimes is just be willing to listen." Another superintendent expressed it by explaining the skills required of the job:

> You . . . have to have the ability to listen to people. A lot of times you come into these jobs and you think people are asking you to lead them and speak to them and somehow provide the answers. Well, that is not really what they are asking for. I think they are asking for you to listen and for you to give thought and consideration to their ideas, and then when it comes time, you have to somehow reach consensus or make the final decision.

A suburban superintendent from the South stressed the need to get multiple perspectives by gathering information and data in a variety of places. He elaborated,

> You want to have as good a cross section of your community [as you can] to get feedback on a lot of issues before you come to a final conclusion,

although you want to have it be informed input and there's a challenge in
that too. . . . It doesn't have to be a formal process, but it can just be
something you do at all the different events that we attend as superintendents. I engage in these assessments all the time—at football games,
basketball games, music events, or whatever. You're talking with people,
getting feedback. . . . In the best way possible, get feedback from groups
that might not be considered sometimes. And maybe it's the kid who did
drop out in high school and is still in your community, and so on.

Once collected, the information is applied in various ways in decision
making. One method focuses on establishing layers of accountability. As
a rural superintendent from the Midwest indicated, "We try to organize
ourselves so that everybody has a reporting responsibility." Establishing
methods of accountability facilitates focus and prioritization. A novice
superintendent explained,

Now I think I'm able to prioritize a little better, to focus energies on issues that we can resolve over the long run and to delegate those issues that
are short term. And just get feedback and collaborate about some of those
issues that we can deal with. And then there are other issues that collectively we make the decision that, "Hey, we can't deal with this." . . . Now,
we're able to say, "Keep a focus on what we're trying to do as a district."

There is no question among the superintendents that the data should
be used primarily to foster student learning. As an urban superintendent from the Northeast noted, "We have a lot of data available to us, and
we have to be able to use that data to identify where those [achieve-
ment] gaps are. So I think it's really important to use the data that we
have . . . to improve student achievement."

USING DATA TO BRIDGE PERSPECTIVES

In order for school districts to meet the increased demand for student
achievement at levels never before obtained by any generation, districts
will have to reorganize and adopt the viewpoint that the district is a single
unit, a school *system*, and not merely a cluster of schools. Furthermore,
teachers and others within the schools should view the school as an inte-

grated system and not a grouping of discrete classrooms. Adopting a systems view carries with it two essential connotations. First, the actions of one are connected to the actions of all others. Therefore, for a teacher to increase achievement within her classroom, she must also take responsibility for what happens in other classrooms because they are all connected. Second, within a well-functioning system, there is synergy. The outcome of the effort taken as a whole is greater than the sum of individual efforts.

Adopting a systems view increases the need to develop collegial groups. Teachers should go from working in isolation to working in cooperative groups sharing their thoughts, ideas, and discoveries about teaching and learning. Through such shifts in thinking, the culture of the district can be transformed from a workplace where everyone is just doing his or her job to a learning community with a strong sense of collective accountability. In writing about competent systems that serve to enhance achievement, Zmuda, Kuklis, and Kline (2004) observed, "A competent system requires several significant shifts—from unconnected thinking to systems thinking, from an environment of isolation to one of collegiality, from perceived reality to information-driven reality, and from personal autonomy to collective accountability" (p. 1).

SUMMARY

We hope that this chapter has provided you with some ideas about approaches you can take with data to meet the challenges of fostering student achievement. Your use of information is critical to meeting this challenge, not just in using data for decision making but also to gain the necessary commitment from everyone involved in helping children learn, as well as using meaningful information to change people's perspectives. Hopefully, the statements and stories of the superintendents we talked with help to clarify the information and provide a sense of authenticity to the ideas presented here. In keeping the link with superintendent voices strong, we end this chapter with a list of the approaches discussed by superintendents to meet the student achievement challenges:

• You can use data to garner commitment from faculty, staff, and community members for student-centered support; this implies that you have an environment that's safe for people to provide feedback—even if it's negative.

- You can use data to hold people accountable and to adjust activities to ensure goals are met; this implies that you continuously collect and use data to inform all your decisions.
- You can use data to reweave patterns of relationships, leading to increases in capacity for teaching and learning; this implies that you treat information as energy that provides the organizing force for the school system to move forward.
- You should establish trust and common ground to clarify the meaning of information; this implies that you and other board members work with the schools and community to develop a shared vision of teaching and learning.
- You should facilitate continuous communication with community members by engaging representative groups in problem-solving activities; this implies that you establish the importance of shared decision making toward facilitating community buy-in to address common problems.
- You should gather and interpret data from multiple perspectives; this implies that you look for feedback from groups that aren't always considered.
- You should use both informal and formal methods to gather data; this implies your willingness to listen and continuously observe.
- You could use data to facilitate change, shift perceptions, and improve how issues are approached; this implies you have a desire to keep educators and the public informed and working together to meet children's needs.

6

SUCCESS STRATEGY: RECRUIT, KEEP, DEVELOP, AND RELY ON GOOD STAFF

Faye E. Patterson

One spends very little time as a leader of an organization before realizing that practically nothing gets done without good staff. Recruiting, retaining, and developing the district's human resources capital is essential to achieving the district's mission. Simply put, without good staff, your ability as an educational leader to make strides in positive directions will be severely curtailed, if not negated.

All district employees must realize their role in working for your district mission, and they must know and understand your commitment to their success. Communicating your commitment to people attracts and retains good staff. Fostering a culture of working together builds both the intellectual and social capital to address your district's toughest issues and resolve its most perplexing problems. In short, district leaders must commit to people's short- and long-term success.

The framers of No Child Left Behind (NCLB) showed their understanding of the significance of hiring good staff by requiring you to have a highly qualified teacher in every classroom. Meeting this requirement can be a huge challenge, as some superintendents made clear to us. Nevertheless, we also heard from them about their commitment to face the challenge; we saw their determination to recruit, keep, develop, and rely on good staff; and we heard their ideas on how to accomplish this, even in the face of obstacles. I share some of their ideas in this chapter.

To begin, I emphasize two points: First, except when you hire the superintendent, it is not generally your job to recruit applicants and screen them for their suitability. It is also not generally your job to provide staff development or to negotiate with individuals for their salaries. You employ the superintendent to take care of those details. It is your job, however, to express your support for the district mission and to emphasize the importance for the district mission of having good staff to implement it. You must keep in front of everyone the realization of the district mission, which will influence the type of candidates you recruit.

Second, the connections between recruiting, keeping, developing, and relying on good staff are not simple and straightforward. Instead, leaders' actions will be interdependent with each step you take, with one action affecting the other conditions for good or ill. For example, hiring the best people you can afford affects your ability to keep them and, of course, your ability to rely on them. Conversely, to the extent that you are unable to recruit staff with all the characteristics you need, you must depend more on the staff you have and develop them over time so that the desired characteristics mature. Providing good staff development may make employees feel valued and more likely to stay. The better staff you recruit and/or develop, the more plausible it will be for you to be able to rely on them; this in turn may well make them feel appreciated, trusted, and committed to stay in your district. Furthermore, the better reputation your district has for appreciating staff and treating them well, the more people will want to work there. This makes your recruiting job easier. So, even though I will write about these efforts one at a time and step-by-step, they do not occur that way in your district—the actions are intertwined with your overall district philosophy of how you treat people.

GET THE BEST STAFF YOU CAN TO FULFILL THE DISTRICT'S VISION

Getting Good Staff

Edith Rusch wrote in chapter 2 about developing and promoting your district vision. Judith Aiken went on in chapter 3 to point out how all your decisions should be examined in light of that vision. Here, I build on their points: Your efforts with staff should be in service to that same vision.

Your first effort to secure good staff comes when you hire the superintendent. A distinct advantage of hiring and retaining a good superintendent is having the same person for an extended period of time to create stability and to institutionalize hiring and selection practices that promote the goals important to the board. You want to attract and keep the best staff available—staff who buy into and share your district vision, who want to develop themselves to be the best they can be, and who are more apt to commit to helping others develop too. Moreover, when you commit to recruiting the best superintendent you can and to supporting his or her development, you can initiate a cascading effect. In other words, the superintendent will be more likely to commit to selecting and developing good principals, and the principals hopefully will take the same perspective toward teachers. This is the most positive possible outcome of your actions and can set the tone within the district for growth, development, and a commitment to people and to ongoing learning.

Once you have selected the superintendent and, as a board, clarified to him or her your values and expectations, you are entitled to expect the superintendent to select staff to carry out those expectations. You are not generally going to participate in the selection process, but you can make clear your desires so the superintendent selects the best possible people for the district's needs and vision. Superintendents described how there is no recipe for selecting the best people. Rather, it is a combination of instincts, standard procedures, and luck. A superintendent of a rural district in the Midwest admitted,

> Oh, I wish I had some—you know, concrete—method of choosing, but it always comes down to the subjective choice that I've made or subliminal reason I've made. You know, I try to look at the gestalt of the person and totality or whatever and come up with something. I do want them to be "Kids first"—to believe that, not just say it. I think we all kind of say that, but it's a smaller percent that actually live "Kids come first." When I find that, that's what I tend to go with.

A superintendent of a district of 16,000 students in the Midwest told of specific characteristics she looked for in candidates for positions:

> I do look for people that know the teaching and learning process and can communicate that and can express themselves well in writing and orally because I think they are out there in the forefront everyday being exemplary

models of what teaching and learning is all about. I also look for people that are committed too—even if there are things they don't know—I don't have a big problem with that if they make a commitment to learn. And I try to foster that by modeling that.

These superintendents made three very important points: one, the need to select the very best staff you can get; two, the part subjective judgment plays in selection; and three, the importance of staff learning and development after they are selected. Before I address staff learning, let me say a few things about the selection process. There are two sides to the emphasis on subjectivity: one is the very valid recognition that judgment about who really is the best person for the job is complex and somewhat impossible to reduce to a formula. Therefore, trusting your own instincts when hiring good people is not necessarily an arbitrary or capricious act but rather, as most superintendents have learned, trusting your instincts draws on a deep sense of knowing and past experiences.

But the other side of the issue about trusting one's instincts also needs to be examined and discussed frankly, and this is when subjectivity can lead easily to bias and discrimination. Björk and Gurley (2005) found that school boards and superintendents hired administrative candidates based on the kinds of leadership styles that they valued themselves. For example, when qualities such as power, control, and hierarchical leadership styles (often considered "masculine" traits) are valued over shared decision making or collaborative leadership styles ("feminine" traits), a male candidate is more likely to be hired than a female candidate. Such (perhaps unconscious) preferences can narrow the range of people you bring in to lead your district and thus have unintended consequences. Perhaps none of us can overcome all of our prejudices in this regard, but we can guard against them by two means: following set procedures and involving others in the selection process.

Set procedures are necessary from a practical point of view to enable you to compare one candidate to another in a fair and impartial manner. They are also necessary to avoid discrimination and other civil rights violations (Hoyle, Björk, Collier, & Glass, 2005; Beckner, 2004). Recruitment efforts must protect the rights of employers and the civil rights of candidates (Beckner, 2004). One way to avoid legal problems in the hiring process is by conducting structured interviews to ensure that all candidates are asked the same questions so that the information can be compared across candidates (Hoyle et al., 2005). Using panels or teams to interview is now the norm. Even when one person conducts the interviews, the questions can be developed by a team. Carefully crafting questions or asking for the same information in different ways helps you avoid being taken in by the applicant who is particularly skilled at being interviewed. A superintendent from the Midwest put it this way:

> We've also developed a set of questions that [are] strictly focused, and we may ask the same question in three or four different ways so that they have to—we get to the heart of whether or not they are just blowing smoke at us.

Involving others in interviewing candidates is another way to guard against one's own biases, that is, to test one's instincts against those of others. Several superintendents emphasized the importance of this. A superintendent from the Southwest told us,

> My administrators are involved in all of the administrative hiring. Because if they don't feel comfortable with that person—and we say that right up front, "We are a team, and we work together." And these people can help you. And so it really works.

Another superintendent from the Midwest noted,

> And the other thing I do through the interview process—I don't just interview them myself. I have our assistant superintendent of personnel and instruction and our elementary director [of] instruction. And I may have an extra person. I may bring [our] finance assistant just to get his take. Because sometimes we can get caught up, and he's got a totally different perspective.

Two superintendents from the South told how they get input from secretaries because of the validity of their insights. One from a district of 8,300 students told of calling people with whom the applicant had worked previously, "I will call the administrators. I will call the secretary of that building, and I will ask questions about the person. I'll find out a lot more about people than I would by calling their supervisor." Another from a district of 1,300 said,

> I often enjoy putting secretaries in that and give them a chance to meet—not interview—but by letting them meet the candidates and have a chance to see the—more perceptive than we often give them credit for as to what the person can do in the job.

As a board member, you can emphasize the importance of administration following set procedures and involving a variety of voices in the selection of staff.

Developing Good Leaders

I would be remiss if I did not note that some districts just do not have access to the quality applicants other districts attract. In that case, you have to be even more resourceful. Several school districts have found success encouraging graduates to return to their districts by offering financial incentives such as tuition assistance or college credits for programs involving dual enrollment in both high school and college courses in exchange for a commitment to teach in their school district for a period of time. But, as I will expand upon in the next section, if you cannot hire the ideal candidate for a position, you can develop him or her into a better employee.

DEVELOPING STAFF TO BE THE BEST THEY CAN BE

First, it would be wonderful if your selection process were infallible and you never failed to get the best person for the job. But, as I said above, there is no formula that will guarantee this. Second, it would also be wonderful if every person came into the job knowing all he or she would ever need to know to contribute to the district vision. But, given the pervasiveness of change that Kathryn Whitaker and Sheldon Watson described in chapter 1, it is unlikely that today's knowledge will be adequate to deal with every future challenge. A third wonderful possibility would be that every employee would decide to educate himself or herself for every contingency the district was likely to face. This also seems unlikely. So district leaders must commit to professional development. A superintendent of a district in the South with over 10,000 students told us:

> We want to make education for kids better. That has not been a problem, but to do the things you need to do . . . to be constantly involved in training and retraining of teachers—for a business, it does not appear to be as big a problem. There seems to be money for that—this is understood that we must retrain our electrical engineers. You just have to do that. For having people to understand that even 1 percent of a major budget—our budget is $60 million and 1 percent is $600,000. We don't spend $600,000 on retraining, and I am beginning to feel that we should be spending a lot more money on retraining.

It should come as no surprise to you at this point that I believe the district's staff development efforts should be aligned with its vision. Nor should it surprise you that I believe the board should take responsibility to see that it is so aligned. Your staff development program becomes a way for you not only to sell the vision but also to enact it.

Setting a Tone for Continuous Improvement

A staff development program focused on the district mission, well supported, and honed for effectiveness sends a strong message that you desire everyone to improve continuously. Of course, you can send this message as well in the hiring process. For example, a superintendent in the Midwest told us of an interview procedure she used:

> I kind of ask a question. One thing, I have a writing assignment. "Tell me the last educational journal you read, and what did you learn from that, and what are the implications for what you currently do?" That question is such a discriminate[ing] question. It discriminates between those that are reading the literature and those that are not. . . . I've never had anyone that I didn't hire come back and say, "Why didn't you hire me?" They know. And I know. And it's right there in the writing.

Once your staff is hired, you can continue to look for improvement. A superintendent of a suburban district in the South responded this way to a question about factors that enabled him to face challenges:

> I think all of us would acknowledge too that a facilitating factor for any of our issues is the presence of a staff which is committed to the concept of continuous improvement. One of the things I find most refreshing (in the 1990s) is that the concept of training and retraining as a lifelong experience appears to be institutionalized in education among our professional ranks today. That wasn't the case 20 years [ago] when there was a much stronger union push to make everyone look the same. I find it refreshing because we can capitalize on that commitment now by demonstrating that we're committed to providing professional resources or resources necessary to support professional training needs and, if we demonstrate that, then we're able to get past a few other problems in the meantime, because we're showing that we're committed to helping them.

The board can affirm the value of lifelong learning for district staff and model this commitment by your own efforts to learn. (Ramón Domínguez provides guidance for your learning efforts in chapter 7). Your commitment to learning and staying open and abreast of new trends and issues makes you much more aware of the overall health of your district and its commitment to lifelong learning.

Staff Development to Keep Good People

As I noted above, recruiting, keeping, developing, and relying on good staff are intertwined. On the negative side, one of the most common reasons given for leaving a school district is a lack of support and professional development. Nolan and Hoover (2004) argued that without professional development, administrators and teachers may become overwhelmed by the job and are likely to resort to survival tactics rather than best practices. They may never realize their potential. Evans (2001) argued that burnout results from a lack of challenge, exhaustion from trying harder, a lack of fulfillment, boredom, and a lack of self-efficacy—all of which can be alleviated by good staff development.

On the positive side, staff development may be one of the best ways to retain enthusiastic employees in the district and to avoid burnout (Wilmore, 2004). One way this became apparent to us was when superintendents talked about staff development as a means to retain good staff. A superintendent of a very small rural district told us,

> I try to give them opportunities where they can grow professionally. For instance, our school district has a no-limit professional growth plan, where they can be gone as many days during a year as seem to fit into their professional growth plan. Not like some districts where you have one professional growth day this year. . . . In our district they can be gone as many days as seems appropriate. . . . We had a policy that didn't cite a specific number of days, and I pushed it. I said we are going to use as many days as we need. Last year I had one teacher out of [a] 150-day contract that was gone 16 days. I just think that we're going to gain, improve the teacher knowledge base so that they are better prepared to meet the needs of the kids.

Staff Development for Personnel Problems

A painful aspect of leading any organization is facing up to and dealing with personnel problems. Sometimes, the ultimate painful action is that you need to terminate someone's employment. A superintendent with 24 years' experience put it bluntly:

> I've been fooled [in the selection process]. And you have to get rid of the cancer quick. So when you've made a mistake, you need to recognize, "I made a mistake, they don't need to be here" and get rid of them as fast as possible. Or it will get worse.

Before you do that, you will provide opportunities for that person to improve his or her performance. For example, one kind of problem personnel is the clock-watcher. The superintendent we just quoted had his own term for them: "With the eight-to-four teachers, I try and give them ways where they can improve their knowledge or skills."

Superintendents pointed out to us that beginners on a job, both teachers and administrators, can have difficulties and be seen as problems until they learn more about the demands of their roles and how to cope with them. Wise leaders will be prepared to provide development opportunities in such cases. A superintendent from the Midwest with 16 years' experience said,

> I look for two things. One, they have a passion for children and teaching and a strong work ethic, and then I can help them become good teachers. I will help them by professional development. With principals, I look for excellent teachers. If they have a good handle on their teaching and learning process and then have the people skills to provide leadership for a group, then I feel fairly successful or fairly comfortable. But you never feel good until they are in that position, and then it's too late. But then you work with it from there.

One superintendent said of beginning teachers,

> I think with the teacher—with the young teacher, and it seems to be an issue of immaturity—a lot of times they are aware and, if they bring that to you and you know they are self-monitoring, I have a little more faith in their ability that they are going to overcome some immature issues and develop better judgment—more mature judgment.

Another told of a beginning administrator who was struggling:

> I had a principal last year, and he moved up fairly quickly through the system as a teacher and then immediately he was an assistant principal. But the principal left and he became the principal, and I think he has all the capabilities by which to become an excellent principal, but I don't think he has the experience in terms of opportunities to look at and model others. And so actually I did take him out of the principalship and put him in the assistant principalship. And I hear that things are going really very well for him. But I just felt he just needed a mentor. He needed to learn. He needed an apprenticeship. He needed to learn at the elbow of a seasoned principal.

In the area of problem personnel as well as other areas, the board can set the tone for the district. You need to terminate problem personnel when it is necessary; until that moment comes, you need to provide them opportunities to learn. There is no magic formula, but I hope the words of these superintendents can help you learn to make good choices in the service of the district mission and the people who will bring it to pass.

RELY ON YOUR STAFF FOR THE DETAILS
OF PROBLEM SOLVING

Though most organizations are far from perfect (a fact that is clear to you if you've spent any time at all in leadership), the virtue of the organization is that it pools the talents and efforts of many individuals toward a common set of tasks. It stands to reason, then, that there is much to gain from allowing those individual talents and efforts to flourish. One step to accomplish this is to realize that you do not have to do everything yourself—that, in fact, some things will be done better if someone else does them. Perhaps board members accused of micromanaging do so because they have not learned this lesson. Superintendents spoke frankly to us about having to discover this truth. Even a superintendent of a district of only 240 students, where superintendents in fact have to do many different tasks, told of how he grew into this realization:

> So that is how it started, with me trying to define my role as superintendent and also with me kind of feeling like I was Superman and I could do everything for everybody. It took a while to understand that there are certain things that I could do better than others and there were other things that they could do far better than I.

He went on with these vivid examples:

> I can't remember, but it seems like it was a principal that had been a principal for many, many years used an analogy of a football player, and said, "When you carry the ball 35 times in each football game, eventually they are going to carry you off the field. You are going to be dazed and confused, perhaps with a concussion. If you learn how to hand off the ball to other people and pass the ball from time to time to those wide receivers, you are going to be much more effective, and so . . .you don't always have to carry the ball." So that was his message to me. Seems to make sense even today. When you have that Superman view of yourself when you first come out, you think you got to do it all. . . . I can remember a picture of [another superintendent], who really never did mature in his job, and he felt like he had to do it all. I can see vividly a picture in the [newspaper] that was one morning sent out across the state where he was helping take off the tires

on the rear wheels of a bus. They were doing bus inspections and he was
there doing that, and some people thought, "There is a man of action." But
at the time I thought, "There is a man that doesn't know his job."

Clearly, as the tire-changing superintendent demonstrates, and as stories of board members' interference illustrate, learning to rely on others
to do what they are best at is not an easy lesson to learn—but it is part
of effective leadership. This superintendent was a particularly vivid sto-
ryteller, but he was not the only one who had come to this realization.
Several superintendents told us the same thing. One from the South, a
superintendent from a rural district, put it this way:

> We have to rely on those principals and the teachers in the schools to pick
> up and help you plan and follow through on it. And in our position, we are
> constantly evaluating and looking at it and extending it and, you know, ask-
> ing those probing questions to keep it going. But I think that the front-line
> folks, the teachers and the principals, are so key in that planning. I believe
> it is the superintendent's responsibility to get it rolling, organize it, and
> then give it to them because they are going to be the ones, because they
> are there every day with the students, they're going to tend to the stu-
> dents' needs.

As I have said, for some people, this is not an easy lesson to learn. But
let me expand on this lesson to present an even more difficult one. Not
only should leaders pass jobs off to people who can do them better, but
sometimes they have to pass some of the thinking off as well. Not only
might any given leader not be the best one to carry out a task, but he or
she might not be the best one to come up with a solution to a problem.
Earlier in this chapter, I described the importance of bringing others' perspectives into the hiring processes. You can expand that notion into other
areas as well. Some of our superintendents described how they brought
others' ideas into solving problems. Board members can do that too.

A superintendent of a district of 5,000 students in the Mid-Atlantic
region told of his approach to vexing problems:

> What I do is confront the issues head on with other people. I put them on
> the table with the different sides of each issue. I say, "These are the prob-
> lems we have" and . . . "I do not have all the answers to these problems.

If I did, I would not be presenting them to you. We have to work together
with these problems." People appreciate this approach but find it frustrating. A lot of people do not want to spend a lot of time with the big issues. The best way to deal with problems is to involve people who can
help make the best decisions and share your frustrations. I certainly would
not want to deal with these problems alone.

Of course, staff will give honest input into problems only if you make it
safe for them to do so. The board and superintendent must establish a
tone in the district that welcomes questioning and critical thinking, even
though it may be painful to hear. A superintendent put his beliefs about
this in colorful terms:

> I think that opportunity has to be nonthreatening too, you know. I tell our
> administrative team that I possess the ability to screw a lot of things up,
> and if I say something and everybody out of loyalty thinks, "That's a hell
> of an idea"—and it may be the stupidest thing that anyone's ever thought
> of—but they don't feel at ease to give suggestions or even constructive
> criticism, some real bad things could happen that could be avoided, and I
> think somehow setting the environment for all people who are in your or-
> ganization to be able to give feedback, even some that's constructive crit-
> icism, feel at ease in doing that is real important.

One way to make it safe for staff to contribute their problem-solving
ideas is to listen carefully to what they say. Eduardo Arellano gives some
practical tips in chapter 12 on how to listen effectively. Another way, one
of the most painful of a leader's roles, is to have the broad shoulders to
take on criticism oneself but pass the glory on to others. In private, you
may confront staff with your concerns, but in public you praise them.
One superintendent from a suburban district in the South called this being a buffer. He said,

> I think it is absolutely critical, and I don't know how many times I have
> said, "You can beat on me, but don't beat on the folks who work with me,
> because it is a buffer." . . . You get paid a few extra shekels to take heat and
> the cheapest, most valuable thing you can give away is recognition.

He gave this example, "I found that if the guy in the mailroom did
something really well, the agency head picked up the award. And if

somebody screwed up near the top, the lightning . . . was probably going to end up in the mailroom." Board members rarely get paid the "few extra shekels" superintendents do, but you can benefit from the same lesson: If you want staff to participate in problem solving, set a tone in the district of appreciation for their efforts and their ideas.

DEVELOPING GOOD STAFF INTO GOOD LEADERS

Education leaders have developed many success strategies to ensure the school district can make improvements. A superintendent argued,

> I think we need to somehow think of a process that will identify our cream of the crop—same thing in identifying principals. You know, we, as superintendents, ought to be finding those people either to replace us or to get into the field. We know who the best teachers are.

Despite their best intentions to recruit candidates from within, superintendents admit they are often their own worst enemies when it comes to recruiting. They warn that care must be taken to avoid inadvertently undermining their own recruiting efforts by complaining about their jobs. In the following quote, the same superintendent explained how superintendents' and administrators' negative self-talk may act as a barrier to attracting good candidates to administrative jobs. He stated,

> Oftentimes, all they hear is negatives about being an administrator or a superintendent. Somehow, we have to turn that around and recruit the highest achieving or most successful teachers to continue to go on into administration, and the same thing with principals. Oftentimes, all they get bombarded with is maybe some of the frustrations . . . instead of really [trying] to recruit and encourage them to come—instead of maybe painting a picture that only a few crazy people like [us] would go in to do it. You know, really, I think that's part of the problem with school administration now and getting people to go into it.

A district that commits to investing in its people attracts and retains high-quality candidates. Your support and encouragement of educators, attracting quality people to the district, and your example as a board member can be an encouragement for others to become a part of your team.

Superintendents identify being an excellent teacher as one of the qualities they look for in recruiting potential administrators. Not all good teachers become successful administrators; however, superintendents perceive that poor teachers are very unlikely to become good administrators. A first-year superintendent discussed why he targeted the best teachers for administration.

> When you're looking for administrators—I've only been doing it for a year, so I don't have a whole lot of experience—but I have found that when you're looking for administrators, unfortunately you have to find your very best teacher and start there. I've been most successful with administrators I have hired who have been teachers that were superb teachers. I hated losing that good elementary teacher or that good secondary math teacher to make them an administrator. But that's the way I think. If you find a poor teacher or an average teacher, you have a chance at having a poor or less-than-average administrator.

Mentoring might be one of the best forms of support a district can provide to educators in the way of professional development. It is mandated by over half of the states for teachers and administrators and is especially important during early career stages (Daresh, 2002; Villani, 2006). Wilmore (2004) argues employees such as principals and teachers must be mentored if they are to succeed.

I hope the ideas in this chapter help you secure and keep the staff you need to meet your district vision. Again, briefly, here are the suggestions:

1. Keep the district vision in mind as you deal with decisions about staff.
2. Get the best superintendent you can to meet the district vision, and emphasize the importance of hiring and developing staff to achieve the vision.
3. Look for staff members who have the following characteristics: a belief in children; a passion for excellence, teaching, and learning; a strong work ethic; good judgment; and good oral and written communication skills.

4. Realize that hiring is a subjective process regardless of the formal processes involved.

5. Establish sound human resource policies and follow the laws governing the recruitment and hiring of personnel to protect the rights of the school district and the civil rights of employees and future employees.

6. Involve others, such as administrators and secretaries, in the process to guard against one's own biases and to ensure the candidates are a good fit for working with current staff.

7. Provide staff development for employees at all levels in the school district based on the needs of the employee, the school, and the district.

8. Provide development opportunities for employees to help keep them in the district and enhance their advancement to other levels.

9. Commit to helping staff become successful even if they initially have difficulty adjusting to the job and the school district.

10. Trust competent employees to do their jobs well.

11. Show staff they are appreciated.

12. Provide for collaboration with staff at all levels of the school district to empower them as leaders and to build trust between the superintendent, administrators, teachers, and other employees.

13. Identify the cream of the crop from within the teacher ranks and grow your own candidates for administrative positions.

14. Focus on the positive aspects of the jobs to attract candidates to the district; avoid negative self-talk about the undesirable aspects of the job, which might deter viable candidates from aspiring to or applying for jobs, especially administrative positions.

7

SUCCESS STRATEGY: LEARN ABOUT EDUCATION AND YOUR ROLE

Ramón Domínguez

As you begin your journey as a school board member, or continue on one you've already started, learning about education and your role on the board may be the greatest challenge you face. This chapter looks at learning as one-third of a triad that defines school board work today. The other two-thirds are change and interpersonal relationships. You will not be able to escape these three entities, so you must learn to deal with them and use them to lead your district toward schools that are both good for all children and good places for adults to work. Kathryn Whitaker and Sheldon Watson gave you in chapter 1 a thorough picture of the changes that affect public education and your role in it. Mary Devin, Teresa Miller, and Trudy Salsberry have dedicated chapter 13 to relationships. My chapter will be about learning. Since we do much of our learning in relationships, however, I will not separate learning from relationships in this chapter.

Leading in a culture of change requires learning. It requires not only appreciating how much you have to learn but also how much you have to teach. You must enter into relationships with the goals of learning as much as you can and teaching as much as you can. One way I think about learning and teaching relationships is through the concept of mentoring, and I will devote much of this chapter to this concept.

YOUR PERSONAL VALUES AND BELIEFS

I will start with a learning task where relationships seem less important: learning about your own most deeply held values and beliefs. A never-ending task in being an educational leader is determining where you stand. Board members, whether appointed or elected, carry a major responsibility in regard to their constituents and definitely to the children within the district. The board member is surrounded by many individuals and groups seeking advice, assistance, and, in many instances, special considerations. A question that you as a board member must wrestle with is how you will respond to constituents, and that begins with how you see your role.

Traditionally, the board member is seen as the community representative and is expected to promote the public interest in education and to uphold the accepted values within the community (Goldhammer, 1964). In explaining this tradition, Enomoto and Bair (2002) point out that schools retain and perpetuate existing cultural values and norms of the society. But in the 21st century, we find many communities that are made up of smaller communities, competing interests, and conflicts about values. The "public interest" and "accepted values" are terms that do not have the clarity they perhaps once had. The question you must ask yourself is, Which component of society and whose interests will I work hardest to represent? This requires that you clarify for yourself your own values and beliefs, what Fullan (2001a) called your "moral purpose" (p. 3).

As a board member, you have the power to influence and affect the experiences of many children, and such power must be taken very seriously. The board and superintendent are not only influencing the economic, political, and social structure of a community, but they are also determining the skills, career opportunities, social/psychological development, and civic formation of each individual child. Commitment, dedication, and a desire to see others benefit and succeed are essential actions needed to meet the enormous responsibility placed on the shoulders of the superintendent and board. Both entities must work together and learn from each other. You must make sense of the complexity of your role. In fact, you will make sense of it, but you must make sense in a way that leads you to create schools that are good for the people who study and work in them. You must decide what that value means to you and how it will play out in your work as a leader. It helps to be introspective and open minded.

Considering the variety of influences, your multidimensional role requires introspection, an open mind, a worldwide view, and reciprocity. The complexity of the 21st century requires you to interpret and challenge all the different voices, ideas, and influences thrust upon you (Bogdan & Biklen, 2007).

Paradoxically, having clarified your own values and beliefs, you must then determine how tightly you will hold on to them and how much you will compromise them for the sake of a smoothly running district. As Fullan (2001a) wrote,

> Moral purpose is about both ends and means. In education, an important end is to make a difference in the lives of students. But the means of getting to that end are also crucial. If you don't treat others (for example, teachers) well and fairly, you will be a leader without followers. (p. 13)

You can draw on many sources to clarify your values and beliefs: seminal experiences you have had, reading and reflection, your upbringing, and religious or cultural principles you have found important. As a board member, you will also learn about your values and beliefs from dialogue with your board colleagues. I will develop this idea further below.

Considering your values and beliefs in the light of those of your colleagues is particularly important to your effectiveness. Mountford and Brunner (1999) conducted a study regarding board member motivation and the decision-making process. Their findings indicated that board members motivated by personal agendas (sometimes referred to as "single-issue board members") inhibited the collaborative and decision-making process among the board. Further, board members working to empower others felt excluded from the decision-making process by the single-issue board member. Discord and conflict arise when board members differ substantially from one another about what actions and policy decisions to expect from the superintendent. In that case, more time is spent on disagreement and ego concerns than on pursuing conscientious decisions.

Similar issues arise in determining district priorities. When board members are able to delineate individual district priorities and work with each other to agree on the best and most effective direction for the district, the school community benefits.

Here is one example of how not being a single-issue board member can make you more effective in leading your district. A superintendent of 24 years from a suburban district told us:

> Once you have a solid board of education who is willing to set aside their personal wants and desires, you have to make sure that those folks are there to assist children and set aside personal agendas to assist all children.

This means, in effect, that you face a dilemma. You cannot get elected or appointed without support from a constituency, and you cannot lead without having strong guiding principles; however, as a member of a board, you may need to compromise your representation of your supporters to work effectively with others. Learning how to compromise well is the work of a lifetime. Each individual board member and superintendent needs to reflect on the following questions:

- Am I willing to forgo my personal agenda in order to benefit the school district?
- Am I willing to listen, compromise, and learn?
- Am I willing to accept change?
- Am I willing to respect others and their opinions?
- Am I committed to respecting the powers vested in me by the state?
- Am I committed to ethical behavior as delineated in the district's code of conduct?

LEGAL DEFINITIONS OF SCHOOL BOARD ROLES

Most textbook and legal treatments call for "board members to function only as members of the board and to make clear in their policies and in their actions the distinction between policymaking (the board's function) and administration (the superintendent's function)" (Ashby, 1968, pp. 47–48). You and your board can lead effectively when you allow the superintendent the opportunity to manage the operation of the district with minimal interference. Micromanagement by the board defeats the premise of a supportive and pressure-free team relationship. This is a principle you must keep constantly before you, but it is not always easy in practice to distinguish policymaking from administration. So, you have one more learning task: to work out the specifics of what it means to make policy and what it means to administer, and how to sort things out when it is not clear where one function ends and the other begins.

Your professional associations can help here, as can attendance at school board professional development activities and reading professional literature. You can also learn about this from your superintendent, whose responsibility it is to assist you in delineating your role.

Two of the major roles of a board are to hire the superintendent and to make policy. Your role should not place you in the position of a micromanager. As a superintendent of a large district in the Midwest put it,

> To function more effectively is to see the whole and not the parts. I think that one of the things I'd like to do with our folks here would be to get them to understand district-level concerns and not just the problems of an elementary school in a certain section of the city.

Again, you may find this a delicate balancing act since you are responsible both for the district as a whole and for the portion of the district that elected you.

Therefore, it is incumbent upon the superintendent to guide you in learning about policy and procedures by understanding these issues: how policy is developed and implemented through procedures, and the effects policy decisions have, not only at the district level but at the departmental level too. You can look to your superintendent, in conjunction with the school attorney, to mentor you regarding the powers and limits granted by the law in exercising your responsibilities.

SHARING VALUES AND BELIEFS WITH YOUR FELLOW BOARD MEMBERS

Learning from Current Board Members

One of your greatest tasks is to learn to dialogue with your fellow board members over values and beliefs. This dialogue takes place within a network of complex relationships. Figure 7.1 reflects the manner in which the board members affect each other. The plus (+) symbol represents an amiable and positive relationship between board members. The positive connection allows for open communication, compromise, support, and in some instances, parallel views on a variety of issues. The negative (−) symbol represents a situation whereby board members may have strong personal, professional, and role-related differences that might heighten disagreement on a number of issues. Negative interactions and relationships sometimes are generated by self-interest, rivalry, and ambition, creating unproductive disagreement and eventually resulting in uncontrollable discord. The neutral (0) position signifies a relationship that allows board members to approach issues with an open mind.

The optimum role adopted by the board member would be the neutral position in that decisions would not be based on the personal or professional relationship but on issues and the effect they have on the district. Kowalski and Keedy (2005) emphasized the importance of "relational communication," defined as a process in which "information is exchanged in multiple directions, and persons influence one another's behavior over and above their organizational role, rank, and status" (p. 215). Figure 7.1 represents an example of a board consisting of three members. Any of the relationships can change and become more positive or negative depending on the different experiences encountered in addressing issues. Fluid personal and professional relationships are a part of serving in the capacity of a board member.

The illustration depicts some of the possible interactions among only those three. Extending to a board with seven members, the complexity

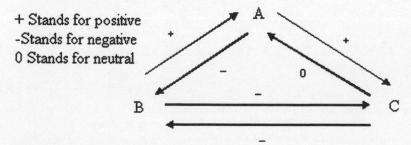

+ Stands for positive
-Stands for negative
0 Stands for neutral

Figure 7.1.   Board interaction relationships

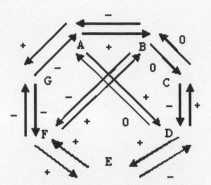

Figure 7.2.   Seven-member interaction pattern

of interactions would definitely increase. A seven-member board is a realistic representative body existing in a number of school districts. Figure 7.2 illustrates some of the possible interactions among members. Simultaneously, each individual board member is subject to influence from multiple constituencies, as shown in Figure 7.3. Finally, putting this all together, we see in Figure 7.4 an incredibly complex web of relationships in which you must work to provide good education for all children.

In this web, you must learn to share your values and beliefs respectfully with your board colleagues. Therefore, one of the first steps in the networking process involves asking other board members to share with you their philosophy of education. As a board member, when you share your understanding of the educational process as well as your beliefs

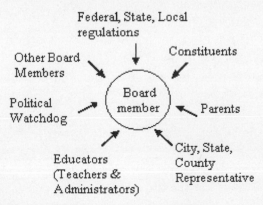

Figure 7.3.   Constituencies influencing board members

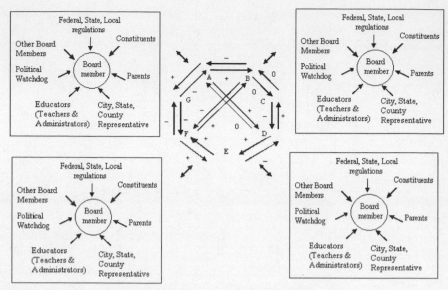

Figure 7.4.   School board member's web of relationships

about students, parents, teachers, and administrators, others can better understand your points of reference. Essential to this process is outlining your concerns and reservations regarding the district. What elements of the district do you value and want to maintain or enhance? Which do you want to modify or change? Disagreement, as an important element of communication, can exist but in a moderate and manageable level, while discussion and questions remain highly valued activities.

The desire to modify or change also needs to be balanced with a discussion of district priorities. What are the district priorities you have set in your mind? What is important for you to address during your term of service? Board members can list and compare their priorities to determine similarities and differences. Awareness of individual priorities is important in understanding at least at a minimal level the reasons a certain board member reacts to board business and issues in a particular manner.

Awareness is further enhanced through the discussion of your individual expectations about the district. What expectations do you have of the superintendent, staff, students, parents, and other board members?

What expectations do you have regarding the district in general? What changes do you want to implement during your term of service? Most important is the discussion about nonnegotiable items. In what areas are you not willing to negotiate or compromise? Discussion about nonnegotiables provides you the opportunity to avoid a variety of conflicts involving the school board and a number of entities: community, superintendent, district employees, and state/national agencies.

Most important is for you and other board members to outline the expectations each has of the superintendent. On these expectations, you must reach some consensus. As a unit, the board provides an agreed-upon set of expectations and requirements. At the same time, individual board members provide input regarding their perspectives on the expectations. The initiative is not a one-time activity but an ongoing learning process since the board/superintendent relationship fluctuates because of time, community climate, change in personal perspective, and the content of issues. You must also understand that the superintendent may well want to protect himself or herself from extreme fluctuations. Therefore, he or she may urge you to establish early the system by which you will evaluate him or her. A superintendent from a very large district in the East described his thinking in negotiating how his board would evaluate him:

> I was fortunate enough with some mentors a few years ago when I negotiated my contract, I negotiated the terms of the evaluation and I negotiated the instrument of the evaluation, and I would recommend that to anyone, I suppose anywhere. Although there tends to be a correlation between size and mischievous behavior, but if someone wants you, they'll get you and they can do it in a number of ways. They can create criteria that are impossible to be met or they can change the rules of the game in the eleventh hour. So I have been very fortunate in the last few years that I have had a solid instrument that has served me very well.

A reciprocal process is important for the board. The superintendent also needs to elaborate to you his or her district priorities and educational beliefs. One superintendent put it this way:

> I think the same thing [board turnover] is true for the superintendent. You know it takes about three years, and sometimes we have such a turnover

that we don't get three years. [You cannot] start [until] your philosophy really come[s] forward in the school system.

Ideally, at some point, the board chair will also initiate an overview of the board's priorities and agreed-upon educational philosophy. Individual board members are encouraged to comment and provide their perspectives regarding the general overview. Even though a basic board consensus has been reached on the priorities and educational philosophy, the understanding still remains that individual board members can cross the consensus boundary on particular board agenda items or issues. The realization exists that board members have stepped into their seat with their individual ideas about education and plans for enhancing the district.

All of this may sound mostly like a venture into interpersonal relationships, but it is a venture into learning as well (see Mary Devon, Teresa Miller, and Trudy Salsberry's chapter 13 for a more complete discussion). Learning about your role comes from listening to multiple constituencies, including the superintendent and other board members. A superintendent from the Southeast said this:

> It is very important, we want to cultivate people and it goes back to the listening, we have to be good listeners and we cannot take offense. Like an old saying, "Everybody can tell us how to do our jobs better than we are doing, and most do." But on occasion they have good ideas and we have to be in tune.

So your ability to listen, garner various perspectives, and balance your perspectives with the needs of your constituents toward what is in the greater public good is a learning process and a daunting one. Learning about each other as well as understanding and supporting each other are essential in reaching decisions beneficial to the district. As board members, you want to avoid micromanagement strategies and the exclusion of other board colleagues in the decision-making process. Instead, a collaborative approach enhances full board participation and a mutual and respectful relationship. Two recent sources may help you bring forth your own ideas in respectful ways and are discussed in different books by the same authors, *Crucial Conversations* and *Crucial Confrontations* (Patterson, Grenny, McMillan, & Switzler, 2002, 2005).

Learning from Veterans

When placed in a board seat, either through election or appointment, board members come to the board with varying backgrounds. Business persons, health professionals, blue-collar workers, community activists, retirees, civil service employees, and a myriad of professionals bring experience and knowledge to the position. Variation in background often means varied perspectives, and this can translate to conflict—but it can also translate to learning opportunities. Board members can learn from each other's knowledge. A superintendent from the Southeast talked about how she drew on others' expertise:

> If you don't feel that you have the skills to address the individual situation, you at least have the skills to know how to find someone that you can ascertain the answers to the questions to help you resolve the situation.

Another superintendent added,

> My best efforts are put forth by the experiences that I get working with my cohorts and associating with people that do things and are good in the fields that I want to take on. If I want to do scheduling, if I want to do finance, or if I want to do building, I always know somebody to go to that can help in that area. And you can rely on those people and do a whole lot of digging in just a little while, rather than have to go back and get it all yourself.

You can take the same approach to your board colleagues. It is especially important to realize that neophyte board members can learn from veterans. A superintendent's description of his own learning from others' experiences applies equally well to new board members:

> You don't know the behind-the-scenes politics that's going on, you don't know some of the—even though it might look bad at one of those public meetings, it really isn't as bad as it looks because it's all orchestrated in order to get votes passed for a budget or some kind of an initiative—and learning about how to get things done and how to weed through all those hurdles so that you keep your focus and your target on kids is really a challenge, and when you work for somebody that knows how to do that and can serve as a mentor for you, that's—I mean, that is valuable.

LEARNING FROM THE SUPERINTENDENT

The superintendent can mentor and support you in a number of categories. These categories include coming to see problems from the perspective of a trained administrator; preparing yourself for board meetings, institutional functions, and public relations/communications; and working within legal and ethical standards.

Seeing Problems from the Administrator's Perspective

One delicate matter you will have to deal with is your relationship with the superintendent. On the one hand, you select, evaluate, and, if necessary, terminate the contract of the superintendent. On the other hand, she or he probably has far more knowledge and experience in education than you do. Because of your role as an overseer of the district, you may believe your perspective should prevail. Because of the superintendent's substantial education and experience, he or she may believe his or her perspective should prevail. One superintendent applied this perspective to the topic of bringing issues before the board:

> Unless there are extraordinary circumstances, I think each of our boards expects us to bring problems to them. They expect us to keep them apprised and to be anticipating what's coming down the pike, but I don't think that they expect us to present them to them as problems. I think they expect us to present these matters to them in a way which demonstrates that we have given thoughtful consideration to the matter and have taken the time and done the proper study to lay out options and alternatives which ideally lead them to the right solution. And quite honestly, that is part of our role.

Learning how to negotiate between these contrary sets of expectations (the board's authority should prevail versus the superintendent's expertise should prevail) is a challenge. Use your superintendent as one source of information about how to proceed. In addition, as always, go beyond the superintendent's perspective to discuss matters with your fellow board members, and use your school board association as a resource to guide you.

Preparing for Board Meetings

One of the best approaches to enhance communication and trust between both parties involves monthly meetings between each board member and the superintendent. The superintendent should take the time to review the monthly board agenda with each board member. Specifically, the superintendent reviews current issues, provides additional information, and answers questions. The essence of the activity is to inform and educate regarding the items up for consideration. A well-informed board member is in a stronger position to react, provide a perspective, and eventually determine the feasibility of voting to accept or reject an item. The superintendent does not place the board member in a position to discuss his or her vote. Both parties can provide their perspectives and opinions on the items. Therefore, the essence of the process is to enhance the networking relationships. By making time to meet and listen to the superintendent, and vice versa, the opportunity develops to open the channels of communication between the superintendent and the board.

Learning from the Superintendent About the District Staff and Operations

You can also learn much from the superintendent about the day-to-day operations of the district. The superintendent needs to provide a detailed and ongoing review of the mission, goals, and organization of the district. Important for the board members to have is an organizational chart displaying departments, and reporting relationships and personnel. Functions and responsibilities also need to be delineated. An additional step involves connecting the organizational chart to the actual personnel and facilities. The superintendent can ask the senior-level managers to provide board members with materials pertinent to their areas of responsibility as well as to conduct a tour of facilities under the jurisdiction of the senior manager.

These visits will allow board members not only to visit the physical plant but to meet the professionals maintaining the daily function of the district. Familiarizing the board members with the function of the district (facilities, personnel, finances) provides an awareness and connection to a real environment rather than to an abstract idea. District employees at various levels are the major contributors to the function of the district. In these visits, you will get the opportunity to know the employees, and they will get to know you.

Genuine communication and respect are important elements in questions and deliberations between the board and staff. Board members must keep in mind that their positions on the board do not supersede their responsibilities to treat staff with dignity. Treating individuals with respect and dignity is important. From one superintendent's perspective, "We have to go back to that one-on-one and looking at people as individuals." Shouting, threatening, reprimanding, or accusing do not have a place in board-staff relationships. The superintendent is again pivotal in mentoring the board on appropriate protocol.

Learn About Operating Within the Bounds of Law, Policy, and Ethics

Board members have important roles. Exercising leadership for the welfare of your community can be very satisfying, but the skills you need to get support from your constituents and to get elected may be different from the skills you need to be a policymaker, leader, and representative of your school district. One superintendent expressed this in blunt terms:

One of the difficulties that I found in the three superintendencies that I've held is the issue of a school board member making the transition from politician to policymaker and the frequency with which I've had to deal with that. That's something that I think I have in place. But it's a constant repetitive kind of difficulty that you have a new board member who comes on and misunderstands the role and, of course, we provide orientation and counseling and nudging, but it's a challenge.

Since you are now an elected official in a fairly well-defined role, your actions need to take place within the bounds of state law. Therefore, it is incumbent upon the superintendent to guide you in learning about policy and procedures regarding the following issues: how policy is developed and implemented through procedures, the effect policy decisions have not only at the district level but at the departmental level, and the importance of utilizing *Robert's Rules of Order* to conduct board meetings.

In working with policy, the superintendent, in conjunction with the school attorney, needs to mentor the board members regarding the powers and limits granted by the law in exercising their responsibilities. Interactions within the board, among individual board members, and with the superintendent need careful monitoring by each entity and the school district attorney. Self-monitoring falls within the requirement of ethical behavior and the commitment to guide and assist the district in meeting its mission, goals, priorities, and expectations. Since laws differ from one state to another, this chapter cannot provide specifics that would apply to all readers. The National School Boards Association provides information in this regard at its website, www.nsba.org/site/page_nestedcats.asp?TRACKID=&CID=381&DID=8622.

As indicated earlier, the board member and superintendent need to be continuously aware of restrictions placed by the open-meeting act in setting their individual interaction in motion. Your superintendent can be an invaluable guide to you in learning the legal requirements of your state. Credentialed and experienced in leading educational institutions, the superintendent has a responsibility to help you succeed in district matters. Mentoring you in matters of policy and ethics strengthens the definition of your role. Appropriate protocol is actually a form of ethical behavior. Taking on the policymaking position on a school board requires commitment to a code of ethics. The superintendent, in coordination with the board chair, has the responsibility to discuss the code with the board and review its importance and implications. Through example and close adherence to the code, the superintendent is the role model for the board and vice versa.

Learning from Your Superintendent About Communication

You will benefit if your superintendent mentors board members in public relations and communication. The experience of a 24-year veteran superintendent from a suburban district spoke to the importance of public relations:

> You are still superintendent in the grocery store as you're going through the checkout line. The checker knows a teacher or has a child in a classroom, and you're still dealing with public relations. So our job never ends.

It may be less hectic in that grocery store, but it never ends because you're selling public education.

The situation is essentially the same for you as a board member. As community representatives, you will definitely be in the public eye during board meetings and at community functions. Constituents, special interest groups, teachers, parents, and other groups will want to communicate with you. A superintendent interested in your success will take the time to prepare you in communication strategies. Realizing the need to possess skills in public relations, a superintendent from a rural district related her experience in learning how difficult it can be to be a good communicator in tense situations:

> We just adopted a new strategic plan and quite frankly it caused me to have ulcers because you would go into a school and have an open meeting and ask all the community leaders to come and they would lambaste everything that you have done, and you know, I would think it really gave me an interesting perspective on some issues.

Learning to apply response techniques is also important. You will be placed in difficult situations. You may be publicly challenged on a specific issue by a political watchdog. How you respond may determine the positive or negative resolution of the issue. Suspending judgment, understanding your audience, and placing a check on your emotions is good advice given by a superintendent from a district of nearly 2,000 students: "I think part of the secret to successful superintendency, principalship, teacher, is knowing your surroundings and identifying and not acting too quickly."

Your superintendent can help you learn this, and one of the most important parts of "not acting too quickly" is understanding how to separate emotion from fact in responding. Holding the emotion in check while providing a factual response can be an effective communication approach. Factual responses are particularly important when working with the media. The board member has an allegiance and responsibility to the other board members, the superintendent, and the district when discussing or presenting district-related matters. Understanding how to relate to the media and, most important, knowing when to refer matters to the public affairs director comes through mentoring by the superintendent. Trust and respect between the superintendent and board members allows information to be genuine and flow without interference. Interference such as a board member conducting a press conference without the input or participation of the superintendent may lead to misunderstandings.

Mentoring board members on methods to develop and ask relevant questions is important to avoid misguided conflict. Refraining from accusatory content, addressing questions with the "I" rather than the "you" reference, controlling tone, and knowing the audience are but a few considerations to be taken into account while asking questions. The superintendent is in a position to provide this guidance. Chapter 12 in this book, by Eduardo Arellano, also provides good advice in this regard.

BOARD MENTORING OF THE SUPERINTENDENT

Up to this point, I have been writing about how the superintendent can guide your learning, but I must point out as well how much the superintendent can learn from you if you are willing to mentor him or her. One superintendent described it this way:

> I was very fortunate with my first superintendency. It was a small, very rural district, with the school board. That board was an appointed board, but they taught me a great deal about politics. I would say that I was not prepared for the political atmosphere when I walked out into that first job. I was very young, and I'm still young, but the school board helped me tremendously in understanding that community and the politics. I had two governing bodies, a city council that I received funding from as well as a county, and they were at odds all the time, and I basically walked into a hot bed and, if it had not been for the guidance of a veteran school board, I would have had difficulties. I very much needed that help at that time. So, as far as my preparation, I wasn't prepared. It was the school board that led me and taught me a great deal.

Another superintendent described the mentoring received from the school board:

> The first school board that I worked with cultivated me in a womb with nurturance and they were an appointed board and leaders in the community

and they served on the board in service. The board did not elevate them, they were already elevated; so they approached the board in terms that it was service and were very nurturing and understood that I would make a lot of mistakes and they would help along the way and I wasn't prepared to be catapulted into the alley of politics and we all have to walk that alley every day and it changes.

I share these stories primarily to make the point that one of your learning tasks is learning how to teach and mentor others. The board as a unit is indeed in a position to assist and mentor the superintendent. As I noted above, each board member networks with, and participates in, a number of entities. The relationships and working partnerships developed within and among these entities expands the scope of knowledge and experience of each board member in the areas of local and state political dynamics, community issues, legislative initiatives, economic and workforce strategies, federal mandates, and awareness of the needs and concerns of parents and school personnel. The combined knowledge base of the board is an excellent source of information that contributes to guiding and assisting the superintendent. As one superintendent told us, "I think [the board members] are working to [help] me to help them, which is a tremendous amount of—well, I think they trust us tremendously and I'm just very pleased."

The key to both learning from and mentoring is to develop a respectful and trustworthy relationship with your superintendent. The board wants to develop a communication environment that promotes respect for the superintendent. The words of one writer from 60 years ago still ring true: "Since he must obtain practically all his powers and duties from the school board, the best qualified superintendent in the world cannot succeed without the cooperation of the board" (Reeder, 1946). In essence, the board can mentor and guide the superintendent through both positive and difficult situations. However, in order to mentor and assist effectively, the board needs to respect the superintendent both personally and professionally. Even though a board member may not connect personally with the superintendent, it is still essential to allow the superintendent to exercise his or her personality. Further, the superintendent should expect a team relationship, support, freedom from special interests' pressure, and open communication (Tuttle, 1963).

Of course, ethical behavior is a must for both parties. Specifically, board members should acknowledge that their individual authority and/or power does not supersede that of other citizens (Educational Research Service, 1975). The board can utilize all of its combined experience to guide the superintendent in a variety of areas, specifically regarding the external political environment. Since the board members are "community representatives," the assumption is that they have been involved to some extent in the political arena. When the board works with a united and conscientious perspective, the superintendent is in a strong position to carry out duties effectively. With a supportive and positive relationship between the superintendent (mentee) and board (mentor) that allows for critical conversations, the superintendent can confidently initiate new innovations and experience professional growth. Through their community contacts, board members can help the superintendent connect not only with a variety of organizations but also with the power brokers in the community. Therefore, mentoring the superintendent in the politics of the community can be accomplished in several ways.

First, in a workshop format under the guidance of the school district's attorney, board members present their perspective of the political environment in the community. The presentation, to some extent, not only allows the superintendent to understand the political decision-making reasoning of each board member but also provides avenues the superintendent can access regarding specific political issues or dilemmas. For example, a board member who is a member of the Chamber of Commerce can assist the superintendent in learning about the business community and working productively with business leaders/representatives.

Second, each board member can agree to introduce the superintendent to several community entities. For example, a board member familiar with state political figures can engage the superintendent in meetings involving local state senators or representatives. The interaction is not only an introduction but also a long-term relationship aimed at addressing the needs of education and the school district. The board member with a background in community activism can be helpful in providing the superintendent a perspective of grassroots organizations seeking a voice in the community. The objective is to give the superintendent an understanding of the different entities and political philosophies affecting future school district decisions. The superintendent's role is not necessarily to align with the different entities; rather, it is to respect their perspectives.

Third, board members possess individual expertise in a variety of areas. A board member not professionally credentialed or possessing a distinct and powerful position can still contribute to the mentoring and learning curve of the superintendent. For example, board members well-connected with parents have been instrumental in gaining favorable passage of school bond initiatives. The superintendent is in a prime position to gain expertise in construction, finance, real estate, bond elections, transportation, negotiation, political strategizing, and many other pertinent areas.

Accepting the position of board member or superintendent requires a definite commitment to public education. Both positions require tremendous learning and the patience and determination to "grow into" the job. Both positions are honorable and only those individuals willing to uphold the highest standards need apply.

8

CHALLENGE:
SHORTAGES OF RESOURCES

Rhonda McClellan, Adrienne Hyle, and L. Nan Restine

Client demographics [have] changed drastically. State and federal mandates have increased. The problem of fiscal resources has become acute. Educational reform continues to be a political issue rather than an educational issue.

—A suburban superintendent

Whether you agree or disagree with this quote, most would agree that many school districts face situations similar to those aforementioned. Shrinking funding, increasing mandates, and unstable school enrollments have led to a shortage of resources, adding to the challenges educational leaders face today. To adapt to today's school environment, many practitioners argue that both schools and boards must become more adept in handling complexity and seeking resources in innovative ways.

The voices of our superintendents reflect concerns about the shortage of resources; we hope that the depth and breadth of their concerns will provide counsel for you as a school board member as you, too, face the issue of resource shortages. If you recognize the relationship between funding and political agendas, you can use your skills and knowledge about how funding patterns influence legislation, attitudes in the community, and professional development to tip the scales in favor of your agenda and goals. We invite you into the world of superintendents to see their challenges firsthand so that you can rethink how best to meet the increased need to use resources wisely for your school district and to help educate others on the most pressing issues at hand.

In this chapter we introduce you to a variety of superintendents' perspectives on the scarcity of resources. Their voices discuss the changing educational needs of your constituents and suggest ways you might become better equipped to prepare students for the 21st century despite resource constraints. Specifically, this inside view gives you an idea about how you might collaborate with your superintendent, other board members, and community members to address the district's resource prioritization so that you can allocate resources to ensure success for all students.

In the following sections, our superintendents speak to the current state of today's schools, their changing communities, and shrinking funds. In a later section, these superintendents refer to strategies that have assisted them in overcoming their resource shortages by working with others and expanding the boundaries of leadership to include board members, community experts, and others who are capable of contributing leadership and needed expertise.

THE LAW AND DOLLARS

A basic understanding of politics, policy, and mandates has helped many superintendents provide stewardship for their schools and communities. To be politically savvy, a school board member first has to acknowledge this savvy as an important attribute for today's educational leaders. Your election to the board demonstrates that you are well aware of this. However, as pointed out by a superintendent of a rural district, rarely are teachers who will become school leaders as knowledgeable about or as educated in legalities as the job may require. She suggests that it is important to educate teachers interested in becoming leaders within their schools:

> Maybe the answer is that the training needs to be back at classroom teachers. . . . All of a sudden, you're an administrator and at 32 credits later you're going to be an expert in all these areas. They need to learn more about the legislative process that we don't even think about as part of teacher prep.

And, yet, we're in the most political business that there is . . . with the funding the way it is. So maybe that is where it needs to be [in] that area. And it wouldn't have to be an extensive amount of time that we spend on [the legislative process]. But maybe it needs to be earlier.

Legal savvy today requires knowing the current policies and policymakers. Furthermore, influencing legislation and informing legislators about what is happening in schools becomes imperative, because, as pointed out by the following suburban superintendent, decision making about education is done by legislators who know little about education: "The other [issue] is the funding issues of public education and the nature that the legislature has taken upon itself to become experts in education and providing legal ramifications on school districts." Legislators may need to understand more about education, but we believe educators also need to understand more about legislative processes.

ERODING FINANCES AND TAX BASES

Scarcity of resources is not a new concern for schools. Familiar shortages and the demands of increasing need have been a topic of concern for a long time. School districts are not independent businesses that manage their own revenue generation and expenditures but are part of a complex, and often difficult to comprehend, state financial system (Glass, 2005). As you continue your service on the board, you will become well acquainted with limited resources to meet unlimited needs. Increasing student populations and the scarcity of resources compound the difficulties of providing services. Superintendents of both large and small school districts experience funding shortages. A superintendent from a suburban district explains:

> [Our] district has grown significantly and with that, you know, the problems get larger; they get more complex. You get more people. There are more human dynamics involved in all of that. You get situations of overcrowding, which—in terms of human behavior, that does a lot of things for students and teachers and staff members. Resources become stretched, and so you—I guess maybe from a superintendent's point of view—the sociology of a whole job has become much more complex.

This superintendent reminds us that growing school districts may not have the tax base to keep up with increases in student numbers while smaller school districts are no longer exempt from the rapid growth urban schools have faced for many years.

In fact, situations are compounded when local support is primarily from a single-property tax base, with little or no industry. A rural district superintendent with 9 years of experience commented,

> Our publics are not accustomed to a growth-oriented school system. . . . All of our schools are 30 years or older. We're now in a position, like many districts in this area of the state, of rapid enrollment growth . . . 7, 8, 9% a year. All of our schools are full. We just do not have any more classroom space. . . . The problem is convincing the public we need the space, and then after that, getting the support for it. . . . There are less than 6,000 people in each town. There's only personal-property tax base; there's no industry in either town—none. . . and they don't want to spend money on taxes. They love their schools, but they don't like to increase property tax revenue.

The consistent shortage of funding dollars, changes in population growth, and an eroding tax base are challenges that affect the difficulty of financing schools.

CHANGING COMMUNITIES

More specifically than just an expanding population, communities are encountering an expansion of population diversity. Changes in demographics and population shifts require different responses from those previously provided by the school district. Although creative solutions for scarcity of funding and flexibility for growth are essential, socially just responses are also essential as school districts are faced with resistance from some of their constituents about the rights of all students to an education. One superintendent commented,

> We are butted up against a large city in our community, in our county, which has a very large African American population. There is resentment in our own community, particularly from the old town residents, for the

influx of those students, and we also get students from some of the other school districts as well. . . . But the bulk of the students do come from the larger inner-city school next to us, and that's a cause for concern.

And he continued,

There are those people who are very supportive, who are what we call the old town and those individuals that we call the new town . . . the new immigrants, if you will, residents to the community. Then we have those who don't want to see anything change. In fact, they would like to see it revert back to where it was of one ethnic group and where there was no diversity in the community, and they hope against hope that's going to happen.

To some degree, trying to obtain funding and resources from their communities drives the objectives of school leaders. To what degree school leaders will serve in educating community members about the meaning of their comments and perspectives about new community members depends upon the passion you and other school leaders have in regards to fairness and your willingness to engage in discussions about entitlement, privilege, and fairness of opportunity and education.

With the constraints of a limited budget and the complexity of serving a population that has a shifting demographic base with rising numbers of students living in poverty, districts have their hands full. But encouraging and often pushing stakeholders to think in terms of sociological, linguistic, and cultural adaptations may be something you were not prepared to do when you became a board member. Superintendents find themselves no longer thinking of their schools as closed education organizations, independent of external influences. Instead, they recognize that their communities' and students' needs surpass the "three Rs" and call for schools to serve as social centers. For educational leaders to supply these services, they are learning to redefine the traditional services of schools and the traditional boundaries of leadership. To address these needs, they are turning to those in the community and school who can, with their various areas of expertise, help compensate for shrinking resources. Encouraging people to step forward and help can be one way you and other educational leaders expand available resources.

Schools are being asked, if not required, to provide expanded services, but with limited resources. The varied and multiple needs of students and communities require that you as a board member ask, "What services can the district afford to provide?" and "How do we convince communities and ourselves that expanding our service is the just thing to do?" As echoed by a suburban superintendent, part of the challenge may be to recognize the needs of students and communities, while the other challenge may be to interrogate and push ourselves and our schools to become socially just. According to this superintendent, with resources dwindling and alternative education needs rising, school leaders are faced with the urgent task of redefining education:

> I think that with all of that said about alternative education, technology, funding of programs, I think we're at a crossroads in public education. We have to really redefine the role of public education, which I think is the bigger issue that encompasses all of those things. Are we going to be parents of the kids? It seems like we're taking on that role more and more with dysfunctional families. That's part of the reason why we have so many more alternative school placements.

This superintendent's words speak to the necessity of schools being able to recognize the needs of their students and the ways schools should be flexible enough to accommodate their needs. He demonstrates how school leaders, the board, and all of us must consider how we address the needs of our students. We cannot escape the idea that not accommodating some students' needs sends a message that their needs are less worthy of our attention.

Expanding resources and budgets to accommodate student and community needs is not easy. Another suburban superintendent talked about the difficulties of balancing the traditional budget with the necessity for schools to create alternative educational services:

> A reoccurring problem, which is more of a contemporary problem . . . [is] that we're spending a greater portion of our budget every year on alternative school placements or meeting the needs of troubled students that we're not capable of providing for in our traditional school setting, and, therefore, they're placed in alternative settings which are terribly expensive and often they are placed as a result of a legal process that has been entered into between the parents, the hearing office, and the district—and the third party is almost dictating to you what you

must do with this situation and almost dictating [to you] as to how you're going to spend your money and it—not gradually, it is the last several years—has significantly taken a larger portion of our operating budget.

What's poignant about this comment is that the superintendent tells us that if schools do not learn how to adjust for the diverse needs of their students, then many students are placed in situations that end up costing the school anyway, but most troubling, these students can be lost in a system that takes them further away from learning.

Deciding to step forward and push for just schooling, however, may not be easy. Holding the line with issues of justice (in fact, any attempts to decide on resources) is difficult. As a superintendent from a small rural school in the West told us,

There are developers that are fighting with landowners that are fighting with council members that are fighting with school board members. So these kinds of interpersonal conflicts certainly do take a toll and it takes people's focus away from kids and learning.

Thus, you and other educational leaders must be prepared for diversity, not only in your student and community demographics but also in the values and worldviews of your peers. Dealing with diversity of opinions and values can be stressful, but not dealing with them may cause you to lose your leadership role and diminish your district's effectiveness.

So the question emerges: When confronting the scarcity of resources and the changes within their community's demography, how do you meet student needs? Despite the increasing pressure toward accountability and assessment, school leaders are being asked by their communities to provide more than academics. Determining what services to provide and how to provide them overwhelms many educational leaders, and it may be just as overwhelming to you now in your district. You may be confronted with what it means to educate *all*.

Furthermore, you may be wondering where the dollars will come from to meet the needs once they are identified, and how you and others will ensure a just distribution of those finances at a school that may

be very different from other schools in the area (Furman & Gruenewald, 2004). One Northeastern superintendent pointed out:

> You still have to garner the votes from board members, but when you talk
> about equity and funding and looking at funding formulas, the whole issue of
> defining the need and how do we define the need, city schools in [two large
> nearby cities] are—[they have] much different needs. Some of the schools,
> even in some of the surrounding counties in [a nearby large city] range from
> very, very wealthy to very, very poor and you look at what are—again, what
> are those needs, where you can say one size fits all in terms of how much
> money should go to a kid? What's the proper amount of money to fund some-
> body—that's, I think, defining need, and clarifying that [is] a challenge.

Resources are diminishing, school populations are shifting, and the need
for a greater variety of nontraditional services is increasing. These three
challenges in resources require creative strategies from our school superintendents and from you. Although these challenges may seem
daunting to you if you are a leader in a district with such limited resources, there is hope. Our superintendents also spoke of how school
leaders are developing strategies for helping kids.

STRATEGIES FOR LEADERSHIP

The perspectives of superintendents in the trenches are also accompanied
by a set of strategies for leadership. Knowing the law, flexible funding, ex-
pansive and inclusive communication, and refocusing on what is good for
all children can give you ideas for how to deal with pressing problems.

Legal Eagles

Despite the importance of funding allocations, our superintendents
told us that few educators know how to or do work with policymakers
who decide on funding and the mandates that are usually tied with the
funding. A rural superintendent noted,

> I think there has to be a lot more done with the lawmaking process that
> governs education. . . . I don't know the best way to do that but we need

to make some connections with the legislative process that are real and relevant, not superficial.

As we heard from superintendents in the earlier section, education is a political business. Thus, to be an effective leader, board members like you should be well versed in legislative processes and government mandates. Furthermore, both school board members and educational leaders must build rapport with those who make legal decisions about education. You should work at educating yourself about the process of funding allocations and government mandates and identify experts who can help you in this regard.

Limited Resources to Meet Unlimited Needs

During our meetings with superintendents, they often commented about their districts' financial status, but some superintendents discussed how to rethink dependence on funding. An urban superintendent stated,

> Superintendents would say the most vexing problem is the lack of stability of finances in the school district. So everything we do is so dependent on the money stream that we have. . . . We are always talking about finances. But we have been doing that forever. So that may be just one of the things we have to endure and deal with, and we may not be able to fix it. So you have to learn how to move around that issue.

Although this superintendent posits that scarcity of money is not a new challenge for schools, she suggests that stakeholders should focus on finding creative solutions for this persistent barrier. School board members and superintendents must identify the greatest untapped resource—the unlimited supply of people who care about and contribute to the use of these resources in education.

Communication

Explaining to stakeholders and to the public why monies are being distributed the way they are is a classic challenge facing superintendents. School board members must present a prudent rationale for resource

allocation that demonstrates to the public that they can have confidence in
how their monies are being spent. Therefore, the ongoing battle to keep
the public informed and willing to contribute to the school's pool of resources is a challenge that superintendents and board members must deal
with daily. A superintendent of a rural district alluded to the importance of
talking about these needs as well as working with others who may have different ideas about how to acquire and allocate resources:

> Our issues are funding, so I would say that primarily our problems are
> geared toward working with the board of supervisors and just the constant
> antagonism of the two—school board, board of supervisors—the political
> issues. They become community issues and how do you convince peo-
> ple—it's a constant PR issue for us—how do you let everyone know you're
> doing well, and therefore they should fund the schools? For us, that's the
> primary issue. It's much easier, I think, to address the issues of achieve-
> ment and—at least in a county and work with the parents—but it's much
> harder when you're trying to convince community members who do not
> have kids in the schools that they should fund the schools.

Learning how to "tell and sell" schooling to community members so that
resources can be secured has become an important issue for successful
superintendents and boards.

You must learn to *talk the talk* proactively, to explain why educating
other people's children is as important as educating your own. Being
able to have these tough conversations rests on your willingness to communicate persuasively. In doing so, not only do you and other educational leaders have to talk about the unique needs of your students and
the responsibility of leading a socially just school but you also have to engage a myriad of people in the conversation and identify opinion leaders
who can influence others. One superintendent proposed,

> [Give them] another aspect in terms of overall district communications—
> and I'm talking about communication internal and external to the organiza-
> tion. Being able to communicate with the employees of the organization . . .
> being able to communicate with the union leadership, with all the employ-
> ees in the district. What kind of communication vehicles you're going to use
> and how to effectively use them. . . . It's done through linkages with an aw-
> ful, awful lot of other people and we have to be able to quickly identify those

individuals and those organizations who can be resources to you. I think that would be very helpful to get a jump start on the job.

The Greater Good

The resources issue has to do with the public support for schooling of all children. When educational decision makers disagree about how to help their students, we can easily forget what is important. Board members and other school leaders are responsible for maintaining a central focus on what is best for all students. One rural superintendent reflected on a situation in which two boards, who shared responsibility for oversight of a school system, struggled over control:

> There's still that belief [in a no-growth, no-tax policy] and the school board—which is elected—and the board of supervisors have maintained an ongoing battle about it, so it really does become an issue of trying to create a culture in the whole community that, first of all, public schools are very good, and secondly, that it is important to educate all children—and that's the culture issue; that's the way it's defined.

The argument presented here is that school board members and other school leaders must work together in creating a school culture that upholds the importance of schools continuing to do a good job for *all* children, and they must remain focused on this vision. And how is this done? Our superintendents would tell you that one key is compromise.

KEYS TO RESOURCE MANAGEMENT

Compromise

If you and other decision makers can stay focused on what is important in schools and how all students can be given equal opportunity, then solving disagreement through compromise may come easier. One urban superintendent spoke of compromise: "The [thing that is] irritating to me is the inability of folks within our organization who should know better to work through compromise situations. Because if they wouldn't dig their heels in, we could get movement on the other side." And, she continued,

> Any time you deal with people, they can be vexing because there are
> needs to be met and school districts cannot meet the needs of all [their]
> constituents. So therefore, I find it interesting to try to work with folks for
> compromise in a situation.

From a different perspective, a superintendent from a rural district offered that the key to overcoming disagreements may also lie in rhetoric
and the skill to use it in overcoming differences. He suggested that educational leadership programs might serve their students well by
"hav[ing] a public speaking course, . . . understanding group dynamics,
conflict resolution, leadership styles. All those skills are important, and
a large part of your job is dealing and working with groups."

When facing the shortage of resources in changing school districts,
school leaders must keep a close guard on communication. The necessity of engaging diverse opinions, staying focused on what's important,
and negotiating toward compromise, our superintendents advise, may
help you and other school leaders overcome the shortage of resources
by inviting and acknowledging the resources you have in people—your
limitless resource.

A Distribution of Authority

To overcome the shortage of resources, school leaders and members
of the board must think beyond the traditional forms of resources and
roles. A veteran rural superintendent spoke about learning to redefine
himself and the position of leader: "I had to get over the 'Ego Thing.' I
thought, 'I am the boss.' I don't think anyone thinks that of me. I found
out that I am not really in charge." Superintendents often talked about
the importance of getting beyond the idea that leadership refers to an
isolated and independent role, filled by a person who alone identifies
what is needed for the district, who alone allocates resources. We suggest that it is imperative that school leaders begin to distribute leadership authority to many people who contribute to the school's pool of resources and therefore to its expertise in solving problems.

Both boards and superintendents need to redefine their resource
bases. Boards will not find the model superintendent who can single-
handedly solve all problems. Superintendents should not aspire to that

role. Both boards and superintendents must be open to participatory leadership, "leading by empowering rather than by controlling others" (Murphy, 2002, p. 188), what might be defined as a "partnership of power" (Snyder, Acker-Hocevar, & Snyder, 2000). In distributing leadership, you must commit to delegating authority and responsibilities.

Helping Others Grow Professionally

Because of varying organizational landscapes, changing demographics and needs, and resources that vary from year to year, educational leaders must remember to continue their education and provide opportunities for others to develop. A suburban superintendent believed that support fostered professional growth and contributed to professionalism:

> Well, one is—with the project that I am working on right now—trying to develop a model for professional development that I think recognizes staff members as being professionals and providing an atmosphere for them to grow, and at the same time there are several staff members who are not treating themselves in the organization very professionally. . . . We expect people to be professional in their growth and provide opportunities for them.

If schools are places of learning, this superintendent reminds us, then learning is the responsibility of everyone in the organization, including board members. Faye Patterson develops this idea further in chapter 6. It is with the personal engagement and development of organization members that schools become professional organizations. Additionally, this professional growth gives the organization new and collective leadership. With the limited resources that schools have historically faced, people have had to meet their own professional growth needs using their own resources. By developing current faculty and staff as the school's chief resource, you have an opportunity to provide a professional model that will inspire and attract future leaders who might now be considering careers in education. One suburban superintendent's words reflect this sentiment:

> I think tied directly to getting new people to come in is the issue of allowing the current administrative team and also our current professional

staff continued growth for improvement, and growth that is not mandated by law but growth that rejuvenates them, keeps them alive. It is a
tough job and people can burn out real quick, and I think we're continually challenged: Where do we find the time and, now, the proper resources to let these people rejuvenate, continue to be excited about
what they're doing as they go face those tough issues on a day-to-day basis, be it a high school—whatever level it is? I think that's a great challenge we have facing us. If we can demonstrate that we are taking our
current administrative team and our professional staff and that there's a
process in place in the school district that renews them, keeps them
alive, keeps the passion going for what our business is all about—that
will be a real indicator to young people looking to that career track,
should they enter that or should they not enter that, and I think that's a
major challenge we have facing us.

A suburban superintendent from a Mid-Atlantic state also spoke about
this need:

> What we have to do, as our responsibility as school leaders, is to ensure that
> there is going to be continuity of leadership to follow and that means that we
> have to nurture and encourage and provide experience[s] for people who
> are—that we identify as our outstanding potential administrators. I don't
> know that we do that very often and we probably don't do it well enough.

New Partnerships

In attempts to overcome the shortage of funding and the rising costs of
providing support and language-learning services, many educational leaders are now looking to their staff and communities for people who may not
hold traditional leadership roles in schools and/or the community to partner with public schools. So it is very important that you are well rounded
and that you keep yourself informed about who in your community may
be a valuable partner, because you want the resources that the community
has to offer to come into the school. A superintendent and board who stay
abreast and connected to key people can also make key community members more informed and, therefore, more knowledgeable about seminal
issues. Furthermore, effective leaders speak of the importance of linking
information, people, and accessible resources.

How can educational leaders position schools to overcome the shortage of resources in times that demand more? Our superintendents suggested that you find good people who are committed to the task of contributing their resources and who have an understanding of how schools work. Additionally, our superintendents suggest you communicate with those key people and your communities about shrinking funds and shifting populations that require an expansion of school services. Your advocacy for social justice is paramount for schools to engage in opportunities for all students to succeed. Furthermore, you can call upon other people to participate as leaders and contribute their own professional expertise so that along with you and other school leaders, you can mutually foster the growth and maturation of school employees so that all become a limitless resource for schools.

Public education in the United States is paradoxical. Its founding ideal was to institutionalize free education as a mobilizer and equalizer of the people. Leaders at the time, however, may have been thinking of "the people" in terms of only one type of student. Today, school leaders must face this paradox. This chapter does not offer any prescriptions for helping superintendents or school board members overcome limitations of resources. It can only describe the perspectives of superintendents and the complexity of those perspectives. It is up to you and other school leaders to determine what you value about education and to work together through difficult times to secure it.

If anything is useful for you in this chapter, please let it be the conflicting voices of our superintendents and a reflection about education as the great democratic ideal. As traditional physical resources become scarcer, you have the authority to disregard those with the greatest need, opting instead to provide them only minimal services. But we argue that the democratic ideal entails providing extraordinary resources to those students with extraordinary needs. Furthermore, you must demonstrate this ideal by valuing its democratic process, one rooted in distributed power. By distributing power to the people who have knowledge and who can contribute to your school, you can tap into an abundant resource. A democracy is only as good as the contributions of the people guiding it.

Additionally, you and all educational leaders have the moral responsibility to suspend self-interest to serve the interest of others. You have the moral responsibility to ask yourself tough ethical questions. We hope this chapter prompts you to engage in democratic process and responsibility, to enlist the expertise of others, to address issues of equity and fairness, and to hold yourself and others accountable by being your "best worst critic."

- Serve and work with others.
- Be fair in doing so.
- Hold yourselves accountable in doing so.

The wealth of your resources depends on your ability to educate others and work with them to use existing resources wisely and to forge partnerships to attract new ones.

CHALLENGE:
MANDATES AND MICROPOLITICS

Cynthia I. Gerstl-Pepin

The roles of district leaders and their relationships to the community have become increasingly political in the past few decades. This chapter provides you with insight into the policy mandates and challenges in which school district leadership operates.

School district leadership is fraught with difficulty in balancing federal, state, and local mandates. Although district leaders such as you seem to have a measure of control over budget, curriculum, and human resources, in actuality state and federal mandates greatly curtail your control. Furthermore, leaders face many political challenges arising from special-interest groups and the complex needs of children, families, and communities. Micropolitics and parental complaints, pressure from different points of view, and the democratic nature of public education also can restrict your freedom to act. Allowing outside voices—both those that demand to be heard and disenfranchised groups who often lack input—into the decision-making processes requires honesty and personal integrity. This chapter explores that component of school leaders' roles.

Some of the insights into these mandates and challenges come from interviews with superintendents and, as with other chapters, superintendents' own words are used to illustrate points. Understanding these challenges and mandates can help you work with your superintendent and special-interest groups to navigate the politically thorny contests over limited resources to ensure that your schools promote success for students, teachers, parents, administrators, staff, and community members. The superintendents' voices reveal their perspectives on the challenges of improving student achievement. I present these perspectives in four themes: (1) context and resource differences; (2) interplay of local, state, and federal policies; (3) balancing equity concerns with special interests; and (4) democracy and public engagement.

CONTEXT AND RESOURCE DIFFERENCES

Some schools serve exclusively high-poverty communities, some serve wealthy communities; some are situated in rural communities, some serve urban or suburban communities; some districts are small, some large; and some are economically and/or racially segregated. Research shows that context plays a significant role in school reform (Anyon, 1997). Because context mediates decision making, an understanding of the social and economic context of a district is essential to understanding the complex political nature of educational decision making.

Urban, suburban, and rural schools share similarities related to funding and curriculum, but at the same time they face resource issues unique to their contexts that can lead to political controversies. Urban schools often serve impoverished inner-city communities as well as wealthy in-town communities, and this can lead to competition over resources such as teachers and programs. Suburban schools can experience tremendous growth due to real-estate development and can be highly racially segregated or racially diverse, while many rural schools often cover vast geographies, raising many issues concerning transportation, whether to consolidate due to dwindling enrollments, or potentially limit course offerings because of their schools' smaller sizes. Additionally, rural schools tend to offer more modest teacher salaries and can have trouble attracting faculty due to their distance from major urban areas. Urban inner-city schools serving predominantly impoverished communities might face problems similar to those of rural schools in terms of attracting faculty. These schools often face more pressure to raise test scores while having fewer community resources and also serve higher numbers of students who need additional support or services.

Resources are another component of context and can also have a tremendous impact on school systems and their leaders. One of the significant tensions in some states is the reliance on local property taxes. This reliance can create discrepancies between the resources that different school districts have and in some cases create confrontational relationships between local citizens and school systems. A district with a higher property base often has more money to spend on education. In states where citizens vote on whether to approve school budgets (such as Vermont and Massachusetts), citizens can challenge school districts and launch campaigns against school budget votes when their property taxes are raised to cover rising school costs. And their challenges can come with great energy. As a superintendent from a rural district in a Southern state noted,

> I think the divisions . . . between various sectors are [greater] than they used to be. I know there is more of a meanness in society than there was when I first took over. People are not as civil, by and large, as they once were.

Given a limited amount of resources to allocate, it is challenging to balance competing interests and needs while maintaining a focus on serving the broad community of students and their families. Rhonda McClellan, Adrienne Hyle, and Nan Restine discuss this further in chapter 8.

Often, educators look to ameliorate resource difficulties through grant writing, and though grants can help, they are not panaceas. Additional federal and state funds are available, but schools have to compete for them and they tend to be available for only a short period. When grant money runs out, a school or district can lose the grant-funded staff and resources and thus must continually apply for new grants or funding opportunities. Often a federal or state grant has a specific focus, such as a particular curricula or programming, so while it brings additional resources into a district, it often also requires additional expenditures in teacher training or purchasing new materials.

For example, the Reading First component of No Child Left Behind (NCLB) requires schools to use particular reading programs, which necessitates that a school purchase new program materials and also pay for teachers to be trained to use these new materials. Reading First may also limit curricular choices to reading programs that might rely on more standardized pedagogical approaches such as basal readers (standardized stories that all students read) rather than a program that might rely more on popular children's literature (Gerstl-Pepin, 2006). Thus, assumptions of funding agencies may not be in sync with those of district curriculum staff.

These factors, coupled with ever-changing state and federal allocations and policies and rising health care costs for staff, mean that budgets can vary significantly from year to year. As a superintendent from a large Midwestern urban district noted,

> I think a lot of superintendents would say the most vexing problem is the lack of stability of finances in the school district. Everything we do is so dependent upon the money stream we have. . . . The problem is that we see this as a funding problem. We are always talking about finances. So that may be just one of the things we have to endure and deal with, and we may not be able to fix it. So you have to learn how to move around that issue. . . . We spend an awful lot of time . . . talking about the thing over which we don't have control.

This superintendent highlighted the challenge that many districts face in working around the many mandates and restrictions placed on them. Given the varying contexts and resource inequities created by those contexts, it is important for you to understand the unique complexities of your district's context when making decisions. Recognizing that context is something that cannot be controlled enables you to focus your attention on issues you can affect, such as seeking ways to generate additional revenue and making tough decisions about how best to use the resources you have.

INTERPLAY OF LOCAL, STATE, AND FEDERAL POLICIES

Levels of government other than local can play a significant role in district leadership, with many layers of policy to wade through, competing interests, limited resources, significant social problems, and politicians who believe they know how best to provide leadership on education. As a superintendent from a Midwestern suburban district noted,

> One [aspect of the superintendency] is the political nature of the position. . . . It seems as though [politicians] have become experts because they've gone to school. So they listen to constituents and all of a sudden they have all of the miracle cures [for education's challenges] . . . , not understanding what is broken, and not fully understanding the ramifications of their solution. . . . Obviously the issues of our society, of race, all those [inequities], may require us to take a look at different solutions. I think sometimes we take a look at public education as a one-size-fits-all operation and we find something that works and say, "Okay, because it works here, we're going to transplant it and use it here," without understanding why things are broken to begin with.

Thus, a problem with mandates and restrictions imposed from above is that they are often not flexible enough to fit the needs of the local context.

The U.S. Constitution gives state governments purview over K–12 education. National moves toward greater accountability and centralization push against state and local control over education. National fears concerning global competition translate into a push for greater national accountability, yet the majority of funding for education comes from state and local sources such as property taxes. The federal contribution amounts to only 6 to 10% of expenditures for elementary and secondary education, while 46 to 48% comes from state sources and 43 to 46% comes from local sources (Marshall & Gerstl-Pepin, 2005). For example, each state has its own unique set of educational standards related to what should be taught in school. NCLB requires that individual states hold schools accountable via test scores. Each state has individually created its own set of standards and negotiated which set of tests to use, yet only within federal mandates.

Thus, schools and districts are often caught in a web of local, state, and federal policies. While chief state school officers serve as the leaders for educational policy in their states, federal laws such at the Individuals with Disabilities Act (IDEA) and NCLB can restrict state options. Federal and state policies can mandate how locally raised funds are to be used. Federal and state policies can direct districts in terms of instructional practices, resource allocation, and policies and procedures. These policies are often written by lawyers rather than educators and can be time consuming to sort through and understand, especially when they may change from one year to the next and often have unintended consequences. As a superintendent from a suburban district in the Midwest noted,

> Ultimately the biggest problems I see have to do with law, rules, and regulations. Just the vast quantity and maintaining it. Our school board policy manual is about four inches thick. I've just gotten an inch-and-a-half thick issue related to changes in the law from a year ago related to student instructional practices. . . . Tied in with law is the whole issue of personnel matters, personnel evaluation, personnel climate culture—everything related to the people that work with the district.

This superintendent gave an example of a law related to instruction that had a component that restricted personnel hiring. And his was only one example in a complex web of federal and state policies that need to be understood and interpreted by district leaders. The context of constantly changing policy mandates can significantly restrict the freedom districts have in deciding what and how students should be taught.

Not only does district leadership have to work within the constraints of external mandates, but they also have to win over teachers, staff, and students to work within these constraints as well. As an urban superintendent from the Southwest noted,

> The inside environment [in the district presents] a different political pressure. . . . In order to successfully lead people, you have to meet their needs. If their needs aren't met, you are not going to last. . . . You have to have some kind of credibility within your staff.

Oftentimes the practical effect is that district leadership feels the need to protect students, teachers, and staff from these external constraints.

Not only do district leaders have to pay attention to the external politics from the federal and state levels, they also have to address internal politics. These politics are often called micropolitics. For school districts, micropolitics are conflicts over control, influence, and power between such groups as teachers, students, staff, administrators, parents, and community members (Willower, 1991). For example, parents can seek to exert power so that their children are placed with certain teachers. Teachers within schools can have disagreements over how to teach, and parents can disagree (with teachers and with each other) over how their children should be taught. Schools within the same district may compete for resources (such as additional staff). Citizen interest groups can work to influence schools. For example, conservative religious groups may advocate against "hot-button topics" such as sex education or the teaching of evolution. Citizen antitax groups can band together to launch negative campaigns designed to vote down school budgets. Specifically, these groups can use tactics such as e-mails and calls to the principal, superintendent, or school board members to garner support for their perspective.

So school boards and superintendents need to serve both the interests and needs of teachers and staff who are professionally trained to deliver education *and* they must address the desires and wishes of citizens who may not be professionally trained but whose tax dollars fund education and whose children attend the schools.

Teaching as a profession often struggles with negative press coverage and public perceptions. Those critical of teaching often cite examples such as the shorter school day and summer break as signs that teaching is not difficult. What these public perceptions miss is the amount of work teachers do outside of their normal teaching day. After-school programs, special events, sports activities, student clubs, meetings with parents and other educational specialists, grading, and curriculum planning are just a few of the activities that require teachers to work at home, come in early, or stay late. Yet the teaching profession is not often accorded the respect of other professions. In order for a district to be healthy and effective, educators need to have good morale and feel supported. Thus, you and other district leaders need to be able to negotiate among teachers and other district staff, state and federal mandates, and local politics.

BALANCING EQUITY CONCERNS
AND SPECIAL INTERESTS

In addition to federal and state mandates, boards and superintendents face an array of political hot-button issues such as budgets, inequitable funding, equity (or the lack of it), school closings, race relations, discipline, and redistricting (Björk & Lindle, 2001). These issues form a complex political web through which district leaders have to navigate. You have to balance the primary mission of educating children with the needs of teachers and staff while serving the potentially competing needs of your communities. As a superintendent from the Southwest noted,

> I think the role of the superintendent has always been one of manager of complex issues. I think, however, through the years it has become tougher. More and more superintendents are talking about how difficult it is to be a superintendent. A terrific amount of . . . political pressure [is] placed upon an individual. The most striking change for me as an administrator would be understanding of the politicization of the administrator's role and the acceptance that one has to have if you are going to be in this kind of position. That it is a political position, and if you don't like it then you are not going to function very effectively and it will take a horrible, horrible toll on you. It is the understanding that there are so many factions within a community. It could be a rural, suburban, or urban community— many, many different needs to be met. . . . Now, can I be all things to all people in all segments of the community? No. . . . So [there are] sets of things that I do particularly well and I keep that match going as long as possible [in order] to survive.

One great and enduring challenge relates to the education of students in the face of issues related to their race, ethnicity, and/or economic background. These students have tended to underachieve in greater numbers and mostly attend underresourced schools (Kozol, 1992, 2005). As a suburban superintendent from the Southeast asserted,

> One problem that we have to deal with is that there are just so many more high-risk students and families in our schools. That creates a whole set of problems as far as what baggage kids are bringing with them to school and how you deal with that in terms of social and emotional needs before you can ever reach the academic side of the ledger. I think we have more poor kids today then we have ever had before. Our free- and reduced-priced lunch counts go up every year. . . . We have drug- and alcohol-abuse counselors in our schools. We have police officers in our schools, all to protect and keep it a safe learning environment. . . . On the other hand, you have some of the best students you have ever had. . . . So you've got these two

groups and it seems like the middle is disappearing. As a school administrator, how do you reconcile that?

While our country is one of the richest in the world, it is also contains extremes of wealth and poverty. Many lower-income families lack access to affordable, quality preschool education, and as a result, many of these children enter school at a distinct disadvantage when compared to students who have had more pertinent educational preparation (Masse & Barnett, 2002). Schools are not immune to the challenges that face society. Rather, they can simultaneously be on the forefront of trying to address social inequalities and find themselves blamed for those inequalities.

One of the most difficult challenges that district leaders face is balancing the desires of powerful parent and community lobbies against the need to serve children who live in impoverished communities. Maintaining a balance often requires a strong ethical commitment to the best interest of *all* children in the district, not just the ones with strong advocates. Furthermore, it is often the children who live in impoverished communities who lack advocates in the district politics. Middle- and upper-class parents have more resources and time to devote to local politics (Brantlinger, 2003). Wealthier parents tend to be the ones who serve on school boards and committees and have a say in district policy. When certain groups (marked by wealth, ethnicity, or race, for example) are not represented on school boards, it is easier to overlook their particular needs since they tend not to have a voice at the table when policy discussions occur (Marshall & Gerstl-Pepin, 2005). So it is challenging to balance the potentially self-serving concerns of those at the table with the long-term needs of all the community, including those who may not be at the table. As an urban superintendent noted,

> [You] have to keep focused on kids. They've got to be [your] number one mission. [You've] got to keep that kind of focus and not get side-tracked by the other things because there are many things that can take you off course—many good-intended people, many prominent issues. Just keep focused on kids and learning and you will be fine. Because there is still a sense of community, still a sense of the common good; that is what keeps me going. I know that it may be hard facing a teacher and telling them that this is not going to work. . . . It may be hard telling a parent that they cannot have exactly what they want [or a] student that they

cannot have their way. But when you do it and say that is for the greater good and for the community, the community of learners, it will make sense.

One of your enduring challenges will be to balance ethically the needs of individual learners with the needs of the larger community (Miron & Elliott 1994). It is easy for any of us to attend to the needs of people who are like us at the expense of those who are not like us. Ultimately, the success of a district will depend on its ability to serve all of its constituents to the best of its ability; when this is not done, then conflicts and inequities occur. At the same time, you cannot ignore powerful lobbies or their viewpoints. This would be tantamount to political suicide. Eduardo Arellano provides good advice about this in chapter 12. The reality is that you have to balance competing interests and try to work out differences, recognizing what you can control and what you cannot. As an urban superintendent from the Midwest noted,

> I would say that when we are talking about vexing problems, the thing that is irritating to me is the inability of folks within our organization . . . to work through compromise situations. If they wouldn't dig their heels in, we could get movement on the other side. [There are] many problems over which we don't have control: the economic situation, the social conditions for youngsters, the level of poverty. We have no control over that. So, we can consume all of our emotional energy dealing with the things over which we don't have control and completely bypass things over which we do have control. I try to get people to refocus.

With such a tremendous number of mandates from above that restrict the freedom of districts, and struggles for power and resources within the community, in order to provide equitable education, district leaders must learn how to maneuver around impediments and to focus on issues that can be addressed by local administrators and overseers of public education. For example, poverty is a significant social issue that has an effect on almost every district and community in the United States. While it is not possible for schools to raise the economic levels of students and their families, they can seek to address inequities through school-community partnerships (Nieto, 1994). For example, some schools have worked with medical professionals to create health and dental clinics on school grounds to ensure students are receiving basic medical attention. Other schools have created innovative programs such as school-based General Education Development (GED) programs for parents at the school site. These are just a couple of ways that schools can seek to ameliorate inequitable issues in the communities they serve by working with other professionals.

Given the need to balance equity concerns with special interests, an additional challenge for district leadership is to be proactive as opposed to reactive (Fritz, 1989). Given the highly political nature of public education, there are constant challenges related to school improvement, professional development, community conflicts, and resources. Many of these issues require immediate attention. Groups within and outside of schools can apply political pressure to support their special interests. The immediate focus is on the issue or controversy at hand, but it is critical to take a broader and more contextual view of an issue. As a rural superintendent from the Northeast noted,

> There is a pattern of thinking about schools that thinks about them one year at a time. It doesn't matter if we are talking about state legislation, formulating school budgets, the way we hire teachers, the way we contract with teachers, the way we promote students, the way we grade them, assess students—everything is done in one-year intervals. And that has us deceived into thinking if we do well in one year, then we'll just think about the next year. It is a very vexing problem to get . . . thinking to shift to long term.

Demographic changes are a prime example. In some districts enrollments could be in steady decline while in other districts there might be explosive growth. Either of these two contingencies requires long-range thinking in terms of future enrollments, building maintenance, and possibly capital improvement projects. One cannot just focus on immediate issues: Future changes in real estate, economics, and population can have a tremendous impact on a school district. Additionally, district leaders can proactively connect to state and federal policymakers to raise awareness of the current issues that districts face. For example, school board and superintendent organizations often work as a collective, and through their professional associations, to raise awareness of current challenges, inequities, and needs.

DEMOCRACY AND PUBLIC ENGAGEMENT

Another challenging aspect of leading school districts is the issue of public participation, input, and engagement. The "public" in public education highlights the democratic aspects of our system, in that schools are publicly funded; the school board governance structure invites citizen representation, and expenditures are often decided through community referenda or bond elections. While democracy is a word used freely, its definition is open to interpretation. Some groups believe in the egalitarian notion of democracy, which asserts that governance should represent the needs of the community regardless of social position. Other groups might subscribe to a more elite version of democracy in which individuals with more education or wealth are elected to act in the best interest of others whose input is not necessarily required. Still others advocate for the notion of deliberative democracy, suggesting that it is critical to invite community input and engage the public over pressing issues, which can lead to decisions that are more representative of the needs of the community or communities in question (Dryzek, 2000; Gutmann & Thompson, 2004).

I argue for the deliberative view of democracy and believe that community engagement and participation are healthy goals for a school district. Engaging community members can create more support for public education particularly in politically contentious times. Democratic engagement and participation requires interactive communication.

In order to foster democracy, not only do district leaders need to communicate with teachers, staff, students, and their families but they also need to communicate with the community members who do not intersect with schools. Space also needs to be provided for individuals and groups to communicate their concerns and ideas with district leadership. Without opportunity for communication, miscommunication and misunderstandings often lead to political upheaval and conflict, so maintaining clear communication among groups within and outside the district is critical. As a superintendent from an urban Midwest district noted,

> One of my biggest . . . challenges is clear and accurate communication. We have a very large constituency, and this plays itself out everyday. I literally see something said here, and it goes through ten people and comes

out completely different on this end, and one of my biggest challenges is to try to organize the district in such a manner so that we get as clear a communication to as many people as possible. For example, . . . if we are going to deal with growth issues, which ultimately result in alternative housing, schedules, or boundaries, or bussing or increases in taxes to bond for buildings or anything like that—I am convinced that if we could clearly communicate the issues to people, 80–90% of them will arrive at the same conclusion that we have arrived at with the same information.

Communication is critical to informing the district community about key issues. An informed public is crucial for the health of a district, particularly since decision making can be highly contentious when district needs outweigh available resources and competing interests vie for those resources.

Although education by definition is set up for public input, many community members' knowledge about education is based on their own experiences in schools. Unlike such other professions as medicine or nursing, citizens have input into education even though they may have no expertise or professional training as educators. This is challenging for educators, as I noted above, because they are often not accorded the same level of respect as other professions such as medicine. Individual community members often base their assertions about education on their children's or their own experience with schools rather than on research or professional training. Many community members or politicians who are not professionally trained as teachers often attempt to influence educational policy and curriculum.

So a key facet of public participation is the need for districts to share information and inform the public about issues in a way that focuses on the needs of students who may not have advocates. District leaders should strive to be inclusive, equitable, and sensitive to the concerns and needs of special interests (Kimpton, 2001; Public Education Network, 2001).

SUMMARY

The purpose of this chapter has been to provide insights into the complex politics (policy mandates and political challenges) surrounding district school leadership. Superintendent and school board leadership is embedded in a complex web of competing interests; resource differentials; federal, state, and local politics; and community and cultural differences. Democratic participation through school board membership, public funding, public meetings, and voting are central components of district educational politics. Unique contextual factors face rural, suburban, and urban communities.

Key to comprehending the challenges to authority and mandates your district confronts daily is understanding local politics, resource challenges, and community concerns and needs, particularly for those groups who do not have advocates. It is also important to gain the ear of political players at local, state, and federal levels. Understanding how mandates and micropolitics have an impact on your district can aid in making decisions that are inclusive, address equity and special interests, and foster community collaboration.

10

CHALLENGE: UNDERSTANDING YOUR SUPERINTENDENT'S PERSPECTIVE

L. Nan Restine, Adrienne Hyle, and Rhonda McClellan

In classical Greek tragedy, the protagonists find themselves thrust into *medias res,* or the middle of things. Stepping into the speeding current of the proverbial river, Greek heroes can never quite gain footing and quickly find themselves over their heads or out of control. Their desire to balance the ideals of life with the currents of the river of life can result in tragedy or triumph. In today's schools, leaders such as you are caught in the same types of conflicts. Generally, educational leaders face the tension of how to develop a vision of the ideal while securing footing in the reality of the speeding and uncertain "river" of school life.

Life in the superintendency and the board has the makings for a great tragedy and also the makings for heroes who triumph over adversity. The superintendent's struggle to balance the ideal with the real is the stuff of which great drama is made. This struggle also has implications for you as a board member. The inability to balance or negotiate the ideal with the real causes tragedy and is often the morass educational leaders must face. If you and other educational leaders collaborate with and advocate for one another, however, districts and actors can sharpen our vision and navigate daily realities within our schools.

Navigating these realities begins with understanding the actors' responsibilities. A major purpose of this chapter is to help you as a school board member to understand the wide range of responsibilities associated with the job of a school superintendent. Specifically, this chapter will help you get an inside view of the superintendent's world, to learn how superintendents think, and to apply your learning to your work with superintendents to ensure student success. We show you the "real" and the "struggle for the ideal" from the perspective of superintendents from school districts across the United States, representing large and small, wealthy and poor, school districts.

Remarkably, the superintendents' stories reflect consistent messages about tensions and their ways of dealing with them. Your knowledge about these challenges and tensions will provide a foundation for exploring similar challenges and tensions in your own districts and with your own situations that arise. This knowledge should help you move forward purposively in your work as a school board member and educational leader.

FINDING YOUR FOOTING

You, as a member of a school board, may be an accountant or a zoologist. You might be retired, self-employed, an employee of a corporation, or own your own business. Your organization may be small and predictable or large and complex, and your work may be planned and coherent or multifarious and disparate. You may have a peer group of work associates within your organization. As a school board member, you chose to serve with few rewards and much accountability, for personal or altruistic reasons, whether appointed or elected. Superintendents, too, have different motivations for choosing to be superintendents and may face demands for accountability that seem out of all proportion to the rewards.

Whereas the reasons for becoming a superintendent vary, so do the expectations regarding the job. Primarily, the specific descriptions and parameters of the superintendency change depending on the current expectations of the school district and the board. Thus, the environment in which educational leaders work has been characterized as "permanent white water," where change is a constant and disruption is anything but temporary (Vaill, 1996). Furthermore, those who currently write about the superintendency have found that the position is now less defined by role and more by responsibilities and relationships (Brunner, 2002; Kowalski & Keedy, 2005).

Superintendents discussed the challenges of finding footing in small districts and their initial lack of awareness about the many tasks required of them. Some rural superintendents also serve in a plethora of other roles—as teachers, coaches, bus drivers, personnel and curriculum directors, maintenance supervisors, and principals. Their responsibilities, though not necessarily more challenging than those of superintendents in urban or suburban settings, are certainly difficult. This perspective was expressed by a rural school superintendent in this way:

> In small districts I will spend my time differently from [an urban district superintendent]. All their lieutenants and all their colonels . . . work under the general. In a small district, you look around and there are not too many people . . . so you end up dealing with a lot of things on a day-to-day management of the school . . . I thought that I would get to be the dealer and the schemer of the school district. You know, the person that helps establish a vision.

One prerequisite to finding footing is for school board members and superintendents to collaborate on defining their responsibilities. Our superintendents spoke about the challenges in understanding others' perceptions of their predecessor, both within the district and in the larger community. Some spoke of succeeding a superintendent who was considered a puppet of the school board president, a very weak superintendent who lacked respect within the district. The National School Boards Association (NSBA) and the American Association of School Administrators (AASA) have worked diligently to define what boards and superintendents should each contribute to leading the district, and these two perspectives (the vision of the community brought by school board members and the professional judgment brought by superintendents) are crucial (Houston & Bryant, 1997).

Collaboration and advocacy are prerequisites for achieving goals. Finding footing toward this end is not without challenge, as described in the following passage by a suburban superintendent in the Southeast,

> Some of us may have gone into our first superintendency believing that our school boards were very wise groups from whom we would learn the

way and the light in our particular school system, but it only takes a series of nonunanimous votes—and then the contingent which comes out of that—for you . . . to realize that you have got to get back into the role of being a teacher of the board to help steer them properly.

Critically important in the work of school board members and superintendents is embracing the understanding that adversarial relationships among you minimize credibility and public confidence and thwart efforts toward any sustained improvement. Finding footing in today's learning organizations requires establishing support and building trust. Clearly, it is extraordinarily difficult to engage the public in education or to garner support for initiatives when mutual respect between school board members and superintendents is absent or when the focus is on individual agendas and not on the superintendent/board team (Castallo & Natale, 2005). As one superintendent in a Southern rural district expressed,

When I came here I was the fifth superintendent in four years. . . . For five years, a different superintendent every year was stressful. So, when I first came here, vision was not as much of an issue as was building trust and confidence, of everybody . . . the board, the press, the teachers, the parent groups. . . . Once I have that, I can move to what I think the better role is, that of launching a vision for the school system.

Study after study of school boards and superintendents suggests that many conditions and structures preclude doing what needs to be done. Traditionally, we think of authority as being commensurate with responsibility, yet many superintendents do not control agendas and are whipsawed by demands of competing sources of power (Fuller et al., 2003) through people, politics, and policy. You, as a school board member, must understand that the tenure for many superintendents is rather brief, that there are considerably more external and internal influences on school leaders than were obvious decades ago, and that sustained growth and improvement requires stability and genuine commitment. This balance in footing is essential to the success of the district. Superintendent and school board members alike need to have a solid footing in terms of responsibilities and must work together at explicitly defining these for involved actors.

THE CHARACTERS: PEOPLE, POLITICS, AND POLICY

According to a suburban superintendent in the Midwest,

> At my level you are constantly dealing with people's problems. After a while you wish you could get an educational issue rather than processing hassles so that someone else can be an educator. The things that take you down in this [job] have nothing to do with academic education. You lose your job over things that have nothing to do with teaching, or you keep your job because you solve problems that have nothing to do with education.

The previous comment reflects much of what we learned from superintendents about their concerns and the challenges faced in relation to people, politics, and policy. Although it might be expected that superintendents should lead initiatives toward change and improvement in schools, the reality is that this is only accomplished with people, that policies can serve as opportunities or as barriers, and that the role of the superintendent is fraught with the potential for political isolation. The challenges that may appear as pedestrian or simple are typically more complex.

As an example, a superintendent in a rural district spoke about inaccurate representations of incidents such as that involving an applicant for a teaching position who did not hold a valid state teaching license.

> [From] that, the word went out that I would not hire this lady and that I did not like her, and there were all sorts of stories that were made up. . . . She called school board members; she called everybody she could think of to force me into hiring her.

A superintendent in an urban Midwestern district expressed her experiences with people as problems in the following:

> I think the things I first encountered when I first became a superintendent were people issues . . . if somebody wants something that either they can't have or we can't give it to them, or we can't deliver the service the way they want. They could get aggressive, and this is within the organization or outside the organization. . . . But the thing that bogs us down and stops us from doing what we need to do are still the people problems.

Separating the issues from the person was often perceived to be more difficult for superintendents in small districts because of increased visibility and fewer players. They spoke about how the inability to separate issues from people can "fractionalize communities" even when involving only "two staff members with different opinions."

Similarly, even when seeking approval for hiring faculty and staff, our participants report that the different opinions held by superintendent and board can create tensions. A superintendent in an Eastern suburban district discussed bringing three candidates to the board for interviews and the board not approving of any of them. "It was almost like you [superintendent and school board members] saw the world completely different. They looked at me as, 'How could I bring these candidates to the board?' I thought they were wonderful." The superintendent implied that the animosities arose from not discussing the reasons for rejecting the nominations.

A superintendent in a suburban district discussed how politics can influence your sense of powerlessness as a school board member. "Today, I think even the school board feels somewhat powerless in the sense that so many others are dictating the agenda, from the state legislature right on through the governor." This sentiment was echoed by an urban superintendent in the Midwest in the comment:

 It seems as though legislators become experts because they've gone to school. So, they listen to constituents and all of a sudden they have all of the miracle cures and collectively come up with how we're going to fix them—not fully understanding what's broken . . . and not fully understanding the ramifications of their solution.

Partisan politics, race, labor politics, and alliances significantly affect the work of superintendents and you as a school board member. What motivates superintendents to seek their posts and school board members to seek their positions are often in conflict. Some select these positions driven by a sense of vision, others as a vendetta. Micromanagement by school boards was often cited as a concern of superintendents, specifically when school boards "stray from policy oversight and budget development into the nuts and bolts of day-to-day administration" (Fuller et al., 2003, p. 18).

Superintendents must address issues involving people, politics, and policy both internally and externally. As one superintendent in an urban Midwestern district stated,

> To function more effectively is to see the whole and not the parts. . . . It is the understanding that there are so many factions within a community . . . many, many different needs to be met. . . . Can I be all things to all people, in all segments in the community?

The answer is most likely "no," at least not all of the time, for superintendents and for school board members as well.

CHALLENGES TO IDEALS: CRICKETS, COMMUNICATION, AND COMMUNITIES

It is important for you as a board member to remember that individuals who enter the superintendency from inside education, having had experience as educators, and those who enter the position from outside the field of education may face different trials in the superintendency. External pressures and demands tend to be more difficult for education insiders to understand or accept while internal pressures are more difficult for outsiders (Fuller et al., 2003). Likewise, perspectives of superintendents hired from within the local community differ in some respects from those hired from outside. As one locally hired superintendent in an urban Midwestern district expressed,

> I was working on committees to help the school system, and I was not some guy who came in from 1,000 or 2,000 miles away. I was right down the street in the middle of the city with my office, and so I thought I knew the city pretty well. . . . Some of these issues are greater than I surmised even being in the town. And the other ones I guess I was not aware of.

It is difficult to fully grasp the magnitude of what might appear to be the mundane in a superintendent's work life. The range of management responsibilities and leadership expectations exists within an organizational structure that is often inflexible and rigid. Student learning and academic achievement, in an ever-enlarged context of standards-based accountability, are the core functions. Yet minor nuisances can cause huge distractions. A superintendent in a rural Southwestern district said,

> I am in the middle of trying to design an alternative education program for our particular school. And that's a problem; there are lots of variables in it. . . . But I enjoy digging into that and doing that. On the other hand, we just had two air conditioners go out and have to get bids for that and . . . have to get the sidewalk built and the gutter was leaking. Crickets . . . the cricket population went bananas on us. And people come to me and say, "Well, what are you going to do about this?"

Communication, or lack thereof, is often praised or blamed as the prime reason for attributing successes and failures. (Eduardo Arellano discusses this in further detail in chapter 12.) What is communicated, how it is communicated, to whom, when, and by what means are all important considerations for your superintendent and you. Otherwise, "speaking to 20 teachers on an issue, [you] have 20 interpretations of that" becomes the typical trend. The importance of communication related to changes in communities resulting from growth and how to avoid taking a defensive posture was expressed as follows by a rural district superintendent in the Southwest:

> One of my biggest challenges is clear and accurate communication. . . . I literally see something said here and it goes through ten people and it comes out completely different on this end. . . . Growth is an example of how critical communication is. . . . Growth issues ultimately result in alternative housing, schedules, or boundaries, or busing, or increases in taxes to bond for buildings. . . . How you do that is absolutely monumental. . . . You are dealing with many other social dimensions. Anger, you are dealing with misinformation, clarifying the district's position, defending.

Engaging the news media and other venues of communication is an important asset. Veteran superintendents spoke about their former practices focused on communicating with parents and the need to reach an increasingly larger proportion of communities with citizens who do not have children in schools. This concern was expressed by a superintendent in a large urban district in the Northeast:

I believe that there is an increase in parent involvement . . . but it is not true parent involvement. What it is, in fact . . . is that individuals—individually interested individuals—claim to be representative of all the parents, and there is no way that they are. They bring individual views and dictates predicated on that.

A superintendent of a rural district discussed understanding what transpires in the community at large to shift focus away from students.

Dealing with conflict that is caused by growth, because we now have some people that say, "I don't want to grow. I want to stay just as we are. I want things to remain the same." There are developers that are fighting with landowners that are fighting with city council members that are fighting with school board members. So those kinds of . . . conflicts certainly do take a toll, and it takes focus away from kids and learning.

Schools and communities are reciprocally influenced. There are those in the community who were served well by the school system and those who were ill served. A superintendent related an incident where three students were expelled from a high school, the first time in 30 or 40 years, and the impact on parents, the school, the school board, and the community. Often, these incidents, as simple as they may appear, place superintendents and school board members in opposing roles, as indicated by this urban school superintendent in the Northeast:

One of the school board members calls, and they wanted to know—because a couple of their constituencies who had worked for them in their political campaign didn't like the fact that their child wasn't being leveled for reading. . . . So the complaint went to the school board and [they upheld the complaint because it came from] a voting population. . . . I find that extremely frustrating.

Reflecting on the primary purpose for schools, a rural school superintendent stated,

Keep focused on kids. . . . Keep that kind of focus . . . because there are many things that will take you off course—many good-intended people, many prominent issues. I know that it may be hard facing that teacher and telling them that this is not going to work. . . . It may be hard telling that parent that they cannot have exactly what they want. . . . But when you do it and say that it is for the greater good and for the community . . . it will make sense.

As a school board member, your role in communicating accurate information and representing the community broadly cannot be underestimated. You serve to represent the interests of many others in addition to your own interests. Both levels of interest can and should be expressed honestly, thoughtfully, and thoroughly. Your role is to advocate for the schools and to engage the community in becoming advocates. Helping superintendents to ask the right questions and assisting them in finding appropriate answers or solutions requires school board members' understanding about what the community values and what the community wishes for children (Houston & Bryant, 1997). Furthermore, you should recognize that the superintendent's day may be more than heady interactions and considerations but as well may involve crickets.

THE TURNING POINT AND CONSEQUENCES OF ACTION

Noted a superintendent in a suburban Southeastern school district:

> Some of us have laughed at times and said that you need to leave with the same thing that you brought—your integrity. We quip, if you tell the truth, you don't have to try to remember what you said yesterday. . . . You have to look down the road and say, "When I finish this thing, do I want to be known for best politics or best practice . . . having provided leadership for best practices?"

The preceding comment reflects many superintendents' perspectives about their work and the realization that there are turning points and consequences for actions. Many of them wondered about their capacity to lead the way toward changing climates and cultures, not just in the schools but in the community. A superintendent in a rural school district with both a school board and board of supervisors offered this comment:

> We are a district of haves and have-nots. There is definitely a culture of those with money sending their children to private schools and a belief

system that they do not necessarily need to or want to fund the public schools. . . . The school board and the board of supervisors have maintained an ongoing battle about it. . . . It really does become an issue of trying to create a culture in the whole community that . . . public schools are very good and . . . that it is important to educate all children.

Superintendents also spoke about vested interest groups, factions determined to maintain the status quo, and changing expectations that permeate their schools. As expressed by one suburban superintendent,

It seems to me that, with the adoption of education in everybody's political agenda, our role has changed depending upon whose agenda we are a part of. When 50 governors meet . . . they changed our role. All of a sudden, we are responding to what is a national issue.

At the district and school levels, superintendents discussed issues having to do with high-risk students and families, providing alternative settings for students, and costly third-party legal processes. Fundamentally, superintendents spoke about spending greater amounts of time and money on fewer students and the profound impact on resources.

Eventually, the responsibilities, the conflicts, and the struggles may cause superintendents to face the turning point, and the idea of defeat confronts them, as stated by this superintendent in a Southern urban district:

I think it is amazing what the state and federal governments expect of superintendents, that our focus and what we are tested on and financed by is student learning and achievement. . . . We want people learning and we want people literate, happy, and giving back to the community, but we are divided, fragmented so much by putting out fires. . . . [We're confronted by our inner voice asking,] "Where in the world did your vision go?" It's just like the man on the Ed Sullivan show with the plates. You are always trying to make sure each plate is going, and then the one that drops is the one that makes or breaks you.

A superintendent of a suburban school district in the West offered:

Those are the days, when the majority of my day has been spent listening to all the reasons and all the things that I am doing wrong, that the district is doing wrong. All the reasons why I am personally inept and incapable. You begin to wonder.

The turning point is a place reached by many school districts. The reminder for superintendents and school board members is that actions have consequences. All educational leaders and specifically board members and the superintendent can and should scrutinize the path being taken and refocus away from turning points that could become negative and toward positive ones.

THE GOLDEN MEAN

In Greek drama, the quest toward achieving the ideal is referred to as "the golden mean." For the Greeks, structure, line, and proportion tie to their ideal—beauty. The golden mean also refers to the ability of the hero, regardless of the torrent of events or the wide range of responsibilities, to remain moderate in action and balanced in thought. To move beyond the turning points and to overcome the many consequences they face, superintendents defined their resilience as professional maturation, particularly the recognition that it takes many people working toward the common good of the school. Part of this maturation requires distributing authority so that more people work at serving schools. One rural school superintendent commented,

> A principal used the analogy of a football player, and said, "When you carry the ball 35 times in each football game eventually they are going to carry you off the field. You are going to be dazed and confused, perhaps with a concussion. If you learn how to hand off the ball to other people and pass the ball from time to time to those wide receivers, you are going to be much more effective and so you don't always have to carry the ball."

At the same time, superintendents note the difficulty of maintaining integrity while involving others in the decision-making processes, as expressed by this superintendent in a Southeastern suburban district:

> Where do you find that common middle ground that your own values aren't subjugated and thrown out the window? How do you act in a moral

and ethical fashion and be true to thine own self and still find a place others can work with you for the common good? . . . There is a tremendous amount of tension and people competing to determine who educates America's children.

Superintendents who were able to further their resilience also relied on the ability to stay focused through harried days, according to a rural superintendent in the Midwest:

> I think they just need to know they have to keep focused on kids. They have got to be their number one mission. They got to keep that kind of focus and not get side-tracked by the other things because there are many things that will take you off course; many good-intended people, many prominent issues—just keep focused on kids and learning, and you will be fine.

When superintendents are confronted by choices and consequences, their decisions are grounded within their ability to balance, manage, and visualize a wide range of responsibilities. Your responsibility as a school board member is virtually the same. You must be able to help superintendents see, manage, and balance their responsibilities for the benefit of students and their education.

THE DENOUEMENT: THE REAL AND THE IDEAL

A suburban school district superintendent stated,

> I think the system really needs to change because society has changed and we really don't have any "first wavers" [those with limited experience]. We're really like the parents; everybody's an expert because they all went through education somewhere. . . . So we're challenged all the time.

Houston and Bryant (1997) echo the above commentary from our superintendents when saying that the public lacks a contextual understanding about schools and schooling, that issues are presented to the public in "such a simplistic way that citizens do not understand all of the dynamics" (p. 757). The gap between public expectations for superintendents and the reality of responsibilities in the position is, more often than not, huge. As a school board member, you can assist significantly in reducing this chasm by contributing to establishing defined, reasonable, and broadly accepted goals for the district that address, most importantly and most fundamentally, student learning.

As a school board member, it is important to understand that pressures from the community and elsewhere can be both burden and blessing for superintendents. However, superintendents must have authority commensurate with the responsibilities of their work, freed from much of the minutia and constraints that bind them in providing stewardship for change and improvement. Very often frustrations abound. As one of our rural superintendents expressed,

> How many of us are going to end up in the hospital thinking we are having a heart attack? It's just phenomenal, the amount of stress in doing these jobs. And then you get board members, and you have to start from scratch with them. . . . That has a significant impact because you could have the momentum on your side. You're doing everything on God's earth to try and improve test scores, and you get the rope jerked out from beneath you.

Clearly, superintendents and school board members must focus on assisting school districts and the people in them to thrive, not merely survive. Strained relationships between stakeholders, superintendents, and school board members contribute nothing helpful toward this end. Given the dynamic nature of communities, the changing nature of policy directives, and the inherent political attributes of schools as organizations, decisions and actions made by school leaders should be examined thoroughly with respect to the effect on relationships and district improvement efforts (Mountford, 2004).

SECURING YOUR FOOTING

If any lesson can arise from looking at the wide range of responsibilities that superintendents face, it is that, as a school board member, you must remember that you and the superintendent are partners in the exceptionally important work of education in your school district.

You will be working together to move the school district from the "real" to the "ideal." This task will be filled with tensions as you work to make your vision of the ideal out of the reality of the speeding and uncertain river of school life. Communication is key to your success. You and your superintendent will need to clarify your roles, responsibilities, authority, and vision. This should result in creating support and enhancing trust across your positions despite the unique demands and concerns. Embrace the notion, as Ramón Domínguez pointed out in chapter 7, that it is virtually impossible to move initiatives forward to completion when mutual respect is missing or when the focus is on fueling feuds between the superintendents and school board members.

At the same time, you must remember that your superintendent may not always see things the way that you do as a member of the board. Despite this challenge, you must work together toward achieving the "golden mean." Together, with clarity of vision and purpose, the two of you are creating the future for your community, your schools, and for the children and adults who learn and live in them. Work together while remembering that your duties and responsibilities may be ever changing in the wide and tumultuous river of opportunity.

●

CHALLENGE:
NEEDING TO BE REELECTED

Thomas Alsbury

Concern about reelection is a necessary part of being a school board member—in fact, of any elected leadership position. No matter how selfless or noble your intentions, you will probably at some point find yourself thinking about your own political survival. Whatever your ideals or integrity, you will still have to think about maintaining the favor of those who put you into office and can take you out. Realizing this has come as a shock to more than one elected official. One superintendent of 7 years from a rural district put it in stark terms:

> The board that I have now struggles so much. They have no courage; they want to be popular; they want to be liked; they are unwilling to take a stand. I even had a couple of them tell me last spring that they don't want to be board members. When their terms are up, they're done . . . because they don't like it. And that's kind of a real disappointment because there's a tremendous responsibility that goes with serving on a school board. I don't know if they were unaware of that responsibility or just unwilling when they finally got on and realized what's involved. But that's been a real disappointment because . . . imagine pulling teeth to get them to come to a board meeting. If they've got three there, two of them figure that they don't have to come, and that's a disappointment.

The political nature of educational leadership challenges all of us. The insights I offer in this chapter come as responses to six questions. Notice that I refer to them as "insights," not "answers": "answers" would imply that I have simple recipes or formulas for success. I do not, but I will give you background information and some general principles that can be helpful. The six questions are as follows:

1. What if I can't find the consensus in my community or communities?
2. How can I tell when the political winds are shifting in my community?
3. Can I be politically effective and still maintain my integrity?
4. What steps can board members take, alone and with colleagues on the board, to accomplish good things for students in the midst of chaotic political situations?
5. Since a board member's role might be seen as more political than the superintendent's (he or she can play the role of expert, but I have to get reelected), how do both of us balance the political and nonpolitical aspects of our roles?
6. What do I consider in selecting a superintendent for my district?

WHAT IF I CAN'T FIND THE CONSENSUS IN MY COMMUNITY OR COMMUNITIES?

The Reality of Politics in School Governance

A superintendent of 10 years in a suburban district told us, "Politics is the art of governing. Politics is not a dirty word. It's an important part of public service. It is the running of government in the service of people." Another superintendent of 12 years in a suburban district noted, "School board members who think they are not politicians are living in a fantasy." Schools, like other institutions, are affected by competition among interest groups seeking to further their own political agendas. Since the design of elected school boards was intended to allow for the influence of citizenry upon school functions, school boards and superintendents must embrace the political realities of their positions. This need is even more pronounced as communities become more culturally diverse.

Cultural and Values Plurality

Cultural and ideological divides in the general community seem to be polarizing communities and making it much more difficult for school board members and superintendents to identify and address public concerns. We now are facing the possibility that, as a citizenry, we no longer have a shared set of cultural and moral values that provide a consistent national identity. In terms of school board member election and turnover, this plurality may make it difficult for you to understand and mirror your community's values, and a disconnection from community interest can lead to election defeat or pressure to resign or retire (Alsbury, 2003).

An increase in plurality means that as a board member you will need to provide more opportunities for two-way communications and substantive input from an ever-widening and diverse collection of community interest groups. The days when board members could simply gather input from a small group of traditionally influential community members, such as business owners, and presume they represented a majority opinion on community values are over. In addition, you will best be served by using open, interactive communications to help the public recognize the reality of the broader and sometimes contradictory demands being placed on the school board. Finally, you will need to work with the superintendent to exercise an increased level of political acuity as you endeavor to respond to the conglomeration of often-conflicting community demands.

As the community becomes more pluralistic in its values, you as a school board member will find it harder and harder to mediate issues. Philosophical ruminations materialize in real policy conflicts: Should you adopt a school policy celebrating multiculturalism or expect cultures to assimilate? Do you support the notion that discipline should be handled at home or involve juvenile services and law enforcement? Should you allow "harmless" hazing/indoctrination or maintain a "no tolerance" policy? Should you uphold a decision to allow students to read literature with profanity and sexual content for the sake of exploring alternative viewpoints and diverse thinking? Is it the role of the school board to protect a student's value set or to expand it, and should that expansion still be pursued if it is in conflict with parental values? Should you write policy requiring athletes to pass all academic classes to play? Should you disallow from playing sports student athletes who engage in a little "harmless" beer drinking on the weekend? Should you support a policy that disciplines a student who was absent from school to care for a sibling, work to raise money with his family, or travel on a culturally enriching family vacation?

These real policy issues face school board members today and can affect their reelection. Unfortunately, when you take a stand on one side of the values fence or the other, you know it can influence ensuing election results. In fact, today it seems that we can categorize many conflicts as being between two polarized groups. Some believe the two groups, orthodox and progressive, are pitted against each other in a "culture war," and as a school board member responsible for drafting policy and procedures to satisfy both, you are often caught in the middle. These two groups disagree on what is right and wrong, how we should live, and other foundational beliefs in moral authority, religion, world politics, and most important, the societal role of public schools.

Societal Role of Public Schools: Orthodox Versus Progressive Views

You, as a school board member seeking reelection, need to be responsive to the citizens who keep you in office. However, currently communities are often split in their beliefs concerning the societal roles of public schools. Therefore, it is crucial for you and your colleagues to recognize and understand basic differences between "orthodox" and "progressive" ideologies to maintain the responsive and equitable representation so critical to reelection.

Orthodox groups generally desire to limit government, and they sometimes view public schools as a monopoly that intrudes on the personal lives of citizens and is responsible for the continuing decline of American values. They often favor instructional methods such as direct instruction of basic skills, standardized content with more traditional historical interpretations, the teaching of phonics, grouping students by ability level, limited homework, traditional scheduling schemes, and strict disciplinary sanctions. Progressives generally desire an activist role for schools, looking to them to intervene and improve society. They support ideas such as cultural pluralism, where values are open to interpretation by different social groups. They often support a literacy approach to English instruction, mixed ability grouping, indirect instruction through projects, journal writing, and cooperative learning groups. As a result, you will probably be faced with these dichotomous community stances on the best educational programs, the most appropriate instructional materials, and the most effective disciplinary policies and practices.

For example, many boards have had difficulty adopting a science curriculum because of differing ideological and religious viewpoints over how evolution is covered in the instructional materials. In the area of discipline policy, orthodox traditionalists will often prefer more systematic and punitive measures while progressives will desire treatment options and alternative approaches that differ from student to student and incident to incident. These differences in position likely will not be casual preferences but instead will represent deeply held orthodox and progressive values and beliefs. You will not likely alter these values and beliefs through discussion and debate.

The two groups also differ in their opinions on how school systems should be reformed. The two reform strategies have been called the *behaviorist* and *progressive* approaches. The behaviorist strategy supports an accountability approach tied to state and national standards and the use of schooling choice to encourage competition between schools as a mechanism for school improvement. The progressive strategy favors reform on a school-by-school basis, teacher professionalism, and the pursuit of social justice.

Some researchers believe polarized forces and an increased plurality of society have heightened the political challenges for school board members, and that this is further exacerbated by the movement for decentralization of decision-making authority in schools (Björk & Gurley, 2005). Scholars argue that these polarized views of the world have led to what at times seems like an impossible task for satisfying a majority of the school district's parents. This culture war has also contributed to the more frequent disconnects between school board and community values that researchers believe lead to increased school board turnover rates (Alsbury, 2003; Björk & Gurley, 2005). This disconnection between community and school board values generally leads to an ever-growing level of dissatisfaction and, ultimately, school board member defeat.

HOW CAN I TELL WHEN THE POLITICAL WINDS ARE SHIFTING IN MY COMMUNITY?

A wry exchange in 1999 among three superintendents from a Southern state illustrated their understanding of politics in school leadership. I prefer the metaphor of shifting winds, but they offered a different one:

> *Superintendent X:* What you should be faulted for . . . is not being able to see when the train is coming down the tracks. If you aren't astute enough to know when that train is coming, then you only have yourself to blame, and I think that comes through a variety of experiences and perhaps maturity, but regardless of how you came to your position, or what you want to do to retain it, you always must be concerned to know whether the train is coming and whether it's time to get off the tracks.
>
> *Interviewer:* I recall when I was appointed superintendent, the executive director of my state association said to me, "There are two kinds of superintendents: ones that are in trouble and ones that don't know they are in trouble." And that speaks to [the] comments of knowing where the train is, . . . because it is always there and—
>
> *Superintendent Y:* How far away it is and—
>
> *Interviewer:* How . . . fast it's moving, right?
>
> *Superintendent Z:* Can you, and are you willing to, make those adaptations, because trains can be detoured, and we have probably all have done that at some point, because [anyone] who has stayed 4 years someplace has adapted and I would say, yes, compromised too, and sometimes you have to do that, too, but you [were] able to build new alliances that changed that direction of that train.

As a board member, you will face similar crises. The Dissatisfaction Theory puts it in less colorful, but perhaps more helpful, terms.

The Dissatisfaction Theory of American Democracy

The Dissatisfaction Theory (Iannaccone & Lutz, 1970, 1994) describes a political cycle in school organizations characterized by long periods of political inaction and punctuated by episodic turmoil of great intensity. The chain of events described in the Dissatisfaction Theory model, as represented in Table 11.1, includes (a) an increase in community dissatisfaction creating a change in your community's values; (b) the defeat of an incumbent school board member, brought on by an increase in your community's participation in the election process and competition for board seats; (c) pressure from the new board members to dismiss the superintendent; (d) your board's hiring of an outside superintendent candidate; and (e) increased pressure from new board members to change school policy. Increased community dissatisfaction that could lead to your defeat or pressure to resign or retire occurs when the ever-growing disconnection between school board and community values becomes a call to action.

In most scenarios, you, as a school board member, will begin your tenure with a clear understanding of the desires of the community, having been elected to represent a set of values and beliefs about how

Table 11.1.   Variables and Indicators of Change in the Theoretical Model as Described by the Dissatisfaction Theory of Democracy

Theory Variables*	Evidence of Change
Change in Community Values	Change in community population
	Change in community demographics
	Increase in elite board behaviors
	Increasing dissonance between board and community values
	Increase in community dissatisfaction
Change in Community Election Participation	Defeat of incumbent board members
	Increase in election voter turnout
	Increase in challengers to incumbent and vacated board seats
	Increase in departure of challengers' values or beliefs from existing board
Change in School Board	Shift of board makeup and personality
	Increased diversity of board values
	Less unanimous support of superintendent
	Less unanimous support of board policy and procedures
Change in School District Policy/Practice	Superintendent fired or pressured to resign

* Note: These operate as a sequenced chain of events

schools should be run. You will likely find that, almost immediately, the quantity and openness of communications with your constituency will diminish as compared to what occurred prior to your election. As a board member, you are now viewed as part of "the system," and thus carry a stigma of positional power that is difficult to shake. A superintendent of 16 years in a suburban district told us, "One of the difficulties that I found is the issue of a school board member making the transition from politician to policymaker." Another said,

> I guess, part of the politics of getting elected is they might have one unique thing that they're—they're going to try to reduce taxes, whatever it is they're coming on board with—and then learning the job, understanding what their role is as a board member, that they're policymakers, not micromanagers.

One superintendent of 12 years from a suburban district proposed questions that you as a board member might want to ask yourself periodically: "Why are [you] on the board? Is it for political gain? Were [you] a single-issue board member when [you] were elected, or are [you] purely there because [you're] committed to quality education and [you] want to improve it?" This brings us to another theoretical perspective that you might find illuminating: elite versus arena school boards.

Elite- Versus Arena-Style Boards

Elite-style boards function in a more closed environment. Elite board members, reasoning that the community knew what they believed in, agreed with it, and thus elected them to represent those values, typically view their election onto the board as a license from their community to represent their own political and ideological values. Elite boards do not actively seek out input from the community. Elite boards often discuss and resolve differences informally and prior to board meetings in an effort to appear organized, strong, and agreeable. Elite boards are characterized by and pride themselves on unanimous board votes.

Arena boards function in an open environment. Arena board members typically believe that they must constantly assess community values and speak for the broader interests. These board members will vote for what they believe are community values even when this may conflict with their own beliefs. Arena boards pride themselves on long discussions and debates in open board meetings and are characterized by split votes. Even though this more open approach may be viewed as the obvious choice of citizens, community members frequently complain that arena boards appear to lack strong leadership, are inefficient, fail to make firm decisions, and flip-flop on their values. Most studies indicate that although communities verbally support arena board behaviors, they actively pressure boards to use elite behaviors, and election defeats increase in boards shifting to an arena style.

This creates a conundrum for you as a board member. Clearly, there is no easy answer along the lines of "Elite is always best" or "Arena style pays off in the long run." The best advice I can provide is for you to attend to conditions in your community and be prepared to shift styles in response to conditions. In times of apparent community disinterest in your work, the elite style may help you plan strategically, stick to your plans, and follow through with efforts to have an efficient and effective district. But in times of community dissatisfaction and activism, an arena style can be more responsive and allow you to deal with difficulties before they cost you your reelection.

CAN I BE POLITICALLY EFFECTIVE AND MAINTAIN MY INTEGRITY?

A superintendent of seven years in a suburban district gave a stark description of encountering political opportunism in a board member:

> I was a very green, naive assistant superintendent and a board member came in and said, "Paul [a pseudonym], you know what my absolute bottom line is, don't you?" And I said, "Of course, children." And he said, "Hell no. Getting elected! Now, once you understand that, and as long as you understand that, we will be on solid ground here. So, everything that you do, I want you to make me look good." That was his message.

Furthermore, some board members run to advance personal agendas. A superintendent of four years in a rural district indicated that one board member had secretly run for the position to settle a vendetta against him for having suspended his daughter from school:

> We have . . . board members that run, because you made them mad—two to three years down the line that's the whole focus—political. It's not what you're doing; it's who you made mad. "And I'm going to run for the board and get you out." That's what they all say.

But political opportunism is not necessarily a bad thing. It is, in fact, one facet of effectiveness. Probably every elected official would recognize the need to strike "quickly while the policy window is open" (McDonnell, 1994, p. 401). The question is not one of whether you should be a political opportunist, the question is how to mix this with service to schools.

Mixing Politics with School Service

A superintendent in a suburban district related this occurrence:

> I've had board members say, "I'm for the budget but, publicly, I'm going to say 'No,' especially if I'm the only vote." If you have eight votes already and they know that, just to get elected a person might say, "You know, out on the street it's going to be a 'no' vote but I support you behind the scene," and you might say to them, "Fine," because you want that board member to be back again. So that's when politics really gets involved.

As a school board member, the motivations for why some of your colleagues ran for school board may differ from yours. Their need to get reelected may motivate them to act in certain ways publicly even though they hold very different views privately. The fact that some board members may mix politics and service in inappropriate ways, as evidenced in the above quotes, can lead you to doubt that some of your colleagues are serving for the correct reasons. The reality of politics' role in school governance is important to understand so you can better ferret out the appropriate and inappropriate role of politics in governance.

Also, remember that you are not faced with a clear dilemma of either being effective or having integrity. In fact, integrity can be politically effective. Integrity often translates into consistency, reliability, and ultimately trust. These characteristics can gain you support when you need it most. A superintendent with 18 years' experience noted,

> Some of us have laughed at times and said you need to leave [the super-intendency] with the same thing that you brought: your integrity. We quip, "If you tell the truth, you don't have to try to remember what you said yesterday." But it is amazing what a value just honesty and integrity has in the middle of the conflict. The truth is, there are some situations when people on all fronts may disagree with you and may be upset with you. But if they think that you have been honest with them—they know that you have been honest with them and that you are consistent—then you tend to weather that.

Another superintendent gave an example of a problem that can cause discontent in the short term but can be overcome if people trust your commitments:

> Teachers realize that we're putting our money where our mouth is. They will appreciate that, and they will let us off the hook for a few months anyway on creeping class sizes, knowing that we're also committed to dealing with that a few months down the road.

Integrity is not a guarantee of anything. History is full of examples of people of integrity who were defeated. That is why to be successful in the long run, integrity helps, but watchfulness and political savvy help too. Switching from an elite style to an arena style and back can also work for you. In short, school board members must be both wise as serpents and guileless as doves.

WHAT CAN I DO WHILE IN THE MIDST OF CHAOTIC POLITICAL SITUATIONS TO ACCOMPLISH GOOD THINGS FOR STUDENTS?

My colleagues' assumption in this book is that you must remain focused on students and their achievements. My assumption in this chapter is that the challenge of facing reelection and other political forces make it terribly difficult to remain so focused. One way to focus on students in the midst of political tension and chaos is to consider carefully your role.

The Role of School Board Members

Understanding your role on the school board might not be easy. In fact, I believe poor understanding of the school board member's role is the primary culprit in the breakdown of school board–superintendent relationships (Alsbury, 2003). There are a variety of ideas about what your role should be as a school board member. Traditional models of school board role include:

1. Guiding the school district toward its purpose, primarily the education of the children, through the development of broad policy statements
2. Screening and supporting key programs and the ongoing operation of the school district
3. Hiring, directing, and evaluating the superintendent
4. Ensuring the fiscal, legal, and operational functions that maintain and protect the staff and facilities
5. Serving as a bridge (or buffer) between the district and the community

The complexity comes in when you begin to do the specific work of these traditional (and vague) descriptors. Some of you may believe that you should take a much more active role in leading school district reform while other board members, the superintendent, and even your state school board association may caution you to avoid micromanaging.

Superintendents (who, like you, are also politically vulnerable, who feel pressured by forces similar to those that threaten you, and who need to be just as wise as you do to survive) often define board members' roles for them through training, agenda setting, and controlling the information provided to board members. Most superintendents support an elite style of board behavior and a strict chain of command. This approach involves (a) the board asking the superintendent to assess something, improve something, or resolve a problem, (b) the superintendent working with district staff to provide data and propose a course of action, and (c) the course of action being approved by the board. If the board votes against the course of action, the superintendent removes the proposal and returns with an alternative. This process continues until the board has a proposal they can accept. The traditional view of school boards holds that at no time in this process would the board be allowed to develop its own proposal or work with district administration or staff below the superintendent.

One superintendent of four years in a suburban district clearly saw his board's role as reactive program-approvers rather than proactive developers. He said,

> Unless there are extraordinary circumstances, I think each of our boards expects us to bring problems to them. They expect us to keep them apprised and to be anticipating what's coming down the pike, but I don't think that they expect us to present them to them as problems. I think they expect us to present these matters to them in a way which demonstrates that we have given thoughtful consideration to the matter and have taken the time and done the proper study to lay out options and alternatives, which ideally lead them to the right solution. And quite honestly, that is part of our role. We are expected to cook it by the time it gets there and to give them all the rationale necessary to feel comfortable with the recommendation that we're making.

Many superintendents also prefer to work one-on-one with school board members to resolve their preferences for a proposal so that by the time the final proposal comes to the board a unanimous vote for approval is expected. Superintendents believe that this approach allows for input from board members while maintaining the public face of a strong, unified board.

This flies in the face of what some board members expected when running for the board seat. Regardless of how you see your role as board member, you should clarify it in your own mind and determine whether it matches with those of your fellow board members and that of your superintendent.

You cannot "fix" this inherently messy situation. Boards and superintendents work from their own assumptions, and they are likely to be contrary assumptions. You can only attempt to navigate the choppy waters as skillfully as possible. As each understands where the other is coming from, you may be able to work together with your colleagues and the superintendent more productively. So I'm going to take just a little space to help you see from the superintendent's perspective. Furthermore, I must point out that perspectives of the superintendency have changed over time.

The superintendent's desire to keep you less involved in program creation and management is mostly due to professional vulnerability. Just as in many professional athletic organizations, the superintendent, like a coach, usually gets little credit for successes and takes most of the blame for failures. Further, your superintendent is likely the only member of the school staff who is not protected by state tenure laws, making him or her easiest to fire. Superintendents know that, just like coaches, they are routinely used as the scapegoat for a district's ills. Your superintendent may seem to maintain excessive control over the information you receive, programs you consider, and policies you approve. This enables him or her to prevent you from making decisions as a board for which *the superintendent* may be held responsible if things go badly.

In addition, superintendents who shift program control to board members often lose favor with their staff, who then respond by exercising strong political influences upon board members, again making the superintendent professionally vulnerable. Furthermore, superintendents know that their responsibilities are only loosely defined, which also makes them vulnerable to the charge of not having carried out those responsibilities. And they have seen those responsibilities change.

HOW DO I BALANCE MY ROLE WITH THE SUPERINTENDENT'S?

The Changing Role of the Superintendent

Björk, Kowalski, and Browne-Ferrigno (2005) indicate that superintendents' roles have changed over time from (1) *teacher-scholar* (1850 to early 1900s), (2) *organizational manager* (early 1900s to 1930), (3) *democratic leader* (1930 to mid-1950s), (4) *applied social scientist* (mid-1950s to mid-1970s), to (5) *communicator* (mid-1970s to present). More recently (1983–2005), a number of factors have influenced changes in how superintendents enact their roles. These factors include a loss of confidence in institutions and leaders, increased levels of interest-group activism, and expanded expectations for public involvement in local policymaking processes. In addition, scholars observe that a growing cultural divide among citizens, more divergent ideologies, and shifting of policymaking to the state and federal levels have created tensions over how power is distributed (Björk & Lindle, 2001; Keedy & Björk, 2003) and strained relationships between school board members and superintendents.

Superintendent–Board Relations

The changing role of the superintendent has changed school board–superintendent relationships. Historically, the superintendent's role has been transformed from a clerk to educational expert, professional advisor, and finally to collaborator. By the 1970s, educational administrators were taking on a more social role focused on the larger system. These trends, as well as demographic and societal shifts, recent demands for systematic reform, accountability, and a focus on issues of equity and social justice, have impelled superintendents to become "social engineers or super social scientists" (Johnson & Fusarelli, 2003, p. 6). Other researchers have discussed a growing need for superintendents to focus on societal inequities and suggest that the shift toward social justice has led superintendents to play a key role as a moral agent.

Consequently, some believe that much of the superintendent's work is now focused upon making value judgments. While the role has changed, superintendents have always been required to orchestrate district responses to multiple forces in changing contexts. Björk and Gurley (2005) suggest that the present-day superintendents should take on the role of *democratic leaders*, a role they say, "may be more apropos in that it reflects enduring citizen demands for voice as well as heightened expectations for working with and through others to accomplish community education goals" (p. 169).

You thus have the task of working effectively with your superintendent despite controversy about your respective roles. There are two points at which you can be particularly effective in maintaining productive relationships with the superintendent: hiring and evaluating.

WHAT DO I CONSIDER IN SELECTING A SUPERINTENDENT?

Hiring and Evaluating the Superintendent

As a board member responsible for hiring and evaluating your superintendent, it is important for you to note that superintendents, just like board members, must have a high level of political acuity tempered by moral principles and the capacity to communicate effectively with a broad range of community-based constituents. Ultimately, they must be able to work collaboratively for the common good. You, as a school board member, are responsible for choosing the right superintendent, setting clear expectations, maintaining positive and productive relationships, and evaluating the superintendent fairly.

You and the other board members must first work toward consensus on the expectations for the superintendent and then make these expectations clear, and you should explore with all candidates the likelihood of a positive school board–superintendent relationship. Superintendent interviews provide you an important opportunity to communicate to the superintendent the vision, anticipated role, and expected board operations. If you cannot achieve consensus on at least some fundamental issues, astute applicants will catch on and may very well withdraw their applications and simply seek a superintendency somewhere else. This is especially true if they are career bound.

Place-Bound and Career-Bound Superintendents

Understanding variations in a superintendent's career pathway is critical for school board members during the hiring and evaluation of superintendents. As you contemplate hiring a new superintendent, it is important for you to understand that while there are numerous superintendent leadership styles, most follow one of two distinct career pathways: place bound or career bound.

These pathways were first identified and researched by Carlson (1972). Place-bound superintendents are insiders who rise through the ranks from teacher, to building administrator, into the central office, and eventually to the superintendency. Place-bound superintendents are selected when school boards are looking for stability and maintenance of the status quo. Place-bound superintendents prefer to avoid conflict rather than resolve it. Research reveals that many place-bound superintendents prefer to resolve conflict by changing behavior, timing the approach, acquiescence and accepting, and bluffing. In fact, Bacharach (1981) suggests that these superintendents avoid conflict by "fence-sitting" and insists that, at times, this is the best and most effective strategy. However, Lutz and Merz (1992) note that conflict resolution could be best accomplished if superintendents and board members worked together using a proactive and arena-style approach. They suggest that many boards handle conflict by resisting public demands and thus "hide conflict under the rug," and that a better method is to "manage conflict" in a way that "kicks up dirt rather than hiding it" (p. 153). They contend that if the district handles conflict early it will avoid increasing dissatisfaction, which eventually will lead to major episodic upheaval and school board defeat. However, place-bound superintendents in very small districts are more likely to exercise peacekeeping measures than to engage in messy and conflict-producing business such as massive school reform.

Career-bound superintendents are typically hired from outside the district and specialize in leading change within a district. They typically do not remain for more than 5 years and often engage in pressing ineffective staff to improve, leave, or retire early. Often career-bound superintendents challenge current practices and are more effective at identifying district areas that need improvement. Career-bound superintendents typically are not as influenced by the threat of community conflict or dismissal and expect conflict and resistance from some staff and community members. Career-bound leaders are often hired when districts are in critical need of change. Thus, you, as a school board, may tend to give these newly selected leaders carte blanche despite staff complaints about such things as major policy and program changes, increased accountability measures, and the liberal use of contractual options leading to the involuntary transfer of staff.

You will want to understand that place-bound superintendents typically follow career-bound superintendents and vice versa, and you

should realize that stability in a district is often a result of this succession pattern. The belief is that following dramatic change in a district under a career-bound leader, the district needs time to implement the reform and establish a new district culture through
consistency and a focus on human relations. If you hire a career-
bound leader to follow a career-bound leader, you will likely experience growing conflict among the district staff and community through
reform overload. Conversely, a series of place-bound superintendents
will likely result in the absence of reform, often referred to as *reform
stagnation.*

Superintendent Evaluation

Superintendent evaluation should focus upon the same criteria used
in the hiring process. Superintendents expect to be challenged as they
lead a system that educates all the children in the district. They do not,
however, want their evaluation to depend on changes (perhaps whimsi-
cal changes) in community desires. Unfortunately, in many of our school
districts, superintendents and school board members may be "trained"
by the community to focus on priorities other than student achievement.
One superintendent in a rural district shared a story:

> I can remember a board meeting that unfortunately was not atypical,
> when my principal was going to share our student achievement scores
> and an award we had received. Also on the agenda was an issue about
> why the girls' volleyball team did not receive new uniforms that year
> when the boys' basketball team did. Well, we had about 80 parents show
> up and speak to the uniform issue, but after the break when the princi-
> pal got up to share, no one was there. They knew about the achievement
> award, and they all went home. I think the board and I both got the mes-
> sage loud and clear about what was important to the parents in that
> community.

As a board member, you should be aware that most research supports the notion that superintendent evaluation needs to be focused
on success in student achievement and instructional improvement—
but community pressures may lead you to focus on noninstructional
issues. Furthermore, even if you can remain focused on student

achievement, and intend to evaluate your superintendent on improving student achievement, you should also be aware that systemic change takes from five to 10 years depending on the district size. Therefore, it is critical that school board members understand the importance of evaluating superintendents on measurable educational goals while providing them the time to achieve real systemic and sustainable change within a district.

Also, you should realize that politically savvy superintendents may be quite willing to be evaluated, if the terms of the evaluation are agreed upon up front. They see it as to their advantage to have everyone agree up front on the evaluation criteria. A superintendent of an urban school district discussed his experience:

> I was fortunate enough . . . a few years ago when I negotiated my contract, I negotiated the terms of the evaluation and I negotiated the instrument of the evaluation, and I would recommend that to anyone, I suppose anywhere. . . . If someone wants you, they'll get you, and they can do it in a number of ways. They can create criteria that is impossible to be met, or they can change the rules of the game in the eleventh hour. So I have been very fortunate in the last few years that I have had a solid instrument that has served me very well.

RECOMMENDATIONS

We have presented a number of issues influencing school board reelection including (a) the rise of cultural and values plurality in your community, (b) balancing stable leadership with being politically responsive, (c) gaining support while being loyal to your values, and (d) maintaining good work relationships with your fellow board members and the superintendent.

From these broad and varied issues surrounding your reelection, several cogent recommendations arise. We believe as a school board member you should do the following:

* Increase your efforts to continually assess and adjust to your community's values and be willing to change to an arena governance

style if you detect increased dissatisfaction in the community. Also be prepared to return to the more stable elite style of governance after the conflict causing the dissatisfaction is addressed. Flexibility in your board's leadership style leads to a decline of election defeats.

- Take notice after an election with one or more politically motivated board changes as this may be symptomatic of an increase in dissatisfaction within your community and lead to further election defeat.

- Determine how you will manage the political nature of your position and ensure that you exercise your role consistently in your actions and comments, balancing how and when to allow politics to influence your actions so that you can increase both your trustworthiness and your longevity on the board.

- Understand that community values and demands may often be incongruous due to increasing values plurality so that you can make decisions for the broader student and community populace rather than attend to special interests. Because community values vary greatly, every decision will likely garner political proponents and enemies. Therefore, you are best served by focusing on student needs; political aggrandizing will likely not protect your position on the board.

- Discuss with your fellow board members and superintendent, and come to an agreement over, your role. Serve, as best you can, within that agreed-upon role. Consistency and a positive board–superintendent relationship lead to less board and superintendent turnover and thus more leadership continuity.

- Carefully consider place-bound and career-bound succession patterns when hiring a superintendent. Districts following these succession patterns tend to enjoy less board turnover.

- Understand that the superintendent's role today is changing rapidly, requiring him or her to satisfy a broad and often disconnected set of interests while simultaneously raising student achievement and addressing social justice issues. By assisting your superintendent in addressing a broader range of demands, you will provide more stability in your own position on the board.

- Hire and evaluate superintendents on instructional goals involving student achievement, leadership, and personnel management as opposed to the current trends toward a focus on facilities, athletics, or politically expedient noneducational issues. While minority interest groups may be quite vocal, board members who lead academically successful schools enjoy greater rates of reelection.

12

SUCCESS STRATEGY: OBTAIN MEANINGFUL COMMUNITY INPUT

Eduardo Arellano

To seek advice from the community, public school boards are required to include in their open meetings a time for "public comments." During this part of a meeting, individuals and groups have the opportunity to provide input to school boards. To put it mildly, you have probably noticed that the quality of this input varies. Sometimes, there are no comments from the community. Other times there are remarks that are not very useful in improving schools. In still other cases, the same people with their limited agendas speak at every meeting, making it tempting to ignore their participation. We should remember, however, that even the views of the most difficult community members can contribute to school improvement. More important, we should also remember that one of the central roles of school boards is to "provide avenues for community input" (Danzberger, 1994).

The challenge is how to separate meaningful community input aimed at improving schools from feedback that does not serve this purpose. Insights from various superintendents, literature on listening and school governance, and my personal experiences as a school board member have aided me in describing strategies in this chapter for obtaining meaningful community input.

When I refer to community, I include residents, students, parents, teachers, administrators, business and government officials, and other interested individuals and groups. I define community in such a way because the vast majority of school boards are responsible to all of these various constituent groups (Campbell & Greene, 1994) who, like school board members, have a stake in improving schools. The strategies I recommend are these:

- Listen effectively.
- Make sure all voices are heard.
- Be patient and understanding.
- Separate the messenger from the message.
- Learn about the community.

LISTEN EFFECTIVELY

According to a superintendent from a rural school district in the South, "I don't care what strategic-planning form you follow, you must give the people the opportunity to tell you what they think is good, what they think is bad, and what they want." A superintendent from a small, rural school district put it more simply, "All you really have to do sometimes is just be willing to listen." Literature on school governance also supports the importance of effective listening (Bartusek, 2003; Campbell & Greene, 1994; Smoley, 1999). While, arguably, listening is an obvious strategy for obtaining meaningful input, practicing effective listening is not always evident. Evidence that effective listening is atypical is clear in the words of the first superintendent just quoted who also said,

> I thought I knew what those people in that school thought, [but] I had no idea what they thought—I was totally way off base. . . . We sometimes assume that we know what people are thinking, or what they feel about what we are doing or, what they feel the future of their community or school or school system should be and we don't give them enough opportunities to tell us.

Many of us believe we know what listening means and how to listen, yet I believe we can all learn more about it. In this section, I suggest reasons for listening, describe types of listening, and then recommend specific skills for effective listening.

Reasons for Listening

There are weighty philosophical and practical reasons why school board members should listen to community input. As of 2003, 96% of school districts had elected board members (Hess, 2003) and so members must be responsive to voters. Philosophically, if public school board members truly value genuine democratic participation in school governance, they should listen to community input. Presumably, democratic involvement is valued as a way of "ensuring that different voices get heard, that the marginalized have someone to appeal to, [and] that different concerns get weighed" (Hess, 2003, p. 38). For practical reasons, school board members should listen to community input because it can help them develop a comprehensible vision that can be transformed into clear goals supported by the community. Input from others illuminates the blind spots of an individual decision maker and thus can promote better decision making. An added benefit is that an organizational climate can be fostered to sustain the district's goals (Tate & Dunklee, 2005). School board members should also listen because it "enhances the ability to learn, incorporate, and adapt new information, knowledge, and skills" (University of Pittsburgh, 2006, p. 3).

Whether we listen for philosophical or practical reasons, we should take into consideration the statement made by Judi Brownell (2006): "The outcome of any encounter is largely dependent on *your* listening behavior" (p. 277).

Types of Listening

Listening effectively is based in part on being able to use skills that are appropriate to the situation (University of Pittsburgh, 2006). As school board members, our task is to "respect minority voices" but know that we "can't please everybody all the time" (Reeves as cited in Colgan, 2004, p. 24). Based on the aforementioned principles and my three years of experience as a school board member, I have identified the need for listening for meaning, critical listening, and empathic listening as indispensable for obtaining meaningful input.

Listening for meaning is aimed at retaining and understanding a speaker's message. It has also been called comprehensive listening, listening to understand, and strategic listening (Tate & Dunklee, 2005). The essence of this type of listening is that you "must sincerely want to listen and must have the patience and willingness to be of assistance . . . , to listen respectfully and attend to the emotions, needs, and concerns of those who are trying to communicate with you" (Purdy, 1997, as cited in Tate & Dunklee, 2005, p. 5). Listening for comprehension demonstrates interest in the ideas and feelings of community members. Listening for comprehension is evident when you are sincerely concerned about the community and you are interested in what community members have to say (Brownell, 2006). Remember, however, that what is considered as listening for comprehension in one culture may be deemed as improper in another (Tate & Dunklee, 2005). That is why school board members must learn about the various cultures within the community in which they serve, as I discuss later in this chapter.

Critical listening describes "situations where the listener makes judgments about the speaker's message" (University of Pittsburgh, 2006). A critical listener pays attention to the credibility of a speaker and his or her sources of information as well as to the structure and support the speaker provides for his or her arguments. Critical listening is vital if you want to respond intelligently to what a person is saying (Tate & Dunklee, 2005).

Empathic listening, on the other hand, focuses on "understanding a message from the speaker's perspective in situations where the speaker needs to be heard or talk through an issue" (University of Pittsburgh, 2006, p. 8). With such a focus, empathic listening takes time, as a superintendent from a small district noted:

> It is sometimes time consuming to get them [community members] to talk through and get through all of the other issues down to the core because they'll never tell you that right off. They always have something else that they focus on, and you have to get down to what's really bothering them.

As much intention, knowledge, and time these types of listening call for, they are all needed. Thus far, I have been describing my first strategy for obtaining meaningful input, which is listening effectively. Let me end this discussion on a very practical note by recommending some skills to practice.

Effective Listening Skills

One of the listening skills that a superintendent from a large school district pointed out was to ask clarifying questions:

> Suppose the board told me in an evaluation session [that] the system needs to do this; we want you to make that work; and then I ask some questions about what they really feel and what it is specifically they want better—and yeah, maybe we can do that—and then we go out and build that up.

By asking clarifying questions, you compare what you think someone said to what they actually intended to say (Brownell, 2006; Mills, 1974; Tate & Dunklee, 2005; University of Pittsburgh, 2006). Checking for meaning is imperative because you cannot assume that messages have the same meaning for everyone, especially when people are from different cultures. By asking clarifying questions, you show positive regard for a community member's worldview and improve your understanding of a situation. Similarly, if you are the one wanting to be heard, clarifying questions can help you determine if your listener has understood you correctly. One superintendent said, "I have learned to ask people, 'How did you hear that? What did you hear me say?'"

Another skill suggested by an experienced superintendent from an urban school district is to be open to views different from your own. She discussed how she learned this valuable lesson:

> You know sometimes . . . I think I know the answers, and I just wait for you to say the answer back to me that I already know is the real answer. . . . I was a high school principal thinking up some ways to give students some incentives. It was some sort of program, and I think I came up with a pizza party or something and some of the students came to see me and said to me, in essence, "You're clueless, you know. We don't want a pizza party. That means nothing to us." And so [I asked], "What would give you the incentive to do what [you are] trying to do?" And they said, "A park-

ing place close to the front door and a top locker." And when we made those the prizes, we had the greatest sale we had ever had—but my point being: never in my life would I have thought that would have been such an incentive to the students.

Brownell (2006) endorses accepting alternative views and asserts that doing so is particularly important in a climate of increasing diversity.

Other practices that are associated with effective listening include mentally preparing and committing yourself to listen, thinking about the issues you are about to face in advance, concentrating, and committing to repeat what you heard to someone else (Barker, Wahlers, Watson, & Kibler, 1991). As a school board member, I mentally prepare myself to think about the issues I am about to face before attending a meeting by setting aside approximately 30 to 60 minutes of quiet time for concentration. Both preparation and concentration can make you a better listener (Tate & Dunklee, 2005; University of Pittsburgh, 2006).

Additionally, there are other practices associated with effective listening: listening for ideas that you share in common, searching for meaning in comments, not arguing about specific words being said, and providing clear responses to community members' comments and/or questions (Barker et al., 1991). Your responses ought to show that you are grateful for the community member's contributions (Tate & Dunklee, 2005).

Last, but not least, is the use of appropriate nonverbal behaviors such as an "attentive posture" (University of Pittsburgh, 2006) and appropriate eye contact (Purdy, 2006; Tate & Dunklee, 2005; University of Pittsburgh, 2006). Tate and Dunklee (2005) point out that up to 55% of a message's meaning comes from facial cues alone and nonverbal behavior. Their insights show that school board members should be sensitive to not only their own nonverbal behaviors but also to those of community members. Tate and Dunklee caution that certain nonverbal behaviors can be interpreted negatively by some ethnic cultures. For example, in some cultures, such as the Mexican culture, direct eye contact with someone considered an authority figure can be interpreted as disrespectful on the part of a community member. All of us need to be aware of and practice continual self-evaluation and improvement to enhance our effectiveness (University of Pittsburgh, 2006).

To advance our listening skills, we should take advantage of professional development opportunities that build listening abilities. However, because one-time workshops have been shown not to make lasting positive impacts on a person's listening capacity, it is better when school board members participate in professional development programs that extend over a period of considerable time (University of Pittsburgh, 2006). If professional development and training opportunities are unavailable, you can simply monitor your listening behaviors and ask friends to monitor your behaviors as well (Brownell, 2006). One way of monitoring your behavior is to analyze when you are more likely to interrupt, whether it is when a certain community member speaks or when a certain issue is raised (Brownell, 2006). Self-monitoring is easier in school districts that televise and record their open meetings because you can watch yourself at home after a meeting and look for behaviors that do not reflect effective listening.

To sum up, in order to listen effectively, school board members should follow these recommendations:

1. Ask clarifying questions.
2. Be open to different points of view.
3. Prepare and commit to listen.
4. Search for commonalities with community members.
5. Listen with your whole body.
6. Continually work on improving listening.

MAKE SURE ALL VOICES ARE HEARD

Outcomes depend on who gets heard, and for that reason alone, school board members should make sure all voices are heard. If we do this, we will represent the entire community we serve, not just a select few. If school board members are to obtain meaningful community input, we need to make sure all voices are heard by getting input from different sources and in ways other than public school board meetings (Smoley, 1999). If community input is sought only through school board meetings, then some students, staff, and other community members may not be able to present problems or solutions.

Still, there are many ways to increase participation in school board meetings, including sending community leaders and other interested individuals copies of meeting agendas, inviting specific community groups to attend meetings, scheduling meetings at times convenient for most of the community, and holding meetings in different schools (Bartusek, 2003). Other suggestions include placing the "public comments" agenda item at the beginning of each meeting to emphasize that community input is a priority to the board. Board members, in turn, can then respond to comments because to do otherwise suggests to community members that their input does not deserve a reply (Sokoloff, 2001). In addition, Sokoloff recommends that districts hold meetings focused on specific topics to which the community can contribute. It may help to think of our conduct at school board meetings as an indicator of how in general we think about our community members. The respect and attention we show them at school board meetings should be an extension of the respect we always show them and our ongoing willingness to hear them.

Another way to make sure all voices are heard is to consider our listening work outside of school board meetings. Some superintendents we interviewed advised that input be sought through one-on-one conversations with students, staff, and other community members. According to a superintendent from a rural school district, these conversations do not need to be limited to formal settings. He offered the following possibilities: "Football games, basketball games, music events. . . . You're talking with people from the local Optimists, Lions Club, Kiwanis." What's more, conversations can take place during school visits (Bartusek, 2003).

Just as it is too often customary to rely solely on school board meetings for public input, it is also common for district leaders to limit our interactions to specific members of the public. A superintendent from a small rural school district advocated soliciting opinions from "groups that might not be considered sometimes," such as high school dropouts. Another seasoned superintendent from a small rural school district contended that students are badly overlooked, yet "they also have very good ideas about what's effective." To this superintendent, the student is "another stakeholder that we don't tap into nearly as we should." As a way of embracing student voices, some school boards have a student serve on the board either in an advisory capacity or as a full-fledged member (Joiner, 2003).

It is also important to communicate with those who do not have children or who do not work in the schools. As one superintendent asserted,

It is important . . . that they understand what the quality of public education means to the value of life in the community and, frankly, what it even means to the property value of the house they own, if that's the only level at which we can reach them.

It is essential to communicate with the whole community because addressing some school district problems requires broad-based support. A superintendent from a rural school district affirmed, "You want to have as good a cross section of your community [as you can] to get feedback on a lot of issues before you come to a final conclusion." Obtaining meaningful community input helps establish "the kinds of communication to allow for honest discussion about improving" schools, as a superintendent from an urban school district added. In sum, according to another superintendent, "Trying to get as broad a base as you can is important for success."

BE PATIENT AND UNDERSTANDING

Educational issues contain built-in conflict, which is why it is imperative that school board members be patient and understanding. One superintendent described his approach to patient listening:

I know enough to keep my mouth shut and listen; I know enough to turn to somebody to find somebody who does know something about [it] so the decisions can be based on something solid as opposed to just gut feelings about it.

A seasoned superintendent from a rural school district offered some good advice:

I found that it was much better to wait until you gather all the facts and have time to reflect over it and then listen to what other people say before you come out with what you think is the best direction. So I think it helped me to learn patience and maybe [become] tolerant of other people with differing ideas. Then also I think it helped me gain a certain tolerance for ambiguity, because very few issues will be black and white.

Once the facts are known, take time to reflect on criticisms and weigh the facts because many times issues are not clear cut. Since in many situations the ideal solution is not obvious, it is essential for you to have *ambiguity tolerance*. Ambiguity tolerance is the ability to work successfully in uncertain circumstances (Rosen, 2000). Ambiguity tolerance is also indispensable if you wish to avoid what a superintendent from a small urban school district called "solving problems that are not the real issues." In addition, you have to recognize that it takes time for some community members, as a superintendent above noted, to "get through all of the issues down to the core" of what is bothering them.

One's patience can be tried with community members who regularly speak at board meetings. After all, we have become very familiar with these members and their perspectives, and because of this familiarity, it is easy to jump to a wrong conclusion about what the person may be saying and the points he or she is making. Therefore, we should listen to the whole idea or message before responding (Barker et al., 1991). Do not interrupt them (Tate & Dunklee, 2005). If we truly want to understand them, we need to "take a look at the world" (Tate & Dunklee, 2005, p. 7) through their eyes. Being patient and understanding are but a couple of characteristics that one superintendent from an urban school district called "human relations qualities" that she believes "have to be as strong as your organizational skills or your systems thinking."

SEPARATE THE MESSAGE FROM THE MESSENGER

In order to ensure that we hear all voices, we must work to hear voices we might not enjoy hearing, including those of people we dislike or at least whose delivery we dislike. A superintendent from a rural school district warned that if you do not separate the messenger from the message, it is very tempting to cast potentially important input aside:

> I have learned not to take it personally. . . . I had a ten-mile run one morning, and I had a major talk with me and came back. And from that day I remembered in every instance, it is not about me. . . . I remember what it

was like being a parent of an elementary child. . . . They are looking to me to do the best job I can to help them, but it is not about me personally.

We can get better at this with personal and organizational approaches.

Personal Approaches

By personal approaches, I mean working on our own personal reactions to things. If we become too emotionally involved because of who brings the information, we can miss the information (Barker et al., 1991, p. 78; Mills, 1974). As our jogging superintendent concluded, more often than not, community input is not about you or me as an individual; it is, instead, about a frustration with a school or the district or some other underlying issue. So it is best to defer judgment on what is being said; empathize with whomever is speaking, and put our feelings in perspective in terms of what is being said and who is saying it (Barker et al., 1991; Mills, 1974; Purdy, 2006). Putting our feelings in perspective is difficult because they can be deep-seated, but we can start by being aware of our strongly held beliefs and temper our reactions when these beliefs are questioned (Banville, 1978; Barker et al., 1991). Equally significant, we should strive to be open minded by recognizing that community members' opinions can be informative even if we do not agree with them (Barker et al., 1991).

Organizational Approaches

Besides working with our own personalities and emotional reactions, we can work on our organizations to improve our chances of hearing all voices. A good start is to establish advisory committees both at the campus level and at the central office level. Principals can appoint campus advisory committees, while boards and superintendents can appoint district advisory committees. For example, to ensure diversity of opinion, one superintendent from a rural school district chose not only "people who say good things" but also those who bring up negative issues, people this superintendent called "truth-tellers." This superintendent found advisory committees helpful in surfacing issues, framing issues, communicating solutions, and generating support for initiatives.

One school district rotated the members of the advisory committees so that the committees would never be made up of all new members. Another superintendent from a small school district discovered that through advisory committees, "you will find out some things that you wouldn't have dreamed of or thought of yourself." One superintendent created a parent advisory committee to "almost compel them to come and listen and exchange, hoping they would be representative of parents in general."

Advisory committees have an added benefit of helping us separate the messenger from the message. For example, a superintendent from a midsized school district suggested having people who are neither school board nor staff members lead community discussions so that the community can feel comfortable pointing out problems. The above organizational approaches might be incorporated into your school district's written policies (Bartusek, 2003) because doing so will provide structure to community input (Smoley, 1999).

LEARN ABOUT THE COMMUNITY

It is crucial that we come to understand the cultural diversity in our communities (Brownell, 2006). Although there are many definitions of culture, Wolvin and Coakley's seems appropriate: "the set of customs, behaviors, beliefs, and languages that distinguish a particular group of people and make up the background, experience, and perceptual filters of individuals within that group" (as cited in Tate & Dunklee, 2005, p. 33). We must work to understand the cultures in our communities because ethnic cultures see the world dissimilarly, and thus see situations dissimilarly. An experienced superintendent from an urban school district claimed, "Our population that we serve is becoming more diverse, not only culturally but socioeconomically [and in their] philosophies."

Thus, being attentive to culture includes awareness of the variety of ethnic, economic, and political perspectives within communities. Given the reality of divergence among groups, we must become skilled in relating to people with disparate needs, values, and ideas. As a superintendent from a rural, midsized school district stated, "I have five communities and every one of them is different and you have to deal with them differently for the most part." A superintendent from an urban school district in the South put it this way:

> Every one of us represents polyglot organizations and counties. There are all kinds of groups competing for time and attention and money and how to educate their kids, that they know how to do it better than you do. And a successful superintendent has to be able to read all those signs and reconcile them and build partnerships where you can.

By learning about our communities, we will not only obtain meaningful input, but we will also build support and trust for our schools.

As you listen to community members, consider the particular culture they represent and their backgrounds, your perceptions of them from prior school board meetings, and even what has occurred to them or their children in school. As Kathryn Whitaker and Sheldon Watson pointed out in chapter 1, it is important to understand change in relation to culture. An experienced superintendent from the Midwest exemplified this when he described his community as one "rooted in tremendous traditions." He understood that his community was likely to resist basic change if implemented too quickly.

A superintendent from a rural school district described how important it is that you, as part of learning about the community, not avoid those who are considered to be "the players" and the "powerbases" in your district. In fact, a superintendent from a rural school district asserted that "in a lot of communities there are a few key people who you really should listen to because they probably do have a pretty good pulse on what's going on." They are people who have either grown up in the community or have been in the community a long time; they may be people of wealth or hold a political position. Bartusek (2003), called these people "opinion leaders" who can tell you what they are hearing about the schools. To lead "public" schools, you must listen both to the opinion leaders and to those who are not.

SUMMARY

This chapter described approaches to obtain meaningful community input. These approaches were listening effectively, making sure all voices are heard, being patient and understanding, separating the messenger from the message, and learning about the community. If the above strategies are implemented, we will obtain meaningful community input that will result in effective policies and practices for our schools and help us lead our communities in positive directions.

13

SUCCESS STRATEGY:
MAINTAIN GOOD RELATIONSHIPS

Mary Devin, Teresa Northern Miller, and Trudy A. Salsberry

As a school board member, you have an incredibly powerful role in ensuring the success of the school community you represent. Central to your work as a board member is an understanding of your role as a member of a team striving to accomplish the work of the "world of education." This final chapter provides some closure to our discussion concerning how you can work with other school board members, superintendents, and the community to prepare students for the future. In short, this chapter is designed to help you to maintain good relationships.

You need relationships to get things done. As elected members of a board of education, you and your colleagues have authority to set policies for the operations of your school district. But the schools will not run on policies alone. You hire a superintendent to implement your policies—but he or she cannot do that alone. The successful operations in your schools will depend on the relationships that you and your colleagues build and maintain with all the parties that make your district work. Through positive relationships, you will be able to get the things done that will make schools operate effectively.

A superintendent from a predominantly suburban school district noted,

I think the superintendency has probably moved to a team of people rather than a person. I mean, there was a time when we all knew principals and superintendents who could administer a program or an organization by their very presence. There was a kind of an aura about them and it didn't mean that they knew everything. It is like the hunting-gathering societies. The chief is always chief but didn't get bent out of shape if the best hunter lived in the hunting and the best fisherman lived in fishing. Yet I think now the superintendency is a group of people and that group of people may change based upon situations—far more of a team. Every now and then somebody will say something [foolish], like "It must be a pretty isolated role." It is the most crowded role I have ever had. The traffic is pretty heavy. But a lot of that is needed, because it is a group of people, not a person anymore.

The relationships fellow board members have with each other influence your board's ability to deal effectively with policy issues. The relationship each of you has with the superintendent affects successful implementation of the policies you adopt. You and other board members will want to consciously work to build relationships that produce a high-performing team focused on the goals of the district. Relationships with staff, peers, constituents, and other power holders in the school community are important, too. Building them is hard work and requires time. Further, maintaining these relationships is no easier and cannot be taken for granted. These relationships must be cultivated, then tended, nurtured, and continually monitored.

As a school board member, you will make decisions that will not make everyone happy, but if you and your colleagues spend time developing and taking care of good relationships, you will be able to move forward with support. This chapter addresses the strategies for developing and maintaining good relationships with the groups that are part of the district and the community it serves.

STRATEGIES FOR MAINTAINING GOOD RELATIONSHIPS

You would not have reached your position as board member if you did not already recognize the importance of relationships. Common underlying themes across both the professional and research literature might be helpful to you and other board members in your work together. This chapter presents successful strategies for maintaining good relationships found in the professional and research literature and, more importantly, echoed in the comments of practicing superintendents. The inclusion of verbatim quotes from practicing superintendents illustrates personal experiences and the reality of maintaining good relationships under a variety of conditions. The most prominent strategies for establishing and maintaining good relationships are these:

1. Share broadly in the creation of your vision.
2. Steer without rowing.
3. Raise difficult issues.
4. Practice systems thinking.
5. Treat your staff with care.
6. Model the image you want for your district.

SHARE BROADLY IN THE CREATION OF YOUR VISION

The importance of a vision was established in earlier chapters. This recommendation reminds you and other board members that how the vision is built influences the relationship between the board and others. A vision that builds and maintains good relationships is a vision that belongs to the school district community, because its members took part in developing it. You and your fellow board members will want to involve others in conversations that establish the vision for your district's future—that is the first step in establishing good relationships with staff and community. As a superintendent from an urban district in the Midwest commented,

> I think community involvement is critical because you have to look at the entire community, not just the school from the standpoint of just being part of the school. I think leadership skills have changed a lot. It used to be that we could pretty much manage our schools and make the decisions and be the go-between between the different people in the organization, and I think now you have to work much more effectively as a team. I think your leadership skills then and now have changed quite a bit.

Engaging a variety of voices and opinions in discussions about what the community wants for its schools and how to best achieve that builds

healthy relationships that you will need when dealing with tough decisions in the future. Participation in such conversations gives staff and
community members ownership in a shared vision. It helps them see the
connection between decisions and what the community wants for its
schools and it protects relationships by increasing the likelihood a decision you make as a board will be accepted, even when it is not the one
others might prefer. You will want to revisit the vision periodically, as
conditions in the district and community change. It is important to continue involving others, reinforcing and clarifying connections between
your actions and the vision, so you do not lose the good relationships established in earlier efforts. The same superintendent last quoted also
noted,

> I've become a better listener. I've become more accepting of those whose
> views might be different than mine. I've changed my leadership style, I
> think, a little bit. I think I've always been positive with people, but I think
> the way I involve people now, the way we involve people as a school dis-
> trict, is different now than it used to be. And I just think my general
> knowledge base has had to become much more—I think it has had to be
> enlarged because it is so much more difficult to lead an organization in to-
> day's times and so I think the skills you have to bring to the table are much
> greater than they used to be.

Strong organizations constantly monitor and evaluate perceptions of
their work. You and other board members will want to know what others think about your decisions, goals, and policies. You can find out by
inviting feedback from stakeholders on an ongoing basis. Developing
and sustaining good relationships requires continual assessment of constituents' perceptions and the use of that information in planning future
communications and interactions. Your board can provide a variety of
formal and informal ways for staff and patrons to share their opinions.
Formal surveys can be conducted periodically. Websites that allow for
questions and answers, letters to the editor, and editorials are outlets
your constituents can use to express opinions related to education. You
might establish a standing item on your board meeting agendas, allowing citizens the opportunity to speak directly to the school board. Such
communication can be very helpful to you in maintaining good relationships.

STEER WITHOUT ROWING

As a board, you and your colleagues will work with your superintendent to steer your district in the right direction. However, if you want to maintain good relationships with those you depend on to do the work in your schools, you will want to take care to recognize the difference between steering and rowing. "Steering" focuses on setting direction in policy and goals that support the vision of the district. "Rowing" is the actual work that takes place in the classrooms and support areas. When you get into rowing, you take on work that is more appropriate for the people employed for their expertise in that area. Staff and others observing your action may interpret the interference as lack of confidence in staff competencies, favoritism or other inequities, or a board member advancing a private agenda. If you row, you risk seeing good staff members or potential applicants avoiding a district where the board has a reputation of interfering with staff as they carry out their duties. A suburban superintendent put it this way:

> I think the school board takes a great deal of care and nurturing and rightly so, because it's not full-time work for school board members and they ought not be involved in day-to-day management of the school system. But they must be kept aware of what is going on in the school system because they're expected to know in the grocery store, they're expected to know what's happening, but I don't think it's a given or an automatic in any way, shape, or form. I think it's something you really do have to work hard. I know there've been some studies done. I was asking colleagues of mine who dealt with elected school boards before I did what was the single greatest difference that they found if they dealt with both appointed and elected boards, and to a person, there's a kind of common thread I found was that I would have to—the warning was you will have to devote more time to the "care and feeding" of the school board than you ever have before because they will have a greater need for knowledge than any board has ever had before because they will be more answerable to their public and I think that's true and I think it's, for the most of us, it's probably not an exaggeration to say that we invest, I don't know, 20% of our working time communicating with, educating with, and working with our school board unlike the corporate environment where a board comes once a quarter or once a year and has a nice chat with the CEO and then goes home.

If relationships are important to you, you will want the board you serve on to remain focused on steering. You can help that happen by asking that your board discuss and reach agreement on appropriate roles for all members in the educational community. You might suggest the board members commit to honoring that role and avoid getting into areas that are responsibilities assigned to staff roles. When tempted to get involved to resolve a complaint brought to you as a board member from staff or patron, you will want to refer your contact to district policies and procedures and inform your superintendent of the contact. It is reasonable for you to expect district staff to know and follow district policies and procedures. It is important for you and your fellow board members to remember that you are held to the same policies and procedures that apply to everyone else, and that the only real authority you have rests with the board as a whole, not with individual members.

RAISE DIFFICULT ISSUES

You need positive relationships with staff, peers, constituents, and other power holders to accomplish your work, so it is tempting to avoid raising issues that might be expected to create conflict. Refusing to acknowledge significant problems is sometimes described as "ignoring the elephant in the room" because we do not want to offend anyone. This problem-solving approach is: If we do not mention it, it will go away. Unfortunately, there is little real-life experience to support the success of this leadership style. Your board's reputation will be notably enhanced by its willingness to open courageous conversations and its ability to successfully manage difficult issues.

If your board wishes to maintain good relationships with constituents even when dealing with difficult situations, you will want to prepare for such situations before one emerges. First, recognize that disagreements and conflict are part of continual improvement and use them to plan the next step for improving the system. As a board, you can reach agreement on how you will conduct business when dealing with conflict. For example, agree to alert the superintendent before bringing up volatile issues in public meetings; to follow established procedures for introducing issues publicly; to focus on the issue (not personalities) and the connection to improving the system; to invite constituents to also bring up issues; and to receive all comments with dignity, treating all presenters respectfully.

Boards in effective school districts recognize it is not the avoidance of these situations but how they deal with them that affects relationships. Knowing you are willing to tackle tough issues and respecting the way that this is done causes staff, students, families, and the rest of the community to form positive attitudes about the integrity and the leadership capacity of the board of education. A superintendent from a Western rural district said,

> But you look for common ground, I guess, and that is kind of what I do as a leader. I try to find ways that we can bring people together even when there are disagreements. Many times we can unite over those things and work together on those.

This is an age of empowered stakeholders and many have strong viewpoints to share with your board and superintendent. The effective board establishes a specific process that includes a protocol for expressing differing viewpoints in a forum designed for that purpose. A protocol is a step-by-step process designed to maintain a uniform practice over time. For example, discussion protocols are designed to keep the discussion focused on its purpose and establish consistent practice in similar group discussions over time. Researchers follow protocols to collect information in focus groups or interview settings. Having such a plan in place for dealing with difficult issues is important because emotions from one or more parties involved in a difficult issue often emerge. This makes it even harder to work through the issue in a way acceptable to as many people as possible. For obvious reasons, it is advisable to have such a protocol in place before becoming involved with a specific volatile issue.

It is important for stakeholders to feel their opinions can be shared, will be listened to, and may be acted upon in some fashion. A typical protocol for discussing difficult issues will designate beginning and ending times for the discussion; allow uninterrupted times for proponents of various perspectives to make comments; provide a structured time for questioning; and maintain an expectation for what will happen next in the deliberations. You must make it clear that the board cannot make all constituents happy but will make decisions based on the shared vision for the district and for improved student learning.

Managing conflict is an integral part of building relationships; it is a healthy component of positive change. A suburban superintendent described his approach and acknowledged the challenges:

> What I do is confront the issues head on with other people. I put them on the table with the different sides of each issue. I say these are the problems we have and that I do not have all the answers to these problems. If I did, I would not be presenting them to you. We have to work together with these problems. People appreciate this approach but find it frustrating. A lot of people do not want to spend a lot of time with the big issues. The best way to deal with problems is to involve people who can help make the best decisions and share your frustrations. I certainly would not want to deal with these problems alone.

As a board, you and other board members must listen to critics, look for the grain of truth in what is heard, and move on. When convinced one's position is the right one, it is easy for one not to bother listening to critics, but critics, especially, need the opportunity to share their opinions. If the goal is maintaining good relationships, the critic needs to feel his or her thoughts were heard. Often good relationships can be maintained even when decisions are not the action the critic sought. If those who really care about the issue are satisfied their position was heard and considered and if the goal is to continually improve, then even the most misguided, confused, misstated, and misinterpreted offerings can be seen to contain a grain of truth or wisdom that can be useful in making improvements to the system. The secret here is to listen and find that grain of wisdom, but make it clear the board and the superintendent will make the final decision. An urban superintendent from the Midwest commented,

> A lot of times you come into these jobs and you think people are asking you to lead them and speak to them and somehow provide the answers. Well, that is not really what they are asking for. I think they are asking for you to listen and for you to give thought and consideration to their ideas and then, when it comes time, you have to somehow reach consensus or make the final decision; but I think what I would say to people is your hu-

man relations qualities have to be as strong as your organizational skills or your systems thinking kind of leadership.

Another superintendent from a rural district puts it simply as, "The bottom line [is] the board and the superintendent have to make the decision and move forward."

Staff and community patrons take note of how the board views and deals with conflict. A willingness to deal with difficult issues and acceptance of conflict with a positive attitude affirms the board's commitment to its purpose, even if the going isn't easy. When board members themselves raise difficult issues, the board models this courageous open climate for all staff and constituents. When the board deals with these issues as opportunities for improving the system, it demonstrates an equally powerful message that the vision for the system will be kept at the center of all decisions, even those difficult to make.

PRACTICE SYSTEMS THINKING

In carrying out their duties, boards make decisions affecting students, teachers, support staff, administrators, parents, and community members. It seems as if no board decision is simple. Wants outnumber resources, and there is always something that must be set aside. Even conscientious boards have made decisions intended to benefit one group and then discovered their action alienated another. How can the board meet the needs of one group and prevent unintentional damage to other good relationships? A rural superintendent from an Eastern state indicated,

> There's a pattern of thinking about schools which thinks about them one year at a time. It doesn't matter if we're talking about state legislation, formulating school budgets, the way we hire teachers, the way we contract with teachers, the way we promote students, the way we grade them, assess students—everything is done in one-year time intervals. And that has us deceived into thinking if we do well in one year, then we'll just think about the next year. This is a very vexing problem to get all the symbolism and authentic thinking to shift to long-term thinking.

This section suggests that a systems thinking approach to decision making is especially important for maintaining good relationships.

You can visualize systems thinking by picturing a square of Jell-O on a plate. If you touch the Jell-O on the top, it jiggles all the way to the bottom. If you stick your fork in the left side, every morsel of Jell-O moves. Or, it can be thought of as the unpredictable number of ever-widening concentric circles that flow from the point of impact when you toss a pebble into the lake on a bright, quiet afternoon. Likewise, in a system such as a school district, every decision has consequences beyond the immediate point of contact, sometimes direct and predictable, sometimes uncertain and unpredictable. Practicing systems thinking helps the board minimize unintended negative consequences of its decisions.

Maintaining good relations with all groups requires the board to keep the entire system in mind at all times. A superintendent from a rural district in the West said,

> The amazing thing about a small town is they revolve around the school. We are the center. We are the focal point of everything that goes on in that half of the county. So as the center point we are sometimes in the flash point where we can make issues grow or diffuse potential problems. I have worked with the town council, and most of those people are just people from off the street, and they do not have a lot of training or a lot of formal education. They look to me and the school for leadership in those areas. So if it's interviewing the new prison warden about contentious issues that we are going to face as a community, by families following their convicted murderers and rapists and child molesters, then I do that. I will ask the tough questions and get the response that we need to hear from those kinds of folks. But it is just basically assuming that leadership role that I've been placed in.

TREAT YOUR STAFF WITH CARE

The most important resource in any organization is its people. The secret to maintaining good relationships is the way the people who do the work feel they are treated. In almost any setting, that means you need to hire the right people, support them by providing the tools they need to perform the responsibilities assigned to them, let them have authority to perform their duties, hold them accountable for results, and stay out of their way. If you want to maintain good relationships, you will want to keep these basics in mind.

Even well-designed practices for hiring, promoting, and separation can unintentionally break down good relationships within and outside the school district. As Faye Patterson pointed out in chapter 6, while hiring practices must comply with applicable laws, regulations, and rules, just as importantly, they must be perceived by others as fair, impartial, and equitable. When these practices are not clearly defined and understood, good relationships quickly take a negative turn. Careful design and clear communication of processes are essential prerequisites for maintaining good relationships.

Supporting staff means putting them in a safe environment and providing them with the conditions and tools required to successfully perform their work, whether that is teaching in the classroom, working in food service operations, or serving on the custodial crew. Tools also include training needed for success in the assignment. Professional development is an excellent investment in building good relationships. A superintendent from a suburban district emphasizes the importance of professional development as a key to improving the system.

> I think all of us would acknowledge, too, that a facilitating factor for any
> of our issues is the presence of a staff which is committed to the concept
> of continuous improvement. One of the things I find most refreshing in
> the 1990s is that the concept of training and retraining as a lifelong expe-
> rience appears to be institutionalized in education among our professional
> ranks today. That wasn't the case 20 years [ago].

MODEL THE IMAGE YOU WANT FOR YOUR DISTRICT

As the official representative of the school operations in the community, everything you and your fellow board members do affects the image of the school district, locally and beyond. As the official head of the local school district operation, what the board does influences the way people inside the system think about their work. Your work, your decisions as a board, and the way you conduct yourself are open to public scrutiny and will shape the image of the district in the community. If you want your schools to be seen as exemplary and professional, then you, the board, must be regarded as exemplary and professional in your actions. In other words, members of the school community often judge the school district by the conduct of its board members. This judgment shapes the image of the district and the quality of its relationships. Thus, the board's actions directly affect those relationships it seeks to maintain.

The relationship between you and your fellow board members is fundamental to building good relationships with others in the school community. A new board will need time to establish its own identity as a governing team and to formulate its own way of working with diverse views among members. When your board reorganizes because of a change in membership or leadership, be ready to repeat the typical developmental stages of forming new relationships on your team, *storming* as you sort through the differences you individually bring to the table, *norming* as you establish the procedures for conducting your business, and finally *performing* as a highly productive team. As board members, you will either form relationships that enable you to effectively conduct the business of the board of education or you will form relationships that get in the way of the results you want.

Your relationships with each other will influence the manner in which the board conducts its business. Proactive boards make sure strategies are in place that maximize the opportunities for their actions to be a positive influence on relationships. Are your meetings positive or negative in tone? Are your meetings effective or ineffective in terms of accomplishing the board's work? Do you and your fellow board members make effective use of time? Does respect for others or personality bashing describe the tone of conversations during your sessions? Does the board consistently act in a respectful manner and conduct its business professionally and with integrity? The descriptors for board meetings set tones of interaction for other parts of the school district.

How you interact with other board members and with the superintendent also influences the climate. Do members of your board pursue individual agendas as though each is "the board"? Or does each board member respect the diverse styles and opinions colleagues bring to the table, exercising authority only as a whole during official meetings of the board? Do staff, parents, and the community think of your board and superintendent as a team, not as individuals who play against one another? Board members should not underestimate the importance of the model their own conduct presents for others.

Proactive boards recognize the important role they play in building a positive climate that leads to good relationships. They begin by establishing clear expectations for board and superintendent roles. Then they publicly recognize what they value—good work by students and/or staff at all levels, community involvement, and personal accomplishments. District award programs that publicly recognize recipients show how the board values good work and recognizes accomplishments. Celebrations of major student gains in performance, or special celebrations honoring retirees, individuals, or building achievements, demonstrate the district cares about the people—students, staff, community—as well as the district goals.

CONCLUDING REMARKS

Building relationships is hard work and it does take time. Remember, what works in one location may not be effective in another. Similarly, since you were likely elected by residents in your area, you may feel you know the values and interests of the community and of the people in that area. If there are parts of the community you do not know well, you may seek more information to help you and your fellow board members implement strategies for relationship building. Therefore, gathering information before taking action is an important tactic for maintaining relationships.

Finally, there is a component that you must never overlook in your efforts to implement strategies for building and maintaining good relationships—and that is to consistently conduct your business and behavior with integrity. Acting with integrity means doing the right thing when no one is there to see what you are doing. It means always keeping students and the welfare of the district at the center of decisions and doing what is right for all students. For you, integrity means remembering your authority exists only when the board itself is assembled and in official session. Unless asked to do so by your colleagues, you do not speak for the board or obligate it on any issue. The board that acts with integrity makes informed decisions and carries through in seeing its decisions implemented. Individual board members who fail to conduct themselves with integrity will find it difficult to build and sustain the relationships that we have discussed in this chapter. A board that fails to make integrity a nonnegotiable component of its work will not build the relationships needed in exemplary schools.

As a board member, your role is important to improving educational outcomes for all students. The challenges of the job are never going away. But if you work with intelligence, integrity, and for the greatest good, using the success strategies in this book, you can make things better for people in your community. We wish you well in that endeavor.

REFERENCES

Alsbury, T. L. (2003). Superintendent and school board member turnover: Political versus apolitical turnover as a critical variable in the application of the Dissatisfaction Theory. *Education Administration Quarterly, 39*(5), 667–698.

American Association of School Administrators. (1988). *Strategic planning* [brochure]. Washington, DC: AASA.

Anyon, J. (1997). *Ghetto schooling: A political economy of urban educational reform.* New York: Teachers College Press.

Annenberg Institute for School Reform. (n.d.). Retrieved May 28, 2006, from http://www.annenberginstitute.org/index2.html

Archer, J. (2005, September 14). Theory of action. *Education Week,* S3–S5.

Ashby, L. W. (1968). *The effective school board member.* Danville, Illinois: The Interstate Printers and Publishers, Inc.

Bacharach, S. B. (1981). *Organizational behavior in schools and school districts.* New York: Praeger.

Bagin, D., Gallagher, D. R., & Kindred, L. W. (1994). *The school and community relations* (5th ed.). Boston, MA: Allyn & Bacon.

Banville, T. G. (1978). *How to listen—How to be heard.* Chicago: Nelson-Hall.

Barker, L. L., Wahlers, K. J., Watson, K. W., & Kibler, R. J. (1991). *Groups in process: An introduction to small group communication* (4th ed.). Englewood Cliffs, NJ: Prentice Hall.

Bartusek, L. (2003, February). Engaging the community around school improvement starts with the board: Role models for achievement. *American School Board Journal*, 38–40.

Beckner, W. (2004). *Ethics for educational leaders*. Boston, MA: Pearson Education.

Bennis, W., Parikh, J., & Lessem, R. (1995). *Beyond leadership: Balancing economics, ethics, and ecology*. Cambridge, MA: Blackwell.

Berliner, D. C., & Biddle, B. J. (1995). *The manufactured crisis: Myths, frauds, and the attack on America's public schools*. Cambridge: Perseus Books.

Björk, L. G., & Gurley, D. K. (2005). Superintendent as educational statesman and political strategist. In L. G. Björk & T. J. Kowalski (Eds.), *The contemporary superintendent: Preparation, practice, and development* (pp. 163–185). Thousand Oaks, CA: Corwin.

Björk, L. G., Kowalski, T. J., & Browne-Ferrigno, T. (2005). Learning theory and research: A framework for changing superintendent preparation and development. In L. Björk & T. J. Kowalski (Eds.), *The contemporary superintendent: Preparation, practice, and development* (pp. 71–106). Thousand Oaks, CA: Corwin.

Björk, L. G., & Lindle, J. C. (2001). Superintendents and interest groups. *Educational Policy, 15*(1), 76–91.

Bogdan, R. C., & Biklen, S. K. (2007). *Qualitative research for education: An introduction to theories and methods* (5th ed.). Boston, MA. Pearson Education.

Bolman, L. G., & Deal, T. E., (2003). *Reframing organizations: Artistry, choice, and leadership* (3rd ed.). San Francisco: Jossey-Bass.

Brantlinger, E. (2003). *Dividing classes: How the middle class negotiates and rationalizes school advantage*. New York: Routledge/Falmer.

Brownell, J. (2006). *Listening: Attitudes, principles, and skills* (3rd ed.). Boston: Pearson Education.

Bruner, J. (1997). *The culture of education*. Cambridge, MA: Harvard University Press.

Brunner, C. C. (2002). A proposition for the reconception of the superintendency: Reconsidering traditional and nontraditional discourse. *Educational Administration Quarterly, 38*, 402–431.

Campbell, D. W., & Greene, D. (1994, January). Defining the leadership role of school boards in the 21st century. *Phi Delta Kappan, 75*, 391–395.

Carlson, R. O. (1972). *School superintendents: Careers and performance*. Columbus, OH: Merrill.

Carver, J. (1990). *Boards that make a difference: A new design for leadership in nonprofit and public organizations*. San Francisco: Jossey-Bass.

Chance, P., & Chance, E. (2002). *Introduction to educational leadership and organizational behavior: Theory into practice.* Larchmont, NY: Eye on Education.

Cherry Creek Schools, Greenwood, Colorado. (n.d.). *Cherry Creek School District.* Retrieved May 28, 2006, from http://www.ccsd.k12.co.us/index.htm

Chula Vista Elementary School District. (2001). *National School Boards Association.* Retrieved May 28, 2006, from http://www.nsba.org/site/page_REN4 .asp?TrackID=&SID=1&DID=442&CID=428&VID=30

Castallo, R., & Natale, J. (2005). A climate of understanding. *American School Board Journal, 6,* 20–22.

Colgan, C. (2004, June). The eternal question: How can school boards improve? *American School Board Journal,* 24–25.

Cronin, J. M., & Usdan, M. D. (2003). Rethinking the urban school superintendency: Nontraditional leaders and new models of leadership. *American educational governance on trial: Change and challenges: 102nd yearbook of the National Society for the Study of Education* (pp. 177–195). Chicago: University of Chicago Press.

Cuban, L. (2004). A solution that lost its problem: Centralized policymaking and classroom gains. In N. Epstein (Ed.), *Who's in charge here? The tangled web of school governance and policy* (pp. 104–130). Washington, DC: Brookings Institution Press.

Danzberger, J. P. (1994, January). Governing the nation's schools: The case for restructuring local school boards. *Phi Delta Kappan, 75,* 367–73.

Daresh, J. C. (2002). *What it means to be a principal: Your guide to leadership.* Thousand Oaks, CA: Corwin Press.

Darling-Hammond, L., & Ball, D. L. (1998). Teaching for high student achievement: What policymakers should know and be able to do. *National Commission on Teaching & America's Future.* Consortium for Policy Research in Education. Retrieved January 2006 from http://www.nctaf.org

Darling-Hammond. L., Hightower, A. M., Husbands, J. L., LaFors, J. R., Young, V. M., & Christopher, C. (2005). *Instructional leadership for systemic change: The story of San Diego's reform.* Lanham, MD: Scarecrow Education.

Davis, S. H. (2004). The myth of the rational decision maker: A framework for applying and enhancing heuristic and intuitive decision making by school leaders. *Journal of School Leadership, 14,* 621–652.

Dryzek, J. S. (2000). *Deliberative democracy and beyond.* Oxford: Oxford University Press.

Ealy, C., Hogan, D., Skrla, L. M, & Hoyle, J. (2000). Superintendent performance evaluation: Its relationship to standards, policy, and quality. In P. M. Jenlink & T. J. Kowalski (Eds.), *Marching into a new millennium: Challenges to educational leadership* (pp. 240–259). Lanham, MD: Scarecrow Press.

Educational Research Service Information Aid. (1975). *Orientation programs for new school board members.* Arlington, VA: Educational Research Service.

Enomoto, E. K., & Bair, M. A. (2002). The role of the school in the assimilation of immigrant children. In S. B. Merriam & Associates (Eds.), *Qualitative research in practice: Examples for discussion and analysis.* (pp. 181–197). San Francisco: Jossey-Bass.

Evans, R. (2001). *The human side of change: Reform, resistance, and the real-life problems of innovation.* San Francisco: Jossey-Bass.

Fiore, D. J. (2001). *Creating connections for better schools: How leaders enhance school culture.* Larchmont, NY: Eye on Education.

Follett, M. P. (1918). *The new state: Group organization, the solution for popular government.* New York: Longmans, Green.

Fritz, R. (1989). *The path of least resistance: Learning to become the creative force in your life.* New York: Ballantine Books.

Fullan, M. (1999). *Change forces: The sequel.* Philadelphia: Falmer Press.

Fullan, M. (2001a). *Leading in a culture of change.* San Francisco: Jossey-Bass.

Fullan, M. (2001b). *The new meaning of educational change* (3rd ed.). New York: Teachers College Press.

Fuller, H., Campbell, C., Celio, M., Harvey, J., Immerwahr, J., & Winger, A. (2003). *An impossible job? The view from the urban superintendent's chair.* Seattle: Center on Reinventing Public Education, University of Washington.

Fulton, M. (1998, April). Investing in performance. *American School Boards Journal.* Retrieved December 2005, from http://www.asbj.com/199804/0498 coverstory.html

Furman, G. C. (1998). Nuts and bolts. In R. R. Spillane & P. Regnier (Eds.), *The superintendent of the future: Strategy and action for achieving academic excellence* (pp. 117–153). Gaithersburg, MD: Aspen.

Furman, G. C., & Gruenewald, D. A. (2004). Expanding the landscape of social justice: A critical ecological analysis. *Educational Administration Quarterly, 40*(1), 47–76.

Gemberling, K. W., Smith, C. W., & Villani, J. S. (2000). The key work of school boards guidebook. *National School Boards Association.* Retrieved May 3, 2006, from http://www.nsba.org/keywork2/guidebook/KeyworkGuidebook.pdf

Georgia district fares well in weathering change. (n.d.). *Center for Public Education.* Retrieved May 28, 2006, from http://www.centerforpubliceducation .org/site/c.kjJXJ5MPIwE/b.1500709/k.45A5/Georgia_school_district_fares_ well_in_weathering_change.htm

Gerstl-Pepin, C. I. (2006). Paradox of poverty narratives: Educators struggling with children left behind. *Educational Policy, 20*(1).

Glass, T. (2005). Management matters. *American School Board Journal, 192*(10), 34–39.

Goldhammer, K. (1964). *The school board.* New York: Center for Applied Research in Education.

Good, T., & Brophy, J. (1987). Classroom complexity and teacher awareness. In *Looking in classrooms* (pp. 26–54). New York: Harper.

Gutmann, A., & Thompson, D. (2004). *Why deliberative democracy?* Princeton, NJ: Princeton University Press.

Hall, G. E., & Hord, S. M. (2006). *Implementing change: Patterns, principles, and potholes* (2nd ed.). Boston: Pearson.

Hess, F. M. (2003). The voice of the people: Maybe what our public schools need isn't less democracy but more. *American School Board Journal, 190*(4), 36–39.

House, E. (1991). Big policy, little policy. *Educational Researcher, 20*(5), 21–26.

Houston, P., & Bryant, A. (1997). The roles of superintendents and school board members in engaging the public with the public schools. *Phi Delta Kappan, 78*(10), 756–760.

Hoyle, J. R., Björk, L. G., Collier, V., & Glass, T. (2005). *The superintendent as CEO: Standards-based performance.* Thousand Oaks, CA: Corwin Press.

Iannaccone, L., & Lutz, F. W. (1970). *Politics, power and policy: The governing of local school districts.* Columbus, OH: Charles E. Merrill.

Iannaccone, L., & Lutz, F. W. (1994). The crucible of democracy: The local arena. *Journal of Educational Policy, 9*(5), 39–52.

Jinkins, M., & Jinkins, D. B. (1998). *The character of leadership.* San Francisco: Jossey-Bass.

Johnson, B. C., & Fusarelli, L. D. (2003). *Superintendent as social scientist.* Paper presented at the annual meeting of the American Educational Research Association, Chicago, IL.

Johnson, S. M. (1996). *Leading to change: The challenge of the new superintendency.* San Francisco: Jossey-Bass.

Joiner, L. L. (2003). The student's voice: Often missing from school board meetings is the very person your policies affect the most, but the trend is slowly changing. *American School Board Journal, 190*(1).

Keedy, J., & Björk, L. (2003). Who will lead? Examining the superintendent shortage. *Journal of School Leadership, 13*(3), 256–263.

Kimpton, J. (2001). *Reasons for hope, voices for change.* Washington, DC: Annenberg Institute for School Reform.

Kimpton, J., & Considine, J. (1999). The tough sledding of district engagement. *School Administrator 56*(8), 6–10.

Kowalski, T. J. (2001). The future of local school governance: Implications for board members and superintendents. In C. C. Brunner & L. G. Björk (Eds.), *The new superintendency* (pp. 183–201). New York: Elsevier.

Kowalski, T. J., & Keedy, J. L. (2005). Preparing superintendents to be effective communicators. In L.G. Björk & T. J. Kowalski (Eds.), *The contemporary superintendent: Preparation, practice, and development* (pp. 207–226). Thousand Oaks, CA: Corwin.

Kozol, J. (1992). *Savage inequalities: Children in American schools.* New York: Harper Perennial Press.

Kozol, J. (2005). *The shame of a nation: The restoration of apartheid schooling in America.* New York: Crown.

Loring, A. K. (2005, September). Achievement: The real business of boards. *American School Board Journal,* 56–57.

Lutz, F. W., & Merz, C. (1992). *The politics of school/community relations.* New York: Teachers College Press.

Marshall, C., & Gerstl-Pepin, C. I. (2005). *Re-framing educational politics for social justice.* Boston, MA: Allyn & Bacon.

Masse, L. N., & Barnett, W. S. (2002). A benefit-cost analysis of the Abecedarian early childhood intervention. In H. M. Levin & P. J. McEwan (Eds.), *Cost-effectiveness and educational policy: 2002 yearbook of the American Educational Finance Association.* Larchmont (pp. 157–176). NY: Eye on Education.

McDonnell, L. M. (1994). Assessment policy as persuasion and regulation. *American Journal of Education, 102,* 394–420.

Mediratta, K. (2004). Constituents of change: Community organizations and public education reform. *Annenberg Institute.* Retrieved May 28, 2006, from http://steinhardt.nyu.edu/iesp/publications/pubs/cip/ConstituentsofChange.pdf

Mills, E. P. (1974). *Listening: Key to communication.* New York: Petrocelli Books.

Miron, L., & Elliott, R. (1994). Moral leadership in a poststructural era. In S. Maxey (Ed.), *Postmodern school leadership: Meeting the crisis in educational administration* (pp. 133–139). Westport, CT: Praeger.

Montoya, N., & Ivory, G. (2005). Competencies for educational technology directors: Perceptions of public school technology directors. *National summit on school leadership: Crediting the past, challenging the present, and changing the future* (pp. 321–328). Lanham, MA: Rowman & Littlefield.

Mountford, M. (2004). Motives and power of school board members: Implications for school board-superintendent relationships. *Educational Administration Quarterly, 40*(5), 704–741.

Mountford, M., & Brunner, C. C. (1999). Motivations for school board membership: Implications for superintendents and district accountability. *Re-*

ports-Research 143. Minneapolis, MN: University Council for Educational Administration. (ED 439480).

Murphy, J. (2002). Reculturing the profession of educational leadership: New blueprints. *Educational Administration Quarterly, 38*(2), 176–191.

Naperville Community Unit School District 203. (n.d.). Retrieved May 28, 2006, from http://www.naperville203.org/

National Commission on Excellence in Education. (1983). *A nation at risk: The imperative for educational reform*. Washington, DC: U.S. Department of Education.

National School Boards Association. (2000). *The key work of school boards*. Retrieved January 2, 2006, from http//:www.nsba.org/keywork2/

Nieto, S. (1994). Lessons from students on creating a chance to dream. *Harvard Educational Review, 64*(4), 392–426.

No Child Left Behind Act of 2001. Public Law No.107–110, 115 Stat. 1425 (2002).

Nolan, J. L., & Hoover, L. A. (2004). *Teacher supervision and evaluation: Theory into practice*. New York: Wiley/Jossey-Bass.

Nussbaum, M. C. (1997). *Cultivating humanity: A classical defense of reform in liberal education*. Cambridge, MA: Harvard University Press.

Oakes, J. (1985). *Keeping track: How schools structure inequality*. New Haven, CT: Yale University Press.

Oliver, C., Conduff, M., Edsall, S., Gabanna, C., Loucks, R., Paszkiewicz, D., Raso, C., & Stier, L. (1999). *The policy governance fieldbook*. San Francisco: Jossey-Bass.

Patterson, K., Grenny, J., McMillan, R., & Switzler, A. (2002). *Crucial conversations: Tools for talking when stakes are high*. New York: McGraw-Hill.

Patterson, K., Grenny, J., McMillan, R., & Switzler, A. (2005). *Crucial confrontations: Tools for resolving broken promises, violated expectations, and bad behavior*. New York: McGraw-Hill.

Petersen, G. J. (1999). Demonstrated actions of instructional leaders: An examination of five California superintendents. *Education Policy Analysis, 7*(18), 1–23.

Pounder, D. G. (1999). Foreword. In F. K. Kochan, B. L. Jackson, & D. L. Duke (Eds.), *A thousand voices from the firing line: A study of educational leaders, their jobs, their preparation, and the problems they face* (p. 5). Columbia, MO: University Council for Educational Administration.

Power to the parents: City of Chicago School District 299. (n.d.). *National School Boards Association*. Retrieved May 28, 2006, from http://www.nsba.org/site/doc_sbn_issue.asp?TrackID=&SID=1&DID=38173&CID=1465&VID=55

Public engagement drives success: San Jose Unified School District. (n.d.). *National School Boards Association*. Retrieved May 28, 2006, from http://www.nsba.org/site/doc_sbn_issue.asp?TrackID=&SID=1&DID=3817 3&CID=1465&VID=55

Public Education Network. (2004). *Taking responsibility: Using public engagement to reform our public schools.* Washington, DC: Author. Retrieved May 5, 2007 from http://www.publiceducation.org/pdf/Publications/Public_ Engagement/Taking_Responsibility.pdf

Purdy, M. (2006). The listener wins. Retrieved February 9, 2006, from http://featuredreports.monster.com/listen/overview/

Quality Schools Consortium (1995). *Continual improvement handbook.* Brentwood, TN: Executive Learning.

Radlick, M. S. (1998). Hardware, software, vaporware, and wetware. In R. A. Spillane & R. Regnier (Eds.), *The superintendent of the future: Strategy & action for achieving academic excellence* (pp. 237–265). Gaithersburg, MA: Aspen.

Ramaley, J. D. (2005). Goals for learning and assessment. In J. L. Herman & E. H. Haertel (Eds.), *Uses and misuses of data for educational accountability and improvement: 104th Yearbook of the National Society for the Study of Education, Part II* (pp. 55–77). Malden, MA: Blackwell.

Reeder, W. G. (1946). *School boards and superintendents.* New York: Macmillan.

Rose, L. C., & Gallup, A. M. (2005). The 37th annual Phi Delta Kappa/Gallup Poll of the public's attitudes toward the public schools. *Phi Delta Kappan, 87*(1), 41–57.

Rosen, R. (2000). *Global literacies: Lessons on business leadership and national cultures.* New York: Simon & Schuster.

Rubin, H. (2002). *Collaborative leadership: Developing effective partnerships in communities and schools.* Thousand Oaks, CA: Corwin Press.

Rudy, D.W., & Conrad, W.H. (2004, February). Breaking down the data: Looking for ways to improve instruction and student learning? Take an informed approach. *American School Board Journal, 191*(2), 1–3. Retrieved May 5, 2007 from http://www.asbj.com/2004/02/0204asbjrudy.pdf.

Rusch, E. A. (1992). *Strategic planning: Looking through the lens of Foucault.* Paper presented at the annual meeting of the American Educational Research Association, San Francisco CA.

Sarason, S. B. (1990). *The predictable failure of educational reform: Can we change course before it's too late?* San Francisco: Jossey-Bass.

Schlechty, P. C. (2000). Leading a school system through change: Key steps for moving reform forward. In *The Jossey-Bass reader on educational leadership* (pp. 182–201). San Francisco: Jossey-Bass.

Schmoker, M. (1999). *Results: The key to continuous school improvement* (2nd ed.). Alexandria, VA: ASCD.

Shaw, J. M. (2005). Getting things right at the classroom level. In J. L. Herman & E. H. Haertel (Eds.), *Uses and misuses of data for educational accountability and improvement: 104th Yearbook of the National Society for the Study of Education, Part II* (pp. 340–357). Malden, MA: Blackwell.

Small groups produce big changes in Westminster, Colo. (n.d.). *Center for Public Education.* Retrieved May 28, 2006, from http://www.centerforpubliced-ucation.org/site/c.kjJXJ5MPIwE/b.1503797/k.FDE1/Small_groups_pro-duce_big_changes_in_Westminster_Colo.htm

Smoley, E. R. (1999). *Effective school boards: Strategies for improving board performance.* San Francisco: Jossey-Bass.

Snyder, K. J., Acker-Hocevar, M., & Snyder, K. M. (2000). *Living on the edge of chaos: Leading schools into the global age.* Milwaukee, WI: ASQ Quality Press.

Sokoloff, H. (2001). Engaging the public: How school boards can call for community involvement in important school decisions. *American School Board Journal, 188*(9), 26–29.

Spillane, J. P. (2006). *Distributed leadership.* San Francisco: Jossey-Bass.

Starratt, R. J. (2002). *Centering educational administration: Cultivating meaning, community, responsibility.* Mahwah, NJ: Lawrence Erlbaum.

Strike, K. A. (2003). Liberty, democracy, and community: Legitimacy in public education. In W. L. Boyd & D. Miretsky (Eds.), *American educational governance on trial: Change and challenges* (pp. 37–56). Chicago: University of Chicago Press.

Superintendent's welcome. (n.d.). *Chula Vista Elementary School District.* Retrieved May 28, 2006, from http://www.cvesd.k12.ca.us/cvesd/superin/wel-come.html

Tate, J. S., & Dunklee, D. R. (2005). *Strategic listening for school leaders.* Thousand Oaks, CA: Corwin Press.

Togneri, A., & Anderson, S. E. (2003). *Beyond islands of excellence: What districts can do to improve instruction and achievement in all schools.* Alexandria, VA: ASCD/Learning First Alliance.

Toth, J. (2004). *Mary Parker Follett.* Hartford: Yale University Press.

Tucson Unified School District board policy. (n.d.). *Tucson Unified School District.* Retrieved May 28, 2006, from http://www.tusd.k12.az.us/contents/gov-board/SectA/A.html

Tuttle, E. M. (1963). *School board leadership in America* (revised edition). Danville, Ill.: The Interstate Printers and Publishers.

Tye, B. B. (2000). *Hard truths: Uncovering the deep structure of schooling.* New York: Teachers College Press.

University of Pittsburgh. (2006). *Introducing listening.* Retrieved February 7, 2006, http://www.cxc.pitt.edu/listeningprint.htm

Vaill, P. B. (1991). *Managing as a performing art: New ideas for a world of chaotic change.* San Francisco: Jossey-Bass

Vaill, P. B. (1996). *Learning as a way of being: Strategies for survival in a world of permanent white water.* San Francisco: Jossey-Bass.

Villani, S. (2006). *Mentoring and induction programs that support new principals.* Thousand Oaks, CA: Corwin Press.

Vision, values and goals. (n.d.). *Chula Vista Elementary School District.* Retrieved May28, 2006, from http://www.cvesd.k12.ca.us/cvesd/superin/vision-values.html

Watson, S. T., & Grogan, M. (2005). Towards a more complex understanding of power to better grasp the challenges of the contemporary superintendency. In G. J. Petersen & L. D. Fusarelli (Eds.), *The politics of leadership: Superintendents and school boards in changing times* (pp. 51–72). Greenwich, CT: Information Age.

Whitaker, K. S. (2003). Superintendent perceptions of the quantity and quality of principal candidates. *Journal of School Leadership, 13*(2), 159–180.

Wiburg, K. M. (2001). Effective planning for technology. In G. Ivory (Ed.), *What works in computing for school administrators* (pp. 225–249). Lanham, MD: Scarecrow.

Willower, D. (1991). Micropolitics and the sociology of school organizations. *Education and Urban Society, 23*(4), 442–454.

Wilmore, E. L. (2004). *Principal induction: A standards-based model for administrator development.* Thousand Oaks, CA: Corwin Press.

Winfield, L. F. (1986). Teacher beliefs toward academically at-risk students in inner urban schools. *Urban Review, 18*(4), 253–268.

Zmuda, A., Kuklis, R., & Kline, E. (2004). *Transforming schools: Creating a culture of continuous improvement.* Alexandria, VA: ASCD.

INDEX

AASA. *See* American Association of
  School Administrators
accountability: external changes,
  public perception, transparency
  and, 5–6; superintendents, school
  board members and, 203; test
  scores and, 4–5, 8
Acker-Hocevar, Michele, xii, xiii
action: superintendents, turning
  point and consequences of,
  158–60
Adequate Yearly Progress (AYP),
  63–64, 65, 77
advisory councils, 33–34
African Americans, 122
Aiken, Judith A., 41, 84
Alsbury, Thomas, 12, 13, 46, 164
ambiguity tolerance, 194
American Association of School
  Administrators (AASA), 23, 151
American School Board Journal, 58

The Annenberg Institute, 30, 32;
  study, 38, 39
Arellano, Eduardo, 13, 39, 45, 95,
  115, 144, 185
authority, distribution of, 130–31
AYP. *See* Adequate Yearly Progress

Bacharach, S. B., 180
Bair, M. A., 100
Bartusek, L., 197
behaviorist reform, 168
beliefs: values and, 100–102
Björk, L. G., 86, 177, 178
board members. *See* school board
  members
Browne-Ferrigno, T., 177
Brownell, Judi, 187, 190
Bruner, Jerome, 74
Brunner, C. C., 101
Bryant, A., 161
burnout, 90–91

Carlson, R. O., 179

Carver, J., 42, 46, 51

challenges: fostering student
achievement, 52–66; leading in
era of change, 1–21; mandates and
micropolitics, 135–48; needing to
be reelected, 164–84; shortages of
resources, 119–34; understanding
perspectives of superintendents,
149–63

changes: collaboration, proactive
vision, news junkies and, 19;
communication, coherence,
receptivity and, 19; external, 2–11;
facilitation and, 20; internal, 2,
11–18; leading in era of, 1–21;
presentism and, 1;
recommendations for, 18–21

Cherry Creek School District, 26

Chula Vista Elementary School
District, 35

class size, 6–7

coherence, 19

collaboration, 19

collectives: growing effective, 39–40

commitment, 85–86, 100

communication, 19, 72–73; ambiguity
tolerance and, 194; crickets,
ideals, communities and, 155–58;
facial cues, nonverbal behavior
and, 190; informing public with,
147; learning from
superintendents about, 113–15;
resources and, 127–29

communities: changing resources
and, 122–26; crickets, ideals,
communication and, 155–58;
learning about community input
and, 196–97; obtaining meaningful
input from, 185–98; reelection

and finding consensus in, 165–69;
reelection and shifting political
winds in, 169–72

community input: comprehensive
inclusion of voices in, 191–93;
effective listening and, 186–91;
learning about community and,
196–97; obtaining meaningful,
185–98; patience and
understanding with, 193–94;
separating message from
messenger and, 194–96;
summary, 197; superintendents
on, 201–2

compromise, 129–30

conferences: parent, 36

confidence: external changes, public
education and declining, 3–5

conflict management, 206

Conrad, W. H., 66

Considine, J., 39

Cronin, J. M., 3

Crucial Conversations (Patterson,
Grenny, McMillan & Switzler),
108

Cuban, Larry, 55

cultural diversity: population shifts
and racial, linguistic and, 8–9

cultural plurality: values and, 166–67

data: AYP and, 77; bridging
perspectives using, 80–81;
collection and programs, 77–78;
decision-making driven by, 67–82;
focusing diverse people on single
tasks and, 71–76; history of
decision-making driven by, 76–78;
multiple perspectives and
interpreting, 78–80; NCLB and,
77; superintendents on, 70, 72–76,

77–80; sustained student achievement and, 67–71

Data in a Day, 77

Data on the Wall, 77

decision-making: considering evidence of success with, 46–49; data-driven, 67–82; history of data-driven, 76–78; policies reflecting district's vision and, 43; policies, vision, actions and, 43–45; prioritizing and, 41–51; study, 101; superintendents on, 42, 44–45, 47–48, 50; sustained student achievement and, 67–71; systems thinking approach to, 208; trust and effective, 49–51

Deming, W. Edward, 76

democracy, 146–47; Dissatisfaction Theory of American, 169–71

Devin, Mary, 13, 99, 199

Dexter, Robin, 52, 67

Dissatisfaction Theory of American Democracy, 169–71; variables/indicators of change in theoretical model as described in, 170

districts: strategies used by highly successful, 68

diversity: population shifts and racial, linguistic, and cultural, 8–9; struggles with racial, 122–23

Domínguez, Ramón, 13, 17, 50, 99, 163

Dunklee, D. R., 190

Ealy, C., 46

Earley, Jim, xiv

economy fluctuations: external changes and national/state, 9–10

Enomoto, E. K., 100

enrollment growth, 122

equity: student achievement and, 63–65

ethics: operating within bounds of laws, policies and, 112–13; school board members and, 117

Evans, R., 90

evolution, 141

external changes: class size, 6–7; declining confidence in public education and, 3–5; growth/decline in district size and, 6–8; legal constraints, student services and, 10–11; minority students/teachers and, 9; model schools and, 8; national/state economy fluctuations and, 9–10; NCLB and, 5; parents and, 6–7, 9; population movements shifts and, 6–9; power and, 2–3, 5; public perception/accountability, transparency and, 5–6; racial/cultural/linguistic diversity and, 8–9; superintendents implementing, 4, 6, 7, 8, 9–10, 11; tax bases and, 10; test scores, accountability and, 4–5, 8. See also changes

facial cues, 190

facilitation, 20

finances: eroding resources, tax bases and, 121–22

Follett, Mary Parker, 40

Fullan, Michael, 21, 100, 101

Fulton, Mary, 58

GED programs. See General Education Development programs

General Education Development (GED) programs, 145

Gerstl-Pepin, Cynthia I., 135
golden mean, 160–61
Grenny, J., 108
Gurley, D. K., 86, 178
Gwinnett County, Georgia, 34–35

Hager, Jim, 25, 38
Hogan, D., 46
Hoover, L. A., 90
"hot-button topics," 141
Houston, P., 161
Hoyle, J., 46
human resources: internal changes
    and reduction in, 17–18
Hyle, Adrienne, 119, 137, 149

IDEA. See Individuals with
    Disabilities Act
ideals: building trust and, 30–31;
    communication and, 30;
    community engagement and,
    29–30; crickets, communication,
    communities and challenges to,
    155–58; sales force for vision and,
    32–34; strategies for marketing
    vision and, 27–34;
    superintendents, reality and,
    161–62
Individuals with Disabilities Act
    (IDEA), 139
integrity: political effectiveness and
    maintaining, 172–74; relationships
    and, 211–12
internal changes: human resources
    reduction and, 17–18; leaders,
    reduction in deference and,
    14–15; NCLB and, 17; political
    activism and, 11–14; school board
    composition and, 14; school
    security/safety and, 16–17;

superintendents implementing,
    12–15, 17–18; technology and,
    15–16. See also changes
Ivory, Gary, xii, xiii, 15

Jinkins, D. B., 45
Jinkins, M., 45
Johnson, S. M., 42

Keedy, J. L., 104
Key Work of School Boards (National
    School Boards Association), 66
Kimpton, J., 39
Kline, E., 81
Kowalski, T. J., viii, x, 104, 177
Kuklis, R., 81

laws: legal eagles and, 126–27;
    local/state/federal policy interplay
    and, 138–41; operating within
    bounds of ethics, policies and,
    112–13; resources, dollars and,
    120–21
leaders: collaboration, proactive
    vision, news junkies and, 19;
    communication, coherence,
    receptivity and, 19; facilitation in,
    19; good staff developing into
    good, 96–98; internal changes and
    reduction in deference toward,
    14–15; resources and strategies
    for, 126–29; superintendents as
    instructional, 56–57. See also
    school board members;
    superintendents
learning initiatives: questions about
    teaching and, 58
legal constraints: external changes,
    student services and, 10–11
legal eagles, 126–27

linguistic diversity: population shifts and racial, cultural and, 8–9
listening, 38–39, 95; community input and effective, 186–91; reasons for, 187; skills for effective, 189–91; types of, 187–89
Loring, Anne, 54, 66
Lutz, F. W., 180

mandates: balancing equity concerns/special interests and, 141–45; context/resource differences and, 136–38; democracy/public engagement and, 146–47; local, state and federal policy interplay and, 138–41; micropolitics and, 135–48
McClellan, Rhonda, 119, 137, 149
McMillan, R., 108
Merz, C., 180
messengers: community input and separating message from, 194–96; organizational approaches to community input and, 195–96; personal approaches to community input and, 195
micropolitics: balancing equity concerns/special interests and, 141–45; context/resource differences and, 136–38; democracy/public engagement and, 146–47; GED programs and, 145; local, state and federal policy interplay and, 138–41; mandates and, 135–48; NCLB and, 137, 139; parents and, 140–41, 143; poverty and, 144–45; property taxes and, 137, 139; Reading First and, 137–38; superintendents and, 137–40, 142–45, 146–47

Miller, Teresa, 13, 99, 199
model schools, 8
Montoya, N., 15
Mountford, M., 101

Naperville Community Unit School District, 26
National School Boards Association, 30, 151
A Nation at Risk, 23, 25
NCLB Act. See No Child Left Behind Act
negotiation skills, 45
news junkies, 19
No Child Left Behind Act, x, 2, 4; data and, 77; external changes and, 5; framers, 83; internal changes and, 17; micropolitics and, 137, 139; student achievement and, 53, 59–61, 63–64; vision and, 22, 25–26, 37
Nolan, J. L., 90
nonverbal behavior, 190
Nussbaum, Martha, ix

O'Donnell, Lorraine, xiv
organizational approaches, 195–96

parents: conferences for, 36; external changes and, 6–7, 9; micropolitics and, 140–41, 143
partnerships, 132–34
patience: community input, understanding and, 193–94
Patterson, Faye, 17, 18, 44, 83, 108, 131, 209
PDCA. See Plan-Do-Check-Act
people: politics, policy and, 153–55. See also staff

personal approaches: improving
  personal reactions and, 195
personnel. *See* staff
Petersen, G. J., 54, 57
Plan-Do-Check-Act (PDCA), 76
policies, 42; interplay of
  local/state/federal, 138–41;
  operating within bounds of laws,
  ethics and, 112–13; people,
  politics and, 153–55; vision,
  decision-making, actions and,
  43–45
political activism: internal changes
  and, 11–14
politics: doing good for students
  while dealing with chaotic,
  174–77; mixing school service
  with, 173–74; people, policies and,
  153–55; reelection and reality of
  school governance, 165–66;
  reelection and shifting winds of,
  169–72; reelection, maintaining
  integrity and effectiveness in,
  172–74; role of school board amid
  chaotic, 175–77. *See also*
  micropolitics
population shifts: changing
  communities and, 122–26;
  external changes and movement
  in, 6–9; growth/decline in district
  size and, 6–8; racial, cultural,
  linguistic diversity and, 8–9
power, 38, 86; external changes and,
  2–3, 5
Power of Parents Conference, 36
presentism, 1
proactive vision, 19
problem-solving: relying on good
  staff for, 93–96
progressive reform, 168

property taxes, 137, 139
public education: external changes
  and declining confidence in, 3–5
public perception: external changes,
  accountability/transparency and,
  5–6

race: population shifts and diversity
  in culture, language and, 8–9;
  segregation of economy and, 136;
  struggles with diversity and,
  122–23
Ramaley, J. D., 53, 54
Reading First, 137–38
receptivity, 19
reelection: considerations for
  selecting superintendents and,
  179–82; cultural/values plurality
  and, 166–67; Dissatisfaction
  Theory of American Democracy
  and, 169–71; doing good for
  students amid political chaos and,
  174–77; elite- *versus* arena-style
  boards and, 171–72; finding
  consensus in community for,
  165–69; maintaining integrity,
  political effectiveness and,
  172–74; mixing politics with
  school service and, 173–74; need
  for, 164–84; questions about, 165;
  reality of politics in school
  governance and, 165–66;
  recommendations for, 182–84;
  role balancing with
  superintendents and, 177–78;
  shifting political winds and,
  169–72; societal roles of public
  schools, orthodox/progressive
  views and, 167–69;
  superintendents and, 164, 165,

169, 171, 172–74, 176, 181–82;
variables/indicators of change in
theoretical model and, *170*
reform: overload, 181; strategies, 168
relationships: concluding remarks for
fostering good, 211–12; conflict
management and, 206; integrity
in, 211–12; maintaining good,
199–212; modeling district's image
of good, 209–11; practicing
systems thinking to foster good,
207–8; raising difficult issues and
good, 204–7; school board
members' and superintendents',
59, 175–77, 178; school board
members' interaction, 104; school
board members' web of, 106;
sharing in creation of vision for
fostering good, 201–2; steering
without rowing to foster good,
203–4; strategies for maintaining
good, 200–201; superintendents
on good, 199–200, 201–3, 205,
206–9; treating staff with care and
fostering good, 208–9
religious groups, 141
resource management: compromise
and, 129–30; distribution of
authority and, 130–31; helping
others grow professionally and,
131–32; keys to, 129–34; new
partnerships and, 132–34
resources: changing communities
and, 122–26; communication and,
127–29; enrollment growth and,
122; eroding finances, tax bases
and, 121–22; greater good and,
129; keys to managing, 129–34;
laws, dollars and, 120–21;
leadership strategies and, 126–29;

legal eagles and, 126–27; shortage,
119–34; superintendents on, 119,
120–32; unlimited needs and
limited, 127; urban/suburban/rural
school, 136
Restine, L. Nan, 119, 137, 149
Robert's Rules of Order, 112
roles: education and personal, 99–118;
learning from superintendents and,
110–15; legal definitions of school
board, 102–3; orthodox/progressive
views, society and public-school,
167–69; personal values/beliefs
and, 100–102; school board
members sharing values/beliefs and
personal, 103–9; superintendents
and, 102–3, 107–10, 112–16;
superintendents' changing, 177–79,
200; superintendents mentored by
school board and, 115–18
Rudy, D. W., 66
Ruff, William, 52, 67
Rusch, Edith A., 22, 43, 84

safety: internal changes, school
security and, 16–17
Salsberry, Trudy, 13, 99, 199
San Jose Unified School District, 36
Schlechty, P. C., 62
Schmoker, Mike, 76
school board members:
accountability with
superintendents, 203; arena-style,
171–72; chaotic politics and role
of, 175–77; constituencies
influencing, *105;* elite-style,
171–72; ethics and, 117; finding
footing with superintendents,
150–52; interaction relationships
of, *104;* learning from current,

103–8; learning from veteran, 109;
needing to be reelected, 164–84;
relationship web of, *106*; *Robert's
Rules of Order* and, 112; securing
footing with superintendents,
162–63; selecting superintendents,
179–82; seven-member
interaction pattern of, *105*; sharing
values/beliefs and personal roles,
103–9; superintendents mentored
by, 115–18; superintendents'
relationship with, 59, 175–77, 178;
tensions between superintendents
and, vii–viii; understanding
perspectives of superintendents,
149–63
school boards: elite- *versus* arena-
style, 171–72; internal changes
and makeup of, 14; legal
definitions of, 102–3; meetings
and increasing participation,
192–93; obtaining meaningful
community input, 185–98;
preparing for meetings with, 111.
See also school board members
school governance: reelection and
reality of school politics in, 165–66
schools: orthodox/progressive views
and societal roles of public,
167–69; resources in
urban/suburban/rural, 136
school security: internal changes,
safety and, 16–17
school service: mixing politics with,
173–74
sex education, 141
Skrla, L. M., 46
special interests: micropolitics and
balancing equity concerns and,
141–45

staff: burnout, 90–91; developing
good leaders from good, 96–98;
developing good staff into best,
88–92; development for keeping
good, 90–91; fostering good
relationships and caring treatment
of, 208–9; hiring good
superintendents to be on, 85;
learning from superintendents
about operations and district,
111–12; mentoring, 97; personnel
problems and development of,
91–92; problem-solving and
relying on, 93–96; recruiting,
keeping, developing and relying
on, 83–99; selecting and getting
good, 84–88; setting tone for
continuous improvement in,
89–90; suggestions for keeping
good, 97–98; superintendents on
hiring/developing good, 85–97
statesmanship, 37
Strike, Kenneth, ix
student achievement: assessing
learning and, 58–61; AYP and,
63–64, 65; challenges to, 65–66;
data and sustained, 67–71;
ensuring quality education for,
61–65; equity in, 63–65; fostering,
52–66; high educational standards
for, 61–63; instructional leadership
and implementing, 56–57;
instruction/learning-focused
vision/mission for, 53–57; NCLB
and, 53, 59–61, 63–64;
superintendents on, 54–57, 59–62,
64–65; teacher qualifications
influencing, 61–62
students: achievement, 52–71;
chaotic political situations,

reelection and doing good for, 174–77; external changes, legal constraints and services for, 10–11; external changes, minority teachers and, 9; fostering achievement in, 52–66; high school journalism, 30; minority, 9, 25; vision sales force and engaging, 32–33

student services: external changes, legal constraints and, 10–11

success strategies: base decisions on data, 67–82; learning about education and personal role, 99–118; maintaining good relationships, 199–212; obtaining meaningful community input, 185–98; prioritize and decide, 41–51; recruit, keep, develop and rely on good staff, 83–99; selling visions, 22–40

superintendents: accountability, school board members and, 203; changing roles of, 177–79, 200; community input and, 201–2; considerations when selecting, 179–82; crickets, communication, communities and, 155–58; data and, 70, 72–76, 77–80; decision-making and, 42, 44–45, 47–48, 50; evaluating/hiring, 179; evaluation, 181–82; external changes implemented by, 4, 6, 7, 8, 9–10, 11; golden mean and, 160–61; good relationships and, 199–200, 201–3, 205, 206–9; hiring, 85, 179; hiring/developing good staff and, 85–97; as instructional leaders, 56–57; internal changes implemented by, 12–15, 17–18;

learning about communication from, 113–15; micropolitics and, 137–40, 142–45, 146–47; needing to be reelected, 164–84; operations, district staff and learning from, 111–12; people, politics, policy and, 153–55; place-bound and career-bound, 179–81; real/ideal and, 161–62; reelection and, 164, 165, 169, 171, 172–74, 176, 181–82; resources and, 119, 120–32; roles and, 102–3, 107–10, 112–16; roles and learning from, 110–15; school board members finding footing with, 150–52; school board members mentoring, 115–18; school board members' relationship with, 59, 175–77, 178; school board members securing footing with, 162–63; seeing problems from perspective of administrators and, 110; selling visions, 25–26; steering without rowing, 203–4; student achievement and, 54–57, 59–62, 64–65; tensions between school board members and, vii–viii; turning point, consequences of action and, 158–60; understanding perspectives of, 149–63; vision and, 25–26, 27, 29–39

Switzler, A., 108

systems thinking: fostering good relationships by practicing, 207–8

Tate, J. S., 190

tax: bases, 10, 121–22; micropolitics and property, 137, 139 tax bases: eroding resources, finances and, 121–22; external changes and, 10

teachers, 91; external changes, minority students and, 9; qualifications, 61–62; vision sales force and engaging, 32. *See also* staff

teaching initiatives: questions about learning and, 58

technology: internal changes and, 15–16

tensions: leading well amid, xi; between superintendents and school board members, vii–viii; twelve kinds of, viii–x

test scores: accountability and, 4–5, 8; declining, 23; rising, 36

thinking: fostering good relationships by practicing systems, 207–8; shifting to long-term, 207

"Thousand Voices from the Firing Line, A." *See* "Voices"

transparency: external changes, public perception/accountability and, 5–6

trust: decision-making and, 49–51

truth, 95

Tucson Unified School District, 26

UCEA. *See* University Council for Educational Administration

understanding: community input, patience and, 193–94

University Council for Educational Administration (UCEA), xii

Usdan, M. D., 3

Vaill, P. B., 1

values: beliefs and, 100–102

values plurality: cultural and, 166–67

vision: action shift: collectives and, 39–40; fostering good relationships and sharing in creation of, 201–2; impetus to outcomes with, 34–37; local visions replaced by national, 25–27; mind shift: power and, 38; NCLB and, 22, 25–26, 37; sales force for ideals and, 32–34; school districts', 26; selling, 22–40; skill shift: listening and, 38–39; statesmanship, 37; strategies for marketing ideals and, 27–34; student achievement implementing, 53–57; superintendents and, 25–26, 27, 29–39; work history, 23–25

vision sales force: engaging advisory councils and, 33–34; engaging kids and, 32–33; engaging teachers and, 32; ideals and, 32–34

vision work: history of, 23–25; NCLB and, 25; strategic planning and, 23–24

"Voices," xii

Washoe County Schools, 25, 38

Watson, Sheldon, T., 1, 54, 88, 99, 197

Westminster, Colorado, 36

Wever, Dan, xiv

Whitaker, Kathryn, 1, 54, 88, 99, 197

Zmuda, A., 81

ABOUT THE CONTRIBUTORS

Michele Acker-Hocevar is a professor of educational leadership at Florida Atlantic University. She has been an elementary school administrator, served as a consultant for a major publishing company, and worked for a Fortune 100 company. Her research focuses on school and organization development, particularly in high-poverty schools. She is co-coordinating, under the auspices of the University Council for Educational Administration, the *Voices* study of school superintendents and principals.

Judith A. Aiken is an associate professor and associate dean in the College of Education and Social Services at the University of Vermont. She teaches leadership courses in the master's and doctoral degree programs and has experience as a principal, curriculum director, and assistant superintendent in both private and public education. Her areas of research expertise are in leadership preparation and development, teacher supervision and evaluation, and women in leadership.

Thomas L. Alsbury is assistant professor of Educational Administration in the Department of Educational Leadership and Policy Studies at North Carolina State University in Raleigh, NC. He spent six years as a high school science teacher and 12 as a K–12 principal, leading his schools to significant and sustained student achievement improvements. His research and consultations focus on organizational theory, the superintendency, school boards, district consolidation, system reform, and leadership preparation programs.

Eduardo Arellano is an assistant professor in Educational Management and Development at New Mexico State University. He is the president of the school board for La Academia Dolores Huerta, a dual-language charter school in Las Cruces, New Mexico. His research interests lie in higher-education policy, minority student success in college, and international higher-education collaboration.

Mary E. Devin served as a public school administrator for 37 years, the last 12 as superintendent in a midsized district, where a very diverse student population was among the highest performers on state assessments. She is an associate professor at Kansas State University in the Department of Educational Leadership and serves as co-liaison for Leadership Academies, which prepare teacher leaders for leadership positions in buildings.

Robin Dexter is the assistant superintendent for Learning with Pittsburg Community Schools, Pittsburg, Kansas. She has degrees in elementary education, deaf education, and educational leadership. She has served 10 years in education administration. She was an assistant professor in the Department of Educational Leadership at the University of Wyoming before moving to Pittsburg. Her research interests are in the areas of school improvement, instructional leadership, and instructionally supportive assessment.

Ramón Domínguez is an associate professor in Educational Management and Development at New Mexico State University, where he has received excellence awards for leadership, teaching, and service. He has co-coordinated the Community College Leadership Doctoral Program and the Educational Leadership Doctoral Program. In higher education, he has experience as associate vice-president of student services, executive vice-president, and president of El Paso Community College.

Cynthia Gerstl-Pepin is an assistant professor at the University of Vermont. Her research exposes social justice issues in education via the intertwining of theory and practice. As a social justice scholar, she uses theory and qualitative inquiry to study educational politics from individual classroom practice to national school reform such as No Child Left Behind. She has coauthored a book, *Re-Framing Educational Politics for Social Justice,* and has published in several major education journals.

Adrienne Hyle is professor of educational leadership at Oklahoma State University. She is currently associate dean for graduate studies, international studies, and research administration in the College of Education. Hyle researches and writes in the areas of leadership, organizational change, K–12 and higher-education faculty and gender issues, and international studies.

Gary Ivory, department head and associate professor at New Mexico State University, has taught in grades 5 through 8. He has been coordinator of research, testing, and evaluation in a school district of 50,000 students. He is editor of the book *What Works in Computing for School Administrators* (Scarecrow Education) and is co-coordinating, under the auspices of the University Council for Educational Administration, the *Voices* study of school superintendents and principals.

Rhonda McClellan received her doctorate in educational leadership from Oklahoma State University. She is currently assistant professor at Texas Woman's University and has taught educational leadership at New Mexico State University. She has also taught composition, literature, and humanities at Northern Oklahoma College. She has master's degrees in English and in Community College English Teaching and has taught high school English.

Teresa Miller is an associate professor of educational leadership at Kansas State University. She has served as a public school educator for 32 years, as a language arts teacher, a gifted-education facilitator, and as both elementary and secondary principal. She has helped plan and develop professional-development schools where a university and a public school district can work together to prepare teachers. She has also facilitated universities and public schools working together to prepare school leaders.

Faye E. Patterson is an assistant professor and director of the School Administrator Certification Program at the University of Tennessee, Knoxville. She has degrees in elementary education, school administration, and supervision. She spent 19 years in public school administration, including 10 years as associate superintendent. Her research interests include educational policies, mentoring new principals, and gender equity in principal preparation programs.

L. Nan Restine served as a public school teacher and administrator and received her Ph.D. from the University of New Mexico. She has served as a faculty member at Western Kentucky University, as a faculty member, associate school head, and associate dean at Oklahoma State University, as associate dean at the University of Alabama, and she is currently the interim dean of the College of Professional Education and chair of the Department of Teacher Education at Texas Woman's University.

William Ruff is an assistant professor of educational leadership at Montana State University and directs a million-dollar federal project to contextualize leadership preparation for the improvement of schools with large concentrations of Native American students. He has taught principal and superintendent preparation courses at major universities. He researches and publishes on instructional leadership, school reform, and the No Child Left Behind Act.

Edith A. Rusch is an associate professor of educational leadership at the University of Nevada, Las Vegas. Her research interests include equity discourse and leadership preparation, PK–16 pipeline issues, democratic praxis, organizational learning, and theories of organizational change. Her work has been published in several journals, and she currently serves as the editor of the University Council for Educational Administration's *Journal of Research on Leadership Education*.

Trudy Salsberry is a professor at Kansas State University in the Department of Educational Leadership. She teaches courses on qualitative research methods, strategies for educational change, and leadership for diverse populations. She conducts research in the area of leadership and underrepresented groups. She is an ambassador for the North Central Association Commission on Accreditation and School Improvement and conducts accreditation visits to overseas school sites.

Sheldon Watson is assistant professor of educational leadership at Central Connecticut State University. His research interests are in collaboration, organizational learning, teacher quality, and educational policy, and on the use and implementation of distributed leadership practices in Connecticut public school districts. He has written book chapters and journal articles and presented at national conferences. He is a former middle school social studies teacher and archaeologist.

Kathryn S. Whitaker is professor and program coordinator of the Educational Leadership and Policy Studies Program at the University of Northern Colorado. She has served as a public school teacher and administrator prior to entering the professorship. Dr. Whitaker's research interests include the principalship, the superintendency, and school district/university partnerships. She has coauthored several books and book chapters and published her research in a number of journals.